AF323415

FINANCIAL SYSTEMS IN TRANSITION

A Flow of Funds Analysis of Financial Evolution in Eastern Europe and Central Asia

ECONOMIC IDEAS LEADING TO THE 21st CENTURY

Series editors: Lawrence R. Klein *(Univ. Pennsylvania)* &
Vincent Su *(Baruch College, CUNY)*

Published

FINANCIAL SYSTEMS IN TRANSITION

A Flow of Funds Analysis of Financial Evolution in Eastern Europe and Central Asia

Editors

Alexander E. Fleming & Marcelo M. Giugale

The World Bank

World Scientific

Singapore • New Jersey • London • Hong Kong

Published by

World Scientific Publishing Co. Pte. Ltd.

P O Box 128, Farrer Road, Singapore 912805

USA office: Suite 1B, 1060 Main Street, River Edge, NJ 07661

UK office: 57 Shelton Street, Covent Garden, London WC2H 9HE

British Library Cataloguing-in-Publication Data
A catalogue record for this book is available from the British Library.

**FINANCIAL SYSTEMS IN TRANSITION: A FLOW OF FUNDS ANALYSIS
OF FINANCIAL EVOLUTION IN EASTERN EUROPE AND CENTRAL ASIA**
Economic Ideas Leading to the 21st Century — Vol. 6

ISBN 981-02-4406-1

This book is printed on acid-free paper.

Printed in Singapore by Uto-Print

This book is dedicated to our children—
Mia and Zoe Fleming and Carla and Juan Giugale.

A.E.F and M.M.G

Table of Contents

Broad Financial Equilibrium

Quasi-Public Sector Deficits

Preface

Lawrence R. Klein

Benjamin Franklin Professor of Economics, Emeritus
University of Pennsylvania
1980 Nobel Laureate in Economics

The economies of the states of the former Soviet Union and the former Council of Mutual Economic Assistance (CMEA) countries of Eastern Europe make up the *transition* economies. This group replaces most, but not all the countries that were formerly labeled socialist economies—the second of the first, second, and third world countries. That classification is now outmoded. People who take a total world view now speak of "advanced industrial countries" and "developing countries." The former socialist countries that were guided by direct central planning have largely vanished, and they are aiming for status as either (i) socialist market economies or (ii) just market economies. The former are basically China and possibly Vietnam, and the latter are those of Eastern Europe and the former Soviet Union.[1] They are all in transition to market capitalism or market socialism. The important aspect is that they are using market-clearing prices instead of administered prices for valuation of their economic activities.

Economies function within an accounting framework, which provides a quantitative tableau for judging operations. The material product framework of the former socialist countries was a derivative of Marxist thinking and not very useful in 20th Century economic analysis. For instance, whenever a socialist country was incorporated into the Project LINK system (where total world economic performance was being monitored for production, trade, and international payments), it was always necessary to transform net material product (NMP) figures into corresponding national accounting figures that were being used for most of the world.

---

[1] North Korea and Cuba are not easily classified.

After the fall of the Soviet Union, the countries that were directly or indirectly involved became free to produce more meaningful statistics and the old accounting system was completely disregarded. Russia, the rest of the former Soviet Union, and the rest of the CMEA countries have all shifted to generally accepted national accounting standards, and, eventually, all will undoubtedly adhere to the UN's System of National Accounts (SNA).

The transition countries had to build on accounts that were in place and develop new kinds of accounts. In some sense, every country needs a set of national income and product accounts (NIPA in US terminology) so that they can have a GDP, by which international market investors can judge their macroeconomic performance. Associated with agreed-upon methods of evaluating GDP, there must be indicative measures of inflation, wage rates, foreign trade prices, exchange rates, interest rates, and other market-clearing variables. These statistical tabulations go along with being classified as market economies.

It is useful to construct national accounting systems around three kinds of accounts, namely (i) NIPA systems, (ii) input-output systems (I/O), and (iii) flow of funds systems. Many of the former socialist countries had both NMP systems and I/O systems. The former were reasonably quickly transformed into approximations to conventional NIPA systems. The I/O systems were widely used in the former socialist economies, but they also needed some transformation, as they portrayed the industrial structures of the centrally planned economies, and these structures changed radically after 1989.

The financial accounting for sectors of transition economies needed significant re-working too. As in the case of nearly all developing countries, there was a serious need for external financing in the transition countries, and a main function of the flow of funds accounts is to reveal the sources and uses of funds that are needed for growth and development. Growth and development, in an international market framework, have indeed been the goal of transition countries.

This, however, is not purely a matter of international financial capital flows in and out of transition countries. Many of these countries are resource-rich, and it has been important—as well as problematic—to trace internal sources and uses of funds for dealing with these resources in order to judge whether they are being used for the good of the individual country's development targets.

In a sense, looking at a country's economy as one giant firm, the NIPA system is the profit-and-loss (or income) statement; the I/O system is an operating statement; and the flow of funds system is a derivative of the nation's balance sheet (or wealth) statement. In fact, the flow of funds statement is a sources and uses statement, based on the period-to-period differences in the balance sheet items. As a flow statement, the flow of funds accounts portray the working of financial operations *during* an accounting period, such as one year or one quarter. The wealth or balance sheet statement refers to an instant of time, for example, the asset or liability *stock* on December 31st or some other relevant calendar day.

The growth and development problems of the transition countries are quite similar to those of all developing countries, except for the fact that the heritage of the transition countries is generally very different from that of most developing countries, and the levels of living or levels of industrialization at the starting point (1989) are quite different from starting values that have faced developing countries when they first embarked on economic expansion. In the language of dynamic systems, one can say that the initial conditions are quite different.

It is not surprising, therefore, that during the 1990s the transition countries encountered some of the same financial and other economic difficulties that the developing economies of East Asia and Latin America faced. The whole world economy had to deal, in search of stabilization, with growing deficits on international current accounts, domestic fiscal deficits, non-performing portfolios of financial institutions (commercial banks, investment banks, brokerages, insurance companies), exchange rate volatility, inflation, stock market volatility, high interest rates, and induced recession.

Many stop-gap measures were introduced. Financial support from outside was often negotiated, but with strong conditionality. To deal with these situations in ways that could restore stability, required an understanding of the economic processes that generated the financial crises.

There is a great deal of evidence that this needed understanding can be greatly enhanced by detailed studies of flow of funds accounts, showing "from-whom; to-whom flows of funds by type of financial instrument". That is the main contribution of this interesting volume. It shows in as much detail as can be made available now, how much light can be shed on each of several transition-country economic experiences of the past few years.

Ultimately one would like to have a complete flow-of-funds matrix like that produced by John Dawson and Steven Everhart in the chapter for Lithuania. They might go more deeply into the subject in the future by separating the banking segment into private banks and the central bank, by splitting the private sector into households and non-financial business. Also, more detail on types of financial instruments involved in the flows of funds would be instructive. They present an annual matrix for 1997, but for understanding crisis situations, an historical and up-to-date series, as in the case of NIPA tableaux, are needed. NIPA valuations are most useful if presented quarterly. Most advanced industrial countries have quarterly tabulations, and many developing countries are doing the same thing. A next goal would be to have quarterly flows-of-fund tabulations, and important entries in such tabulations at a more refined frequency.

As a user (not a producer) of economic information, it is easy to ask for a great deal of refinement. Such refined estimates are not available in the present volume, but what has been accomplished is an important first step.

Rationale, Organization and Acknowledgements

When the former Soviet Union collapsed and the countries of Eastern Europe and Central Asia (ECA) abandoned central planning in the early 1990s, fertile new ground for economic analysis opened up. Transition presented policy-makers with a whole array of formidable problems, both in nature and dimension, from sudden disappearance of entire production structures and major relative price changes to unfunded social liabilities and total absence of capacity in core public institutions. Thus, in the early years, much of the economics of transition was focused on providing governments with answers to urgent priority issues.

Almost a decade later, enough country experiences have accumulated to allow for a more reflective study of the transition period, both in terms of past performance and likely future developments. A critical component of any such study should be the evolution of financial systems in the transition countries, something that gained further relevance in the aftermath of the international financial crises of 1997 (East Asia), 1998 (Russia) and 1999 (Brazil).

This book reviews the evolution of financial systems in eight ECA countries (Estonia, Hungary, Kazakhstan, Latvia, Lithuania, Poland, Russia, and Romania) since transition began and, to the extent possible, provides a broad picture of their medium- and long-term outlook. This outlook is based upon flow of funds projections that were undertaken for the most part on the basis of data up to end-1997 and have not been updated. However, in the context of this book the importance of the projections rests not so much in their accuracy, or in how up-to-date they are, but rather in illustrating the consistency and rigor that the flow of funds framework imposes on the process.

The book looks at financial systems not simply as the collection of institutions, markets, and market trading prices but, more generally, as the structure of financing relationships among main sectors of the economy (the government, the banking industry, the private non-financial sector, households, the rest of the world, and so on). This permits a more thorough understanding of the linkages between macroeconomic performance and financial flows. Policymakers, academics, financiers, and development practitioners working in the region will hopefully benefit from the new perspectives on the financial system offered in this book.

The country studies presented here are based on flow of funds dissections of national accounts, monetary statistics, and purpose-built sector saving/investment matrixes. This allows for a detailed analysis of sectoral imbalances and their interplay within the overall framework of an economy, as well as for the interpretation of the resulting macroeconomic trends. While flow of funds accounting is a common technique in macro-financial analysis, it had seldom been applied on a comparative cross-country basis to the study of transition, possibly because data paucity made it all but impossible before. Gradual accumulation of data since 1991 and a series of country-specific estimations, make it possible now.

A brief technical introduction to flow of funds methodology is presented in Chapter 1. Chapter 2 then provides a summarized overview of how financial evolution took place in the ECA countries and how it may continue in the future.This is followed by the eight country specific chapters. These chapters were commissioned for, and delivered in a technical seminar held at the World Bank in the Fall of 1998. While they carry a common theme (inter-sectoral financing structures during transition), the chapters are not standardized to attain a common focus or methodology. Rather, they are adapted to highlight the issues that are most relevant for the country in question and to fit the information available in that country (sometimes very limited). The projections contained in the country cases are meant to indicate broad trends (sometimes under alternative scenarios), rather than to predict specific values.

The research effort behind this volume is part of, and has been partly financed by, the World Bank Research Program. However, the findings and opinions reflected in this book are the authors' own, and do not necessarily reflect the views of the World Bank, its Board of Executive Directors, or its member countries.

Many people within and outside the World Bank have contributed to this effort. In particular, we would like to thank the participating authors for the excellence of their technical contributions, Lajos Bokros for his help and encouragement in launching the work, and Lawrence Klein, Frank Lysy, Pradeep Mitra, and Marcelo Selowsky for their suggestions. Michael S. Geller ably led the production team. Sylvia Torres was in charge of organizing the October 1998 seminar. Caroline McEuen provided editorial services.

Alexander E. Fleming and Marcelo M. Giugale
Washington, D.C.
May 2000

1.

The Flow of Funds in a Transition Context

Alexander E. Fleming and Marcelo M. Giugale

Background

Flow of funds accounts have been used in the OECD countries for many years as an aid to analyzing money flows around financial systems and to assist in the framing of monetary policy. The founding father of the flow of funds approach has generally been considered to be Wesley Mitchell who wrote on "The Flow of Payments, a Preliminary Survey" in an unpublished work in 1944. Later, in 1952, Maurice Copeland wrote a path-breaking book entitled "A study of money flows in the United States". This book paved the way for the regular preparation of the flow of funds accounts in the United States by the Federal Reserve System. In the United Kingdom, the Radcliffe Committee Report in 1959 gave an impetus to the collection of flow of funds data in the United Kingdom. Subsequently the other OECD countries have collected financial data in flow of funds format.

This chapter describes the flow of funds accounts and their usage in the financial analysis of the real and financial sectors of the economy. By highlighting the specific benefits—as well as problems—associated with the use of the flow of funds approach in OECD countries, and then in transition economies, it provides the foundation for the rest of the book.

Objectives and coverage of flow of funds accounts[1]

The flow of funds system of accounts brings the main financial activities in the economy into focus by setting them in statistical relation with one another and with the more familiar national income and expenditure accounts. The aim is to help identify both the role of finance in the generation of incomes, savings and expenditure, and the influences of economic activity on the financial markets. The accounts provide a statistical framework that can be used in a general way to analyze financial developments; to trace, for example, certain broad effects of monetary policy, such as how the enterprise sector as a whole adjusts its financing to a credit squeeze.

The Elements of the System

The flow of funds accounts divide the economy along behavioral and institutional lines into broadly homogeneous groupings, or sectors. For each sector the accounts show and classify its financial transactions within a consistently defined system, linked to the national income and expenditure accounts. Each sector account identifies and measures the main sources and uses of its funds. It sets out the flows of payments and receipts, not only for goods and services, but in particular for financial instruments of ownership and debt, and so encompasses net borrowing and lending.

The flow of funds system is one of several complementary ways of accounting for the total transactions or activities in the economy. The national income accounts measure output, incomes and expenditure. Input-output tables measure the technological relations between industries in terms of expenditure (inputs) and receipts (outputs). Then there is the national balance sheets which show the holdings of assets and liabilities of each sector corresponding to the flows. Finally, the balance of payments accounts provide a means of measuring economic activity vis-à-vis the rest of the world. The flow of funds accounts complement all of these accounts by measuring money-flows around the economy.

To elaborate on the flow of funds approach, it is useful to start with the traditional national income identities. The basic accounting identity of national income analysis may be expressed as:

---

1. This section draws heavily on Bank of England (1972).

$$Y = C + I + X - M$$

or, incomes earned by the factors of production (Y) are equal to the sum of income-generating expenditures: consumption (C), physical investment (I) and exports (X), less imports (M) (which are included in expenditure, but which generate income abroad, not at home).

Each of the elements in this identity may be broken down and allocated to one or other of the various sectors of the economy. Take a simple case with three domestic sectors:

(1) the household sector;

(2) the enterprise sector;

(3) the government sector;

and a sector representing the rest of the world

(4) the rest-of-the-world sector.

Dividing up income, call Y_1, the factor incomes earned by households (wages and salaries, rent, etc.), Y_2 enterprise profits plus rent, and Y_3 the profits of government enterprises plus rent. Expenditure can be similarly divided up: C_1, being consumer expenditure and C_3 current expenditure on goods and services by government authorities; while I_1, I_2 and I_3 are investment expenditures on goods and services. In addition, transfers (interest payments, grants and taxes) take place between sectors; for all sectors together, including those paid and received by the rest-of-the-world sector, they add to zero. Call the net receipts or payments of transfers by each sector T_1, T_2, T_3, T_4. The identities may then be set out thus:

Table 1

	Income	Trans-fers (net)	Consump-tion	Invest-ment	Balance of goods and services		Financial surplus/ deficit
Household sector	Y_1	$+T_1$	$-C_1$	$-I_1$		=	F_1
Enterprise sector	Y_2	$+T_2$		$-I_2$		=	F_2
Government sector	Y_3	$+T_3$	$-C_3$	$-I_3$		=	F_3
Rest-of-the-world sector	Y_4	$+T_4$			$-X+M$	=	F_4
Total	Y	$+0$	$-C$	$-I$	$-X+M$	=	0

Reading across the rows, it can be seen that for domestic sectors factor incomes plus net transfers less current and capital expenditure on goods and services equals the financial surplus or deficit (F). A surplus measures the total amount a sector has available to add to financial assets or to reduce financial liabilities, and a deficit measures the net amount it has to raise by selling financial assets or by borrowing. The financial surplus or deficit of the rest-of-the-world sector is equal to its net receipts of interest, dividends, taxes, etc. plus imports less exports of goods and services, and is equal in amount and opposite in sign to the balance on the country's balance of payments current account. The transactions of the domestic sectors can be divided, as in the national income accounts, between current and capital items. The difference between income, current transfers and current expenditure—that is saving—is carried to the capital account, and set against investment and capital transfers, to arrive at the financial surplus, or deficit.

The sum of the financial surpluses and deficits is shown in the table as zero, which does no more than express the fact that a change in one sector's financial liabilities is matched by that in another sector's financial assets. In fact, as recorded, financial surpluses and deficits sum to the residual error in the national income accounts.

Flow of funds tables themselves—see Table 1B below for the basic format—simply set out the particular routes along which funds pass between the sectors' capital accounts in a particular period, covering, say, a year or a quarter. They show each sector's net transactions in each particular financial instrument or market (for instance, the market for government bonds). The convention is adopted that the acquisition of an asset or the reduction of a liability is a positive flow, the reduction of an asset or the incurring of a liability is a negative one. The flows in each market then add to zero, and the sum of the flows for each sector equals its financial surplus or deficit. The markets and instruments shown are chosen to reflect, as far as possible, the institutional framework, but this aim is sometimes in practice frustrated by the form in which the data become available.

Table 1B. Illustrative Flow of Funds Matrix (basic format)

Financial instrument/sector	Household sector	Enterprise sector	Government sector	Rest-of-the-World sector	Banking sector
Investment	0	10	20	–	–
Saving	10	5	5	10	–
Financial Surplus(+) Deficit(-)	+10	-5	-15	+10	0
Government Bonds			-5	+5	
Bank Deposits	+10			+5	-15
Bank Lending		-5	-10		+15

There are a number of important features embedded in the flow of funds framework illustrated by the table above:

- The system is closed, so that the sum across sectors for each transaction (that is, the sum of each row) is identically equal to zero, as is the sum of the resource gaps. The current account of the rest of the world is necessarily the mirror image of the country's current account, since the world as a whole is a closed economy. Specifically, the country can run a current account deficit if, and only if, the rest of the world is running a surplus of an equal amount.

- Transactions in the rest-of-the-world sector are entered from the point of view of the rest of the world, not from the point of view of the country.

An alternative way of presenting flow of funds accounts (used in some chapters of this book) is to break down each flow according to whether it represents a source or use of funds. Thus, each sector would have a "sources" and a "uses" column. This is illustrated below in Table 1C.

The sources and uses format disaggregates financial flows in a way that highlights the inflows and outflows of funds to each sector.[2]

---

2. The sign conventions differ in the sources and uses format from that in the basic format. By way of an example, an increase in bank deposits (looked at from the perspective of the banking sector) would carry a positive sign in the sources column. A decline in deposits would carry a negative sign in the sources column of the banking sector.

Table 1C. Illustrative Flow of Funds Matrix (sources and uses format)

	Government sector		Banking sector		Private[1] sector		Rest-of-the-World sector		Total	
	Use	Source	Use	Source	Use	Source	Use	Source	Use	Source
Investment	20				10				30	
Saving		5				15		10		30
Surplus/deficit	-15				5		10			
	Δ Fin assets	Δ Fin liab.	Δ Fin assets	Δ Fin liab.	Δ Fin assets	Δ Fin liab.	Δ Fin assets	Δ Fin liab.	Δ Fin assets	Δ Fin liab.
Δ Government bonds		5					5		5	5
Δ Bank deposits				15	10		5		15	15
Δ Bank lending		10	15			5			15	15
Total	20	20	15	15	20	20	10	10	65	65

Note: [1] For simplicity, the enterprise and household sectors have been amalgamated into one private sector

Presentationally, the financial surplus (or deficit) is the link between national income (above the dotted line) and financial analysis (the lower portion of the matrix). Much of the analytic interest in the flow of funds technique stems from the interaction between general economic activity (upper portion of the matrix) and financial conditions (the lower portion).

The observation and measurement of the changing sectoral patterns of financial surpluses/deficits over time, and the accompanying changes in financial flows, can yield analytic insights into the nature of economic change (Chapter 2 seeks to do this for the transition economies).

While the flow of funds matrix is at the core of the analysis of the financial sector set out in this book, a wide range of other tabulations and analytic formats are derived from it or associated with it. The flow-of-fund approach might, at its broadest, encapsulate any type of analysis which takes as its starting point a sectoral view of the financial sector. This is evidenced by the variety of modes of analysis represented in the ensuing chapters.

The Purpose and Value of Flow of Funds Accounts.

Historically, the flow of funds system is the offspring of the national income concepts and cannot properly be understood in isolation from them, because financial flows, its chief concern, are the complement of the flows of income and expenditure. The national income accounts express the circular nature of economic flows. Output, on the one hand, generates income for each of the factors of production while, on the other hand, it is used to meet the demand generated by various forms of expenditure. The principal links between national income accounting and financial transactions stem from the fact that those who receive income are not necessarily those who spend (spending can come out of past savings or out of borrowing). Furthermore, those who save are by no means the same as those who invest in physical assets such as buildings and machinery. This explains the existence of financial institutions and means that finance has a crucial role in the determination of incomes and expenditure. There are not only the markets in goods, labor, and so on to be cleared, but also, and simultaneously, the financial markets in which funds are channeled from those who are persuaded to save to those who think it profitable to invest.

The flow of funds approach aims to account in the end for the factors which contribute to the generation of income, and to do so in a way which encompasses all the very many different types of financial asset used in the financial system.

Difficulties can arise in the application of the flow of funds approach, however. As discussed later, this is particularly the case in transition economies. But against this its comprehensiveness has several practical advantages. For example, flow of funds accounts can give insights that are not possible within the more aggregate national income accounts. In particular, changes in monetary and fiscal policy, the effects of which can be observed in the national income accounts only very indirectly, can in principle be traced more explicitly through sectoral flows to changes in financial positions which affect spending decisions. This is not to say that flow of funds accounting explains the mechanism of monetary (or fiscal) policy, but rather traces some of the channels through which it works. The accounts include many items which have no place in the basic presentation of national income and expenditure though they affect the development of economic activity: purchases and sales of financial assets, government borrowing, activities of banks and those of other financial institutions. These transactions are interesting in themselves to those concerned with financial markets and are set out in a consistent framework.

The more elaborate sectoral breakdown usual in flow of funds analysis, as compared with national income statistics, also has its advantages. The institutional framework of the accounts makes it possible to observe and measure the effects of changes in these institutions. More precisely, money and credit flows are highly sensitive to such factors as the laws determining the forms of business organization, the kinds of credit institutions operating and their regulations, tax laws, and so on. Flow of funds accounts can measure or indicate the effects of changes in these factors upon the structure of financial transactions in the economy, by making it possible to observe the evolution of the financial structure over a number of years.

Among the difficulties that may be encountered, there are significant gaps in the statistics, giving rise to a certain amount of arbitrary allocation by sector and to the existence of an unidentified balance of flows for each sector. Figures become available only after a delay, and sometimes after a long delay. Significant movements may take place within a sector and so be excluded from the accounts—such as any lending among enterprises. In practice, moreover, some sectors are not strictly homogeneous, but lack of data and considerations of manageability alike may prevent the use of as many sectors as would otherwise be desirable—the example of financial institutions was mentioned above.

A danger for a student of the accounts is that they inevitably focus attention on sector surpluses and deficits. But to 'draw the line' at a balance of this kind rather than consider the whole spread of sources and uses of funds is to some extent arbitrary.

Using Flow of Funds Accounts in a Transition Context

The application of flow of funds accounts in OECD economies to describe financial activity is not an exact science. It is much like piecing together a jigsaw puzzle with some of the parts missing. Even with some parts missing, however, it is possible to gain a fairly comprehensive picture of developments. In transition economies there are more missing pieces and it is not possible to disagregate financial flows into as many sectors and instruments as in the more mature economies. However, as will be seen from the papers that have been collected as part of this book, it is still possible to deploy the technique with some success and use it to shed light on many of the problems faced by transition economies.

Insights into the Transition Process.

In the transition economy context the flow of funds approach can yield a number of important insights. As noted above, observation of the emerging pattern of funds flows can illuminate the changing structure of the economy in general and the financial sector in particular. The transition economies are changing rapidly in response to the forces of stabilization and structural change. The shift in real sector activity from a public sector orientation to a private sector one, the evolution of a banking sector coupled with an emerging capital market, and the changing linkages between the real and financial sectors can be tracked through the lens of the flow of funds accounts. In many transition economies certain markets—say the capital markets—or segments of markets, such as a government debt market, may be completely absent. Comparing flow of funds matrices across countries can therefore throw into sharp relief the structural differences between economies.

The changing patterns of financing can also be identified through the deployment of the flow of funds framework and this can provide insight into emerging financial imbalances and constraints that could impinge on the development of the real sector. This could point to weaknesses in the legal and institutional underpinnings of the financial sector.

The flow of funds accounts have been used effectively in OECD countries also as a framework for forecasting financial sector developments. They can similarly be used in the transition economy context to provide a financial feasibility check to expected movements in the financial positions of the main sectors of the economy. The internal constraints imposed by the structure of the flow of funds matrix ensure that an internally consistent outcome results.

The flow of funds accounts can help answer such questions as whether an emerging current account deficit can be financed or not. The shifts in sectoral positions can be quite significant in size over a relatively short time period. It is also possible to use the accounts effectively to answer "what if" questions, for instance discern the short-term impact of a sudden withdrawal of access to external private financing. The ensuing chapters deploy the flow of funds framework in this way in the context of a range of transition economies.

Problems in Application.

While the range of questions that the flow of funds approach can address in the transition economies is perhaps wider than in the more mature OECD economies, the problems associated with its application are also more pervasive. The most obvious weakness is the lack of data that limits the degree of disaggregation in the matrix. Typically, and as evidenced by the following chapters, the size of transition economy flow of funds matrices are smaller, both in terms of sectors and instruments. In some countries, the data itself can be of dubious quality and different data sets can lead to inconsistent conclusions. This curse can also be a blessing in as much as inconsistent data sets forced together within the flow of funds matrix can help transition economy statisticians to refine statistical series in an effort to gain consistency.

The essence of transition, of course, is that the composition of the sectors themselves will change significantly over time. The privatization of state enterprises will, for instance, gradually shift segments of the government sector into the private sector. This shift can lead to statistical problems but if it is properly accounted for can provide insights into the speed and nature of the process.

Delays in collection of data can also blunt the use of the flow of funds technique for short-term policy making. Technical assistance that has been provided to the transition economies by western agencies has served in some instances to help put in place effective data collection systems that rival, in terms of their availability and accuracy, the data of their OECD neighbors.

One of the most difficult issues to address in the transition economies is the measurement and interpretation of financial flows in a high inflation environment. This is particularly problematic before stabilization programs fully take hold. There are approaches that can be used, however, to normalize flows in high inflation periods: express flows in terms of shares of GDP, for instance. This approach is used extensively in the ensuing chapters.

Another feature that characterizes flow of funds in transition economies is the large "errors and omissions" that appear in the balance of payments accounts (the rest-of-the-world sector column). Their size can dominate the identified flows in the accounts and it is difficult to interpret the economic activity that they represent. In the case of Russia, for instance, much of the large "errors and omissions" are thought to be capital flight. Finally, the flow of funds accounts are unable to shed light on transitional problems such as currency substitution—specifically the strong moves towards dollarization that take place, especially at times of economic and financial crisis.

On balance, however, the flow of funds accounts can complement well the national income accounts and other data series that are increasingly becoming available in transition countries. The accounts can moreover facilitate the analysis of the enormous historical shifts that are taking place in the real and financial sectors in these fast evolving economies.

References

Bank of England. 1972. *An Introduction to Flow of Funds Accounting: 1952-70.* London: Bank of England, Economic Intelligence Department.

Board of Governors of the Federal Reserve System. 1980. *Introduction to Flow of Funds.* Washington D.C.

Copeland, Morris A. 1952. *A Study of Moneyflows in the United States.* No. 54. New York: National Bureau of Economic Research.

Dawson, John C., Editor. 1996. *Flow of Funds Analysis: A Handbook for Practitioners.* New York: M.E. Sharpe.

Dawson, John C. 1991. "The Flow of funds Accounts, the United Nations System of National Accounts, and the Developing Countries," in Vincente Galbis, Editor.

The IMF's Statistical Systems in Context of Revision of the United Nations' System of National Accounts. International Monetary Fund, Washington DC.

Mitchell, Wesley. 1944. "The Flow of Payments, a Preliminary Survey" mimeo.

Ouanes, Abdessatar and Subhash Thakur. 1997. *Macroeconomic Accounting and Analysis in Transition Economies.* International Monetary Fund, Washington DC.

Radcliffe. 1959. The Radcliffe Committee Report, London.

2.

The Evolution of Financial Systems in Eastern Europe and Central Asia: An Overview Through the Lens of the Flow of Funds

Marcelo M. Giugale and Alexander E. Fleming

Introduction

The abandonment of state-controlled, centrally-planned, development models in the formerly-socialist countries of Eastern Europe and Central Asia (ECA) during the early 1990s brought about significant (and unavoidable) economic dislocation[1]. Factories were closed down, production slumped, large numbers of workers were made idle, prices rose sharply, money savings evaporated, and elaborate public networks of social welfare all but disappeared. These were the visible symptoms and costs of transition to a market-led, private-sector-driven economic system.

However, behind those visible symptoms, a new structure of financial relationships between the various sectors of society was being forged. Under newly-market-determined prices, the flows of financial resources among the state, enterprises, households, banks, the rest of the world, and other agents were drastically changing. The underlying financial system of the transition countries was changing or, in other words, new "flow of funds" patterns

---

1. See, for example, World Bank. 1996. World Development Report 1996: From Plan to Market. New York: Oxford University Press.

13

were emerging. Economic transition in the financial systems was, in effect, a switch from one pattern of flow of funds to another.

This book provides country-by-country accounts of how the financial systems of a representative sample of ECA countries evolved during the early stages of economic transition through 1997 and, within broad macroeconomic projections, examines how those systems are likely to evolve in the coming years. This chapter distills the common features of those accounts, identifying regularities and seeking to draw policy conclusions that are relevant for the region as a whole.

At the outset, it is important to note that the country analyses presented in this book, and distilled in this chapter, define financial systems in a flow of funds sense, that is, as the complete matrix of inter-sector financing flows, rather than simply as a set of institutions (banks, stock markets, and the like) trading financial products. This has permitted a deeper understanding of the financial forces at work during a period of vast change in the countries in question. The analysis sheds light not only on the large fluctuations in nominal prices (like interest and exchange rates) but also on the sectoral adjustments that were driving those fluctuations (like sector deficits and financing needs). By looking at the likely evolution of those adjustments, it also provides for a more robust forecast of how those countries' economies may behave in the future. Furthermore, through its discipline of internal accounting constraints, flow of funds analysis of financial systems filters out inconsistencies in the data, a welcome feature for economies whose statistical offices and information gathering agencies were not spared the initial convulsions that followed the end of central planning.

Transition: A Story of Shifting Financial Imbalances

A common feature characterized the macro-financial evolution of all countries that underwent transition in ECA: a large initial fiscal imbalance caused, on impact, by a combination of collapsing tax bases and inflexible social welfare expenditures. On the one hand, a whole range of production activities became unviable and ceased to pay taxes, virtually over-night, as both input and output market prices were liberalized and aligned to international equivalents. Annual contractions in real GDP of 15–19 percent and three-digit annual inflation rates were then typical for the region. On the other hand, and perhaps for political support reasons, public social welfare programs could not be formally dismantled, although their real value did shrink. As a consequence, fiscal deficits of 6–10 percent of GDP became common.

The manner in which governments handled the mismatch in the relation between fiscal revenues and expenditures, coupled with other sectors' reactions to that mismatch, proved crucial for the success of macroeconomic stabilization. From a flow of funds point of view, transition has been an intersectoral financing game, where prices just reflected the balance between the sectoral demands for and supplies of funding.

While strict taxonomies are difficult, five broad flow of funds patterns arise from the eight country studies presented in this book, all of which followed deep, initial fiscal imbalances: continuing disequilibria in both the public and private sectors (Kazakhstan and Romania); continuing disequilibrium in the public sector with equilibrium in the private sector (Hungary, Russia); public sector equilibrium with private sector disequilibrium (Estonia); public and private sector equilibria (Latvia, Poland); and disequilibrium in the "quasi-public sector" (Lithuania). Each pattern led to distinct macro-financial consequences in the period up to 1997 (high/hyper-inflation, unsustainable indebtedness, external dependency, banking crises and so on) and presents specific policy challenges over the coming years.

Kazakhstan and Romania: Twin Deficits—Public and Private Sector In Disequilibrium

Since transition began, **Kazakhstan's** public and private sectors both experienced deficits. These have been financed by foreigners, presumably, on the expectation of forthcoming natural resource riches.

Kazakhstan failed during the transition years to establish an effective taxation system. This caused expanding fiscal deficits (about 3 percent of GDP, on average, between 1993 and 1998), even though public investment levels were modest (around 2 percent of GDP). Unable to find funding for those deficits, and to restructure non-viable public enterprises, in 1994, the government sought to monetize its financing needs. Simultaneously, it tried to dilute, through an increase in inflation, the stocks of accumulated arrear of its public enterprises. In that year, inflation reached over 1,800 percent.

To stabilize the economy, the government tightened monetary policy in 1995 and replaced money financing of its deficit with, primarily, foreign loans. Most of that lending came from official sources, supported both by the country's low initial debt position (like other former Soviet republics, it did not assume responsibilities for the Soviet Union's liabilities) and by its potential oil revenue (pending construction of adequate transportation means for its Caspian Sea crude). This brought about an overall sense of macroeconomic stability (inflation fell to 17.3 percent in 1997), and created an opportunity to introduce needed policy reforms to raise tax collection and/or reduce expenditures. Up to 1998, that opportunity was not being taken. This kept the country highly dependent on foreign capital flows, an arrangement that proved less than reliable in the aftermath of the Russian crisis of that year.

A similar financial imbalance was present in the private sector accounts. With continuous deficits (worth 2–3 percent of GDP), the sector was not only unable (and perhaps unwilling) to cover the government's funding needs but also added to the country's external financing requirements. This again is particularly noteworthy for, as a percentage of GDP, private investment in Kazakhstan has been low relative to other ECA countries (around 10–12 percent in 1996 and 1997). Plainly, the country's private sector was grossly under-saving. In the event, the sector's funding needs [net of its own internally generated finance and government lending to (semi) public enterprises] were met through direct foreign investment, primarily into the oil and minerals area.

With a transition period marked by low investment, even lower saving, and high external financial dependency, how is the Kazakhstani economy likely to evolve in the coming decade? Short of a major, and unlikely policy reform effort capable of altering the domestic saving patterns of both the public and private sectors, the answer will be given by two factors over which Kazakhstan's policymakers have little or no effective control—the speed with which a (geopolitically) viable pipeline out of the Caspian Sea is in operation and the economic evolution of Russia. But, even in the most optimistic scenario (no delays in pipeline construction and limited contagion from Russia), Kazakhstan is unlikely to grow fast (3 percent p.a. at the most), will see scant increase in economy-wide productivity, and will remain dependent on oil.

Given these projections, an unsustainable sectoral, or flow of funds financing structure is expected to result: a government that is incapable of increasing its tax revenues fast enough (if at all) will continue to exhibit large deficits (of more than 5 percent of GDP), a private sector that can internally finance only about half of its planned investment, and a banking industry that will play at best a marginal role as financier. This keeps the country heavily dependent on foreign savings that are primarily oriented to the energy-related sector.

If, instead, the pipeline's construction is delayed and Russia's economic troubles spread to the rest of the region, Kazakhstan's prospects are much bleaker. Both growth and investment paths will be further depressed, simply because none of the country's domestic sectors will be able to attract enough foreign capital or to generate enough internal finance. In other words, no matter which scenario is assumed, from a flow-of-funds point of view, Kazakhstan does not appear to fully emerge from the market transition process in the medium term.

While less dependent on single energy commodities, ***Romania's*** transition path has been somewhat less foreign-finance dependent than Kazakhstan but probably more unstable. Romania's initial recession was not as deep as in other parts of the region (about 13 and 8.8 percent contractions in real output in 1991 and 1992), and the country's GDP started growing again as early as 1993. Likewise, its inflation rates in the early years were not among the highest among formerly planned economies (albeit, at some 200 percent p.a., still large). By 1996, the Romanian economy had four years of positive growth and declining inflation, and was expanding at about 4 percent p.a. (with inflation down to about 30 percent p.a.). Throughout, the government's accounts had been highly volatile, fluctuating between large net financing needs and temporary equilibria (in 1993 and 1995). The non-financial private sector had witnessed this high volatility as well, adding to the economy's persistent balance of payment's current account deficit and to the country's prime source of funding—foreign inflows.

Yet, much of the relative ease of the initial transition was based on the postponement of key adjustments in the public sector accounts (especially among state enterprises). That adjustment effectively began in 1997, sending the economy into a sharp, lasting recession, causing a major inflationary surge (150 percent in 1997), and raising the government financing needs to over 6 percent of GDP. With no increase in private saving to match, Romania's current account problem worsened (to about 8 percent of GDP).

This exacerbated twin (government, non-financial private sector) deficit position will dominate Romania's prospects over the coming decade. Even with moderate growth recovery in later years (3 percent in 2001), the country will remain heavily dependent on foreign financing (as its current account expands to over 10 percent of GDP). The reason is that neither the government nor the private sector are expected to generate positive net saving. Even if some reduction in fiscal deficits does take place over time (to, say, 3 percent of GDP), recovering private production will have to be financed primarily and increasingly from abroad. This does not appear to be a sustainable solution and highlights the role that public policy and, more generally, confidence (particularly confidence in the country's financial system) will have to play in raising domestic saving rates.

Hungary and Russia: Continuing Fiscal Imbalances, With Very Different Results

A large fiscal deficit and vast moral hazard problems in the banking sector characterized ***Hungary's*** early transition years. By the time it peaked in 1994, that deficit was just under 10 percent of GDP. While a new legal framework (put in place in 1992) and subsequent bank restructuring efforts gradually brought discipline to bank lending, the macroeconomic stabilization package launched in 1995 delivered only a relatively modest improvement in the fiscal position. In 1998, the fiscal deficit was still at about 5 percent of GDP. Who was paying for it? And, did it prevent Hungary from turning around the high-inflation, deep-recession environment of its initial transition years?

In essence, Hungary's government borrowed heavily throughout the transition period, both from foreigners and from the domestic household sector (in the latter case indirectly through the banking system). The confidence in the country's repayment capacity that underpinned that borrowing is somewhat puzzling; after all, Hungary entered transition already heavily indebted (external debt to GDP in 1990 was equivalent to some 40 percent of GDP) and it showed worrisome balance of payments' current account deficits during most of the 1990s. The strong prospect of accession to the European Union (EU) and, hence, the prospect of enhanced financial backing certainly played a major confidence-building role. But, more importantly, Hungarian households remained committed savers that on average delivered financing to the domestic economy worth about 6 percent of GDP per year, even in the face of fluctuations in external flows. As discussed elsewhere in this chapter, that "domestic confidence" was scarce in Romania and patently absent in Russia.

With resilient financing and the stabilization effort of 1995 noted above (which partially, but effectively, reduced the fiscal imbalance), Hungary managed to recover growth (in the order of about 5 percent p.a. in 1997 and 1998), reduce inflation (to some 10 percent p.a.), and boost its exports (roughly doubling them as percent of GDP between 1995 and 1998). Barring major policy slippage or external crisis, the country is well placed to meet the Maastricht criteria (fiscal deficit, inflation, debt, exchange and interest rate stability) and join the EU in the next decade. Whether accession happens early (through a "high-growth" path of 5 percent p.a.) or later ("moderate" growth of 3 percent p.a.), it will have to continue to be underpinned by not only foreign financing (worth about 3–4 percent of GDP p.a., half of which in the form of FDI) but, more importantly, by Hungarian households' saving (of 7–9 percent of GDP p.a.). In contrast to the transition years, that saving will not be primarily directed to finance the state (whose deficit will be bound by the accession criteria) but a growing private enterprise sector.

Russia's transition performance and outlook appear far bleaker than Hungary's despite similarities in their fiscal situation. Data sets comprehensive enough to assemble flow of fund accounts for Russia date back only to 1993 and, for the analysis in this book, extend through 1997, the year before the country entered a serious financial crisis. From these accounts, it is clear that the country's inability to tax had sealed its macroeconomic fate long before the 1998 crisis actually took place. With average annual central government deficits during the 1993–97 period around 7 percent of GDP, and current savings of -3 percent of GDP, the evolution of Russia's financial system was clearly unsustainable.

In the early years, private sector reluctance to absorb the fiat money printed to finance the fiscal accounts translated into very high inflation. With real money demand (M2) at just over ten percent of GDP, additional nominal balances drove inflation above 300 percent in 1994. In effect, the additional, explicit, and targeted taxation that could have closed the fiscal deficit was replaced by implicit, untargeted taxation through inflation.

To stabilize price growth, in 1996 the Russian authorities started to switch their fiscal financing more heavily toward domestic debt (rather than money printing). Ruble-denominated treasury bills were sold to both the local banking system and, later on, to the rest of the world. To make those bills attractive, their interest rates were allowed to reach extremely high levels in domestic real terms (about 30–40 percent per year, on average, in 1996) and exorbitant levels in dollar terms (with the ruble/dollar exchange rate fixed by the central bank, ex-post dollar returns on short-term ruble-denominated Russian treasury bills exceeded 30 percent in 1997).

That government funding mechanism was patently unsustainable because the economy's growth could not match the real interest rate being paid (the economy was actually shrinking) and the real exchange rate's appreciation (which reached more than 60 percent between 1995 and 1997) was not being validated by productivity gains in the tradable sectors. Public debt ballooned out of hand—less than US$ 40 million worth of treasury bills were sold to foreigners in 1995, compared with over US$40 billion in 1997. The government had no choice but to default on this debt in 1998, triggering a wide-spread financial crisis in the country and sending shocks to emerging markets world-wide.

Remarkably, from a flow of funds perspective, the Russian private sector remained fairly stable, running a financial surplus position throughout the transition period. Saving and investment to GDP ratios stood at around 24 and 20 percent, respectively. However, the private sector was patently unwilling to finance the government's expenditures. It resisted formal taxation. It avoided holding domestic money balances. And while foreigners poured funds into the country's treasury bill markets which would eventually see default, Russia's private sector channeled its excess savings abroad (in the order of US$35 billion in 1997).

That mismatch between the public expenditure level, and the private sector's unwillingness to pay for it, has been the underlying force driving the evolution of Russia's financial system during transition, and has led to the various visible symptoms of macroeconomic instability. While flow of funds accounting helps single out and quantify that mismatch, it will take supreme political will to address it in the coming years.

Estonia: When the Private Sector is the Problem

Like other countries emerging from the former Soviet Union, Estonia faced an immediate, sharp recession primarily associated with the sudden realignment of relative prices and the ensuing reallocation of resources. More unusually, that recession was accompanied by an early (1992–93) and severe banking crisis. But, both the recession and the banking crisis were short-lived. These events would, however, shape the growth path for the Estonian economy during the rest of the transition process, not least because they profoundly affected the objective function of public policymakers.

Since 1994, Estonia's government has maintained either a balanced budget or a budget surplus, anchored price stability on a currency board, and shied away from public indebtedness (by 2000, the country is expected to have no net public debt). At the micro level, it embarked on perhaps the farthest-reaching and speediest structural adjustment performed in the region, ranging from total trade liberalization to strict banking regulation.

Sound public policy, combined with increasing prospects of early accession to the EU, led to a strong growth recovery and an all-out investment boom, both driven exclusively by the private sector. By 1997, the economy was growing at 10 percent p.a., domestic credit to the private sector expanded by the equivalent of just under 20 percent of GDP, and foreign capital inflows to that sector amounted to about 17 percent of GDP. With private saving falling rapidly (to just under 10 percent of GDP in 1997) and accelerating asset inflation, a major balance of payments current account deficit (of 12 percent of GDP) was both unavoidable and difficult to sustain. This unsustainability quickly became an issue when confidence-driven reductions in foreign funding materialized, following the East Asian (1997) and Russia (1998) crises. Interestingly, and from a flow of funds perspective, the Estonian policymakers, with their three-fold objectives of no fiscal deficits, no discretionary monetary policy, and no public debt found themselves almost powerless to influence the saving and investment balance in the private sector.[2]

This links Estonia's economic prospects to a single financing issue: for how long will foreigners continue to finance—either directly or through the domestic banking system—annual private investment levels worth 25 percent or more of GDP, levels that can sustain the fast growth observed during the late transition years? The likely answer will be a mixed one: Estonia's growth (and in particular the growth of its private sector) will have to decelerate (to a more manageable, but still high 6 percent p.a., according to the projections set out in this book), net foreign financing flows will remain forthcoming but more moderate (about 10 percent of GDP in the medium-term), and annual domestic credit by the banking system will slow down (to about 6 percent of GDP).

---

2. As a back-up mechanism to the currency board, the Estonian authorities created a Stabilization Reserve Fund in which fiscal surpluses were accumulated as a potential tool of monetary policy outside that board. But, given the various political and market signaling implications of drawing down the Fund, it has not been actively used.

Latvia and Poland: The Achievement of Broad Balance

Estonia was not alone among transition countries in bringing its fiscal accounts into balance following the drying-up of tax resources in the years immediately after central planning was abandoned. After running major fiscal deficits early in the transition, Latvia and Poland also achieved a degree of financial balance (or close to balance) on their government accounts. More importantly, the strengthening of their fiscal positions was accompanied by fast, but sustainable, private sector growth, in large part financed from abroad, but also funded out of domestic savings. This places those economies on a solid foundation for medium-term growth, even though their structural reform record may still be incomplete.

By the time its banking industry went into crisis in 1995 (eliminating some 40 percent of the industry's assets), *Latvia's* transition-induced recession, hyper-inflation, and (mostly) large fiscal imbalances were all but over. However, the crisis effectively triggered a new policy stance (not least in terms of tight banking regulation) that, from a flow of funds point of view, would eventually put the economy on a more sustainable growth path. A major contraction in the government's financing needs (the fiscal accounts reached a surplus worth about 2 percent of GDP in 1997), allowed for a re-orientation of available funding from the domestic banking system toward the non-financial private sector (about 6 percent of GDP). This was augmented by confidence-driven inflows of foreign finance (equivalent to some 10 percent of GDP in 1997). In turn, that allowed for a domestic investment level of about 20 percent of GDP and a growth path of about 6 percent p.a., supported by a flat gross saving rate and a balance of payments current account deficit of 14 and 6 percent of GDP, respectively.

Latvia's economic development should be sustainable in the medium-term, if the government manages to maintain its fiscal balance. This, together with a gradual increase in private domestic saving and continuing (but not necessarily large) net foreign inflows, should accommodate a 5–6 percent real growth path. This growth path could feasibly be met even if foreign financing of the Latvian private sector turned temporarily (1–2 years) scarce, both because of the possibility of repatriation of the domestic banking system's current accumulation of assets abroad and the government's low level of sovereign indebtedness (and ensuing borrowing capacity).

Two, very distinct sub-periods can be identified in *Poland's* transition flow of funds pattern. The first is 1992–94 when the government absorbed the lion's share of available domestic financing. Contrary to common perception, foreigners provided little funding, either through debt or through FDI (although the Paris Club of official creditors provided substantial sovereign debt forgiveness to Poland in 1991, and rescheduling negotiations with the London Club were not concluded until 1994, something that dampened private investors' confidence in the Polish economy). The second sub-period is 1995–97 when adjustment in the fiscal accounts freed resources for private production financing and significant foreign capital began to enter Poland, fostered by the increasing prospects of EU accession. Thus, comparing the two sub-periods, net flows to the government fell from over 8 percent of GDP in 1992 to about 1 percent in 1997, while those going to the non-financial private sector increased from about 1 to more than 10 percent of GDP. Throughout, the household sector remained a stable, net supplier of funding (on average, providing 5 percent of GDP per year) through the domestic banking system, a remarkable phenomenon given that Polish banks were plagued with solvency problems and eventually needed a government-sponsored recapitalization effort (over 1993–95).

The resilience of household confidence in the domestic banking system, coupled with foreign investor's enthusiasm for Poland's prospects within the EU, will shape the country's post-transition development path as both sectors will still be required to fund the country's private sector growth. That confidence will, in turn, be dependent on the government completing the pending structural reform agenda before joining the EU, notably in terms of privatization and banking sector reform. In other words, it will determine whether Poland replicates the accession experience of Greece (fiscal deficits, low savings, moderate growth, high indebtedness, and EU-financed current account deficits) or of The Republic of Ireland (fiscal prudence, high saving, fast growth, declining public debt, and a relatively minor role for EU transfers).

Lithuania: A Tale of Quasi-Public Sector Deficits

Like other countries in the former Soviet Union, Lithuania experienced both hyperinflation (410 percent in 1993) and recession (-16.2 percent growth in 1993). Thus, in 1994, it implemented a comprehensive stabilization program, anchored on a currency board arrangement. This brought inflation down almost immediately, and laid the ground for growth recovery. That stabilization program was, however, based on the prospects of a rapidly-declining path for the government's fiscal deficit (which in 1993 was worth about 6 percent of GDP). Cut off from money printing, the state was to bring balance to its financial accounts while resorting to borrowing in the meantime, primarily from abroad (and especially from official sources). That balance was to be achieved by tackling, through policy reform, the array of sector-specific structural problems that drained budgetary resources, that is, by tackling the deficit in the so-called "quasi-public sector." This is defined as the aggregate financial position of the general government, the public energy sector, strategic public enterprises, farmers, pensioners, and the other sectors and interest groups that were, in effect, financially dependent on the state. Even in 1996, after successive reforms, that deficit was estimated to be three to four times higher than the posted financial deficit in the general government accounts (and roughly equal to the country's money base).[3]

The reduction in the posted fiscal deficit in the central government accounts did take place (from the previously referenced to -6 percent of GDP in 1993, to -4.7 percent in 1994 and 1995). However, it was based less on a genuine contraction of expenditures (and enhanced revenue collection) than on shifting sector support off the budget and onto state-controlled banks (the government owned shares in all banks). In effect, the initial stabilization effort was financed out of the capital stock of the banking system. This led to a major banking crisis in 1996, and to ensuing changes in the country's political leadership. A renewed effort to tackle sector-specific problems was then initiated, aimed at bringing lasting balance to the fiscal and quasi-public sector accounts, and putting the economy on a more sustainable growth path.

Whether that balance has since been achieved remains unclear and, from a flow of funds perspective, is the key to Lithuania's economic prospects over the next decade. By the end of 1998, the posted fiscal deficit had been almost eliminated and the economy had experienced strong real growth (on the order of 4.4 percent in 1998, in spite of the Russian crisis of that year). More importantly, contrary to the pre-1996 situation, four-fifths of the net foreign flows entering the country to finance its large balance of payment's current account deficit (equivalent to about 10 percent of GDP in 1997) began to go to the fast-growing private productive sector, while only one-fifth of the rest went to the government. For this pattern to be sustainable, two inter-related conditions need to be met: foreigners' confidence in Lithuania's repayment capacity has to remain strong and the real-side

---

3. See M. Giugale, "Lithuania: Macroeconomic Issues and Prospects for a Transition Country at a Junction" (prepared for Lithuania's Agricultural Strategy Workshop, April, Washington, D.C., 1997, processed).

adjustments in the various deficits within the quasi-public sector need to materialize.

Should structural reform adequately address those underlining sectoral deficits, Lithuania's economic prospects are sound. Long-term growth of 6 percent p.a., driven by enhanced and more efficient private investment, would take place; inflation would resemble EU averages; the balance of payment's current account deficit would become manageable (under 3 percent of GDP by 2007); and, the country would not critically depend on foreign financing (its external debt to GDP ratio would increase from 14 to 20 percent through the year 2007). This would likely make Lithuania a prime candidate for EU accession. Alternatively, if continuing deficits on effectively-state-dependent sectors remain and, thus, confidence in the macroeconomic stability of the country is lacking, growth is unlikely to surpass 3 percent p.a. Furthermore, domestic investment as a proportion of GDP will stay virtually constant (at some 21 percent), inflation will not converge to EU standards (hovering around 8 percent p.a.), the current account will stay heavily in deficit (7 to 9 percent of GDP), and the country (especially its private sector) will have to rely heavily on external financing (its total external debt to GDP will more than triple in a decade). Such performance would likely leave Lithuania on the fringe of the EU.

Some Additional Cross-Cutting Issues

While flow of funds patterns have differed substantially across ECA countries during transition, several common issues have arisen. First, *foreign capital dependency*. The need for external financing (initially from official sources) was a common feature of the early years of transition. With collapsing production structures and, hence, tax bases and mounting social needs, it was expected that economies in ECA would require significant injections of foreign capital. The basic flow of funds projection analysis presented in this book shows that the region will likely not be able to generate enough domestic savings to support its own growth over the coming decade either. Financial deficits in either the public sector, the private sector, or both will remain a post-transition feature.

Second, *saving enhancement*. In the light of the external dependency, and the proven volatility of international financial markets, providing a conducive framework for saving will remain a central policy issue in the region. That framework will involve efficient taxation of saving instruments, confidence in the domestic banking systems, pension reform, capital markets development, and, critically, balanced public accounts supporting sound monetary policy.

Third, ***investment sustainability***. Much of the rationale for transition to a market-driven development model was based on the assumption that the private sector would undertake production activities that the state was performing under central planning, but with much higher efficiency, spurred in part by increased private investment. Governments were thus swift in reducing public investment budgets (for example, Russia to about 4 percent of GDP; Kazakhstan, 2 percent), motivated also by the need to implement fiscal adjustments that would anchor price stabilization programs. However, on average, the speed of private investment response did not always match the speed of public divestment. In effect, part of the transition and of its parallel stabilization efforts was financed through the accelerated depletion of the countries' capital stock (outdated as those stocks may have already been), especially in infrastructure. The underlying reason is not difficult to find: it takes longer to establish the frameworks (legal, regulatory, institutional) and the confidence in which private investment can thrive than to stop allocating public funding to investment projects. Whether that speed mismatch proves sustainable in the medium- and long-term remains less clear.

Fourth, ***fiscal dependencies***. Many of the ECA countries have brought discipline to their government accounts, and have curtailed or eliminated fiscal deficits. However, many have not cut the links between the budget and the financing needs of selected sectors of the economy. Excessive depositor compensation, restitution schemes, loan guarantees to state companies, credit allocations, implicit subsidizations through underpricing, and the like remain a feature of the way public business is conducted in the region. While many of those actual and contingent expenditures are usually not shown in the fiscal budget, they will continue to condition that budget's sustainability and may still derail on-going stabilization efforts.

Fifth, ***new financial agents***. The financial systems of all of the countries covered by the book remain very small in comparison to countries in the OECD. The flow of funds analyses reveal that the banking sector has grown the quickest of all the elements of the financial system. But this growth has not taken place smoothly. Virtually all the countries began the transition with the formation of a myriad of small banks. Over time, and under the pressure of tightened regulation and supervision, a consolidation has been taking place in the number of banks. The capital market has also begun to develop. Trading in the equities markets has been spurred by the privatization process. However, relatively few new issues have taken place to finance corporate expansion. Bond markets have been dominated by government issuance but maturities, for the most part, do not exceed five years. Over the next decade the orientation or flows in the financial system are likely going to reflect a strong growth in the activities of non-bank financial institutions, specifically pension funds (in the wake of pension reform in several transition economies), insurance companies, leasing companies, and asset management companies. Hence the structure of flow of funds matrices in transition economies will look significantly different from what they do today by the end of the first decade of the new millenium.

Finally, *disclosure*. Both because of the need to attract foreign capital in order to encourage domestic saving, and to maintain institutional arrangements conducive to fiscal discipline, the ECA countries will have to put in place major initiatives to make country information more available and more transparent. This will have to cover fundamental accounting and auditing standards, public expenditure and revenue information at central and local government levels, financial statements of public enterprises and agencies to upgrade systems of national accounts, industrial surveys, and household data.

Public and Private Sector Disequilibrium

Kazakhstan
Romania

3.

Kazakhstan—Financing Imbalances in a Resource Rich Economy

John Dawson and Stephen Everhart

Kazakhstan's Financial Evolution during Transition: A Flow of Funds View

The transition period in Kazakhstan has involved the whole range of serious problems now associated with the shift from Soviet economic management to a free enterprise system. These include major inflation in the years through 1994 and declines in production that accelerated until 1994, and continued through 1995. In the same period, the economy was undergoing a complete structural reform and institutional change dictated by a future reliance on private markets. Macroeconomic stabilization policy may be said to date from 1993, but adequate data to interpret the macroeconomy can only be obtained from 1994 onwards.

In spite of the troubled times, some domestic investment did take place, and it was financed. This chapter will examine how the saving/investment process operated during the transition period. The broad saving and investment patterns will be examined first, sector surpluses and deficits will be derived from them, and flow of funds data will be used to analyze the borrowing and lending flows. What can be inferred about the private sector financing of investment will then be considered, followed by an investigation of the banking sector in Kazakhstan's financial system.

29

By way of background, gross domestic investment is shown in Figure 3.1, together with domestic and foreign saving. Real investment—as suggested by the percent of GDP data on the lower panel of the figure—declined through 1997. This decline can be related to a number of factors. Foremost would be the low level of profits, which in turn relates to disorganized markets, the slow abandonment of state controls, and the development of arrears among financially stressed firms. Another major factor would be the rapid decline—especially in 1996—of state enterprise investment. In addition, a major industrial reallocation was taking place toward the electricity, fuel, and metallurgy sectors, and away from light industry and agriculture. Investment recovery is shown by the 1997 and 1998 increases in investment as a percent of GDP. In the upper panel, where investment appears in nominal terms, it is elevated in 1994 and 1995 by residual inflation, but its recovery is clear in recent accelerated growth.

A major feature of the saving situation is also revealed in Figure 3.1: the rise in rest-of-world saving, which began as early as 1996. As will be seen, this rise in foreign saving is a key factor in the lending and borrowing pattern that is developing in Kazakhstan. The large gap between investment and rest-of-world saving must be filled by domestic saving, especially in the form of earnings retained by businesses.

In order to derive sector surpluses and deficits, the economy is divided into sectors in Figure 3.2, presenting general government, the private sector,[1] and rest-of-world. The general government and the private sector each contain sector estimates for gross investment and saving; below, on a separate axis, the difference between the two is shown, that is, the deficit for each sector. The overseas or rest-of-world sector—which does no investing in Kazakhstan—has only a saving curve on the upper axis (the Kazakhstan balance of payments current account deficit), which becomes the sector surplus on the lower axis. The basic structure of the Kazakhstan financial system is immediately apparent in the lower set of curves: A large and growing rest-of-world surplus is financing the two domestic deficits, that of the private sector and (especially) the growing deficit of the general government. The next three figures will supplement Figure 3.2 by providing a flow of funds account analysis of each of these three sector

---

1. The private sector is an omnibus residual sector, including provincial and local government, nonbank financial institutions, enterprises (including government enterprises), and households. A separate banking sector is computed but not shown on Figure 3.2.

surpluses/deficits. The ultimate task, after inclusion of the banking sector, will be to understand *how*—that is, by what borrowing and lending means— the rest-of-world surplus ultimately finances these two domestic deficits.

Figure 3.1. Savings and Investments in Kazakhstan

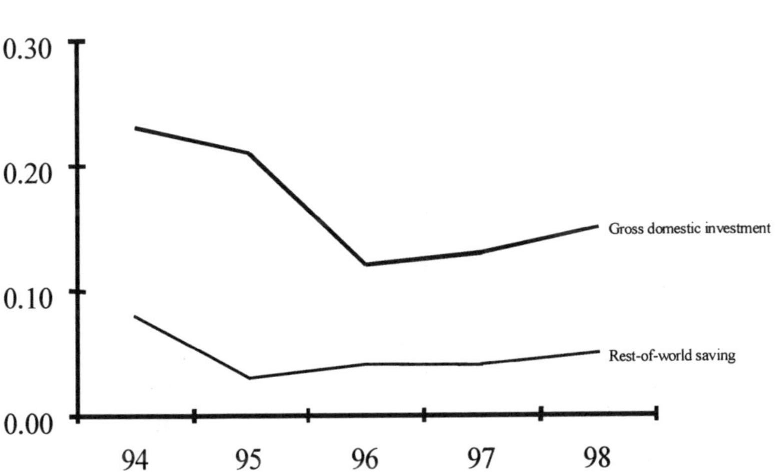

Note: 1998 data are projections.

Figure 3.2 Sector Investment, Saving, and Surplus/Deficit (flow data as percent of current GDP)

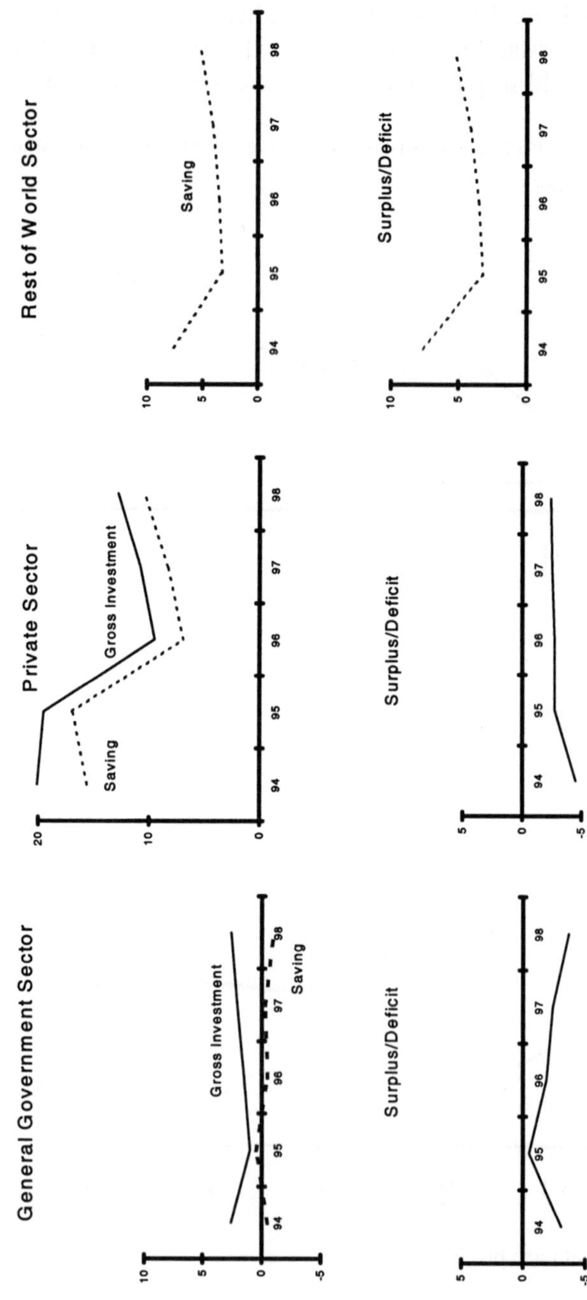

Figure 3.2 illustrates features of the general government finances. With its declining curve for government saving, the figure reflects a key fiscal problem. During transition, Kazakhstan has had great difficulty in establishing a modern fiscal revenue system; as a percent of GDP, revenues declined from 18.8 percent in 1994 to 15.5 percent in 1996, and only now (with major tax reform) have stabilized at about 16 percent.[2] With vigorous restraint, current expenditures have remained in the range of 16–17 percent of GDP since 1995. But the resulting negative government saving, when combined with the financing needed for budgetary gross investment, yields the growing general government deficit on the lower axis of Figure 3.2.

Figure 3.3 is a flow of funds analysis of this deficit. Total borrowing of the general government must finance the moderately growing government lending (at the bottom of Figure 3.3) as well as the deficit, so it is a rapidly growing total, especially in 1997 and (projected) 1998. As Figure 3.3 reveals, the bulk of the borrowing is from the rest-of-world, largely from official sources for projects and pension reform. The additional financing from the banking sector in recent years reflects Treasury bill absorption by the deposit money banks; direct government borrowing from the central bank (NBK) is being phased out.

The balance of payments analysis starts with the rest-of-world saving curve in Figure 3.2—that is, Kazakhstan's current account deficit. This deficit has been rising in recent years, from 3.1 percent of GDP in 1995 to 4.2 percent in 1997. Increased imports of goods and services—primarily reflecting service imports associated with foreign direct investment—have outpaced the generally buoyant exports. From the rest-of-world viewpoint, this deficit is rest-of-world saving, a surplus that becomes rest-of-world net lending to Kazakhstan. A flow of funds analysis of this net lending flow is presented in Figure 3.4.

The rest-of-world net lending at the top of Figure 3.4 is analyzed into the capital inflow—total lending to Kazakhstan—and the net increase in Kazakhstan's international reserves at the bottom of the figure.[3] The total capital inflow is larger than net lending, so the increases in reserves are positive. This reflects the rather comfortable overall balance of payments of recent years. NBK gross international reserves have exceeded three months

---

2. These estimates include substantial amounts of privatization revenue.

3. The curve for international reserves consists of the net international reserves of the NBK, plus the net foreign assets of the deposit money banks. Because of the statistical uncertainty of the latter, the estimates for reserves are subject to large estimation errors.

of imports in both 1996 and 1997. Furthermore, the external debt stock remains modest, at about 20 percent of GDP. The breakdown of total lending to Kazakhstan in Figure 3.4 shows about one-third going to general government in medium- and long-term loans, and almost all of the flow to the private sector consisting of direct foreign investment. The pattern is not complex.

The analysis of the private sector differs somewhat from that for the sectors previously mentioned. This is because the primary focus is on the financing of private investment—that is, the activities of the business portion of the private sector. It will be assumed that all private sector borrowing is for the purpose of investment finance, and that all household saving is equal to, and is used for, financial asset acquisition by the sector. The remainder of private sector saving is assumed to measure the internal business finance used for investment. This picture of the finance of private investment appears in Figure 3.5.

Note that the internal finance curve—after the aberrations of 1994 and 1995—maintains a strong growth trend, parallel to the recovering private investment. This would reflect the recovery and growth of private business profits and retained income. There is, however, a substantial financing gap to be met by borrowing, and the curve for total private borrowing also shows substantial growth in recent years.

Among the borrowing components in Figure 3.5, two are already familiar: the large flow from abroad (from Figure 3.4) and the flow of lending from general government (from Figure 3.3). In addition, there is the credit flow from the banking sector. The banking data, however, are unreliable, especially for 1994—96.[4] The high 1994 flow is a result of directed credits that were part of an attempt by the government to clean up arrears among enterprises, an effort that was unrelated to investment finance. These were also years of turmoil in the banking sector, with many banks closing and large portfolio write-offs. These events help account for the negative levels of bank lending in 1995 and 1996. What is significant in this curve is the low level of lending in 1997 and (projected) 1998, when the data are better. The undeveloped state of the domestic financial system is also indicated by the private sector reliance on foreign borrowing, which is almost entirely direct foreign investment.

---

4. Various data sources disagree; there are little data on the deposit money banks; the errors and omissions item in the banking sector account is large and variable.

Figure 3.3 General Government Finance (flow data as percent of current GDP)

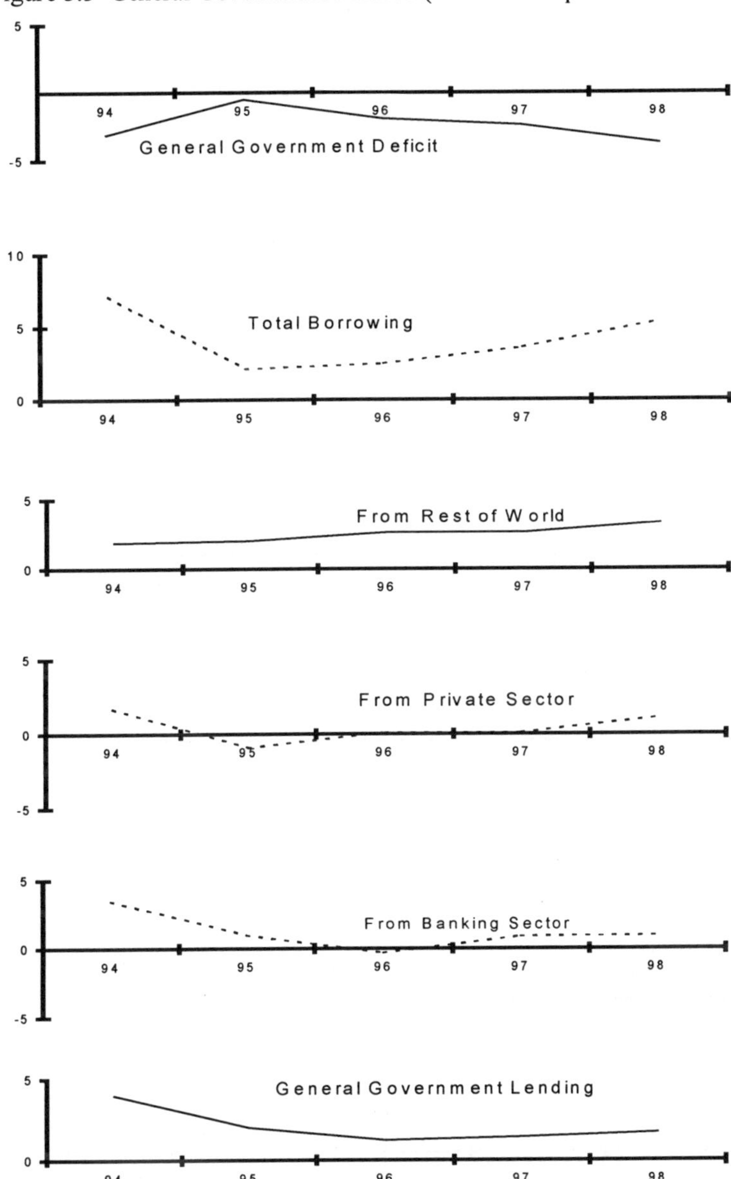

Note: 1998 data are projections

                                                          Financial Systems in Transition

Figure 3.4 Rest-of-the-World Net Lending to Kazakhstan (flow data as percent of current GDP)

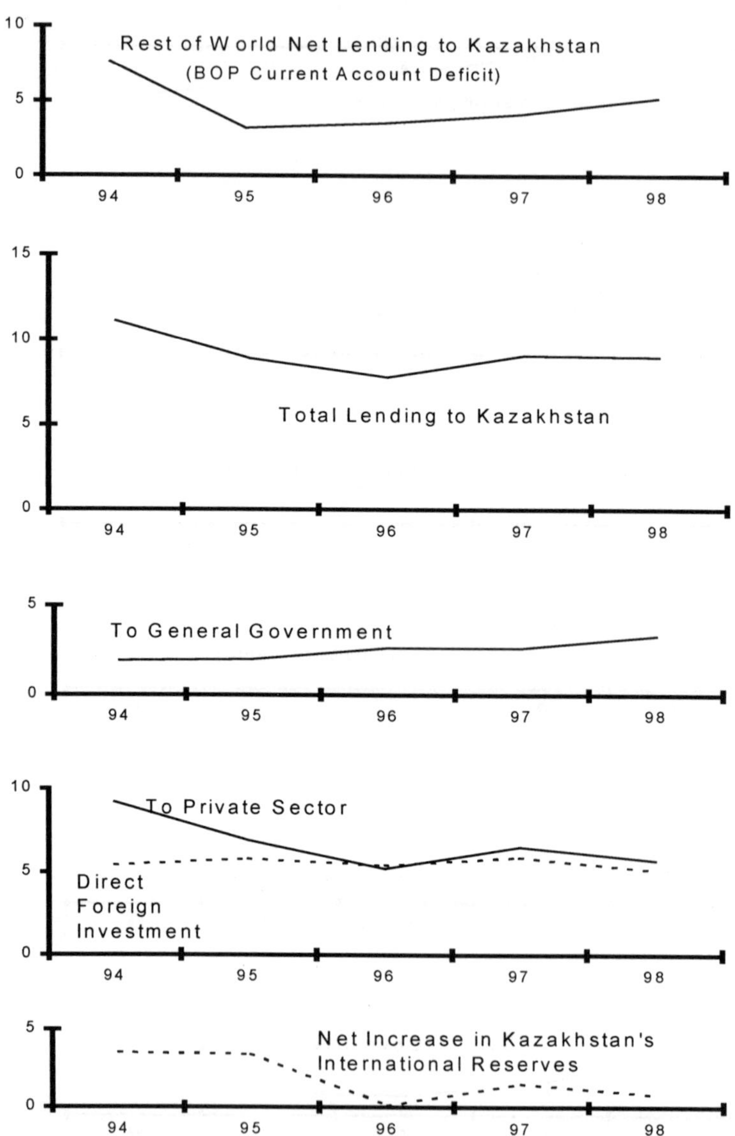

Note: 1998 data are projections.

Figure 3.5 Private Sector Investment and Financing (flow data as percent of current GDP)

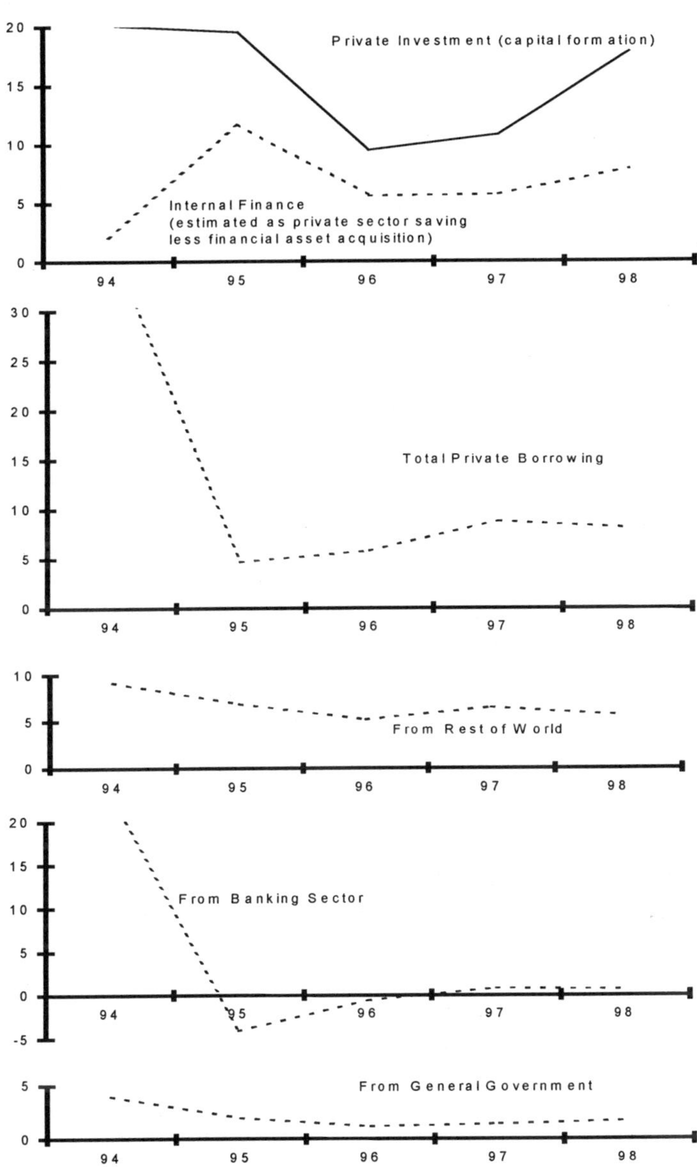

Note: Note: 1998 data are projections

The banking sector is considered next—the monetary authorities and the deposit money banks. The banking sector of the Kazakh economy is small; at year-end 1997, total banking sector capital (including the National Bank) was only US$2.23 billion, and total banking sector assets represented just 9.9 percent of GDP. The Kazakh authorities have encouraged consolidation in the banking sector, and the total number of banks has fallen from 230 in 1994 to 76 today, including 5 state-owned banks, 1 international bank, and 20 banks with a foreign interest. Six banks with negative net capital were closed by the authorities in 1998. It must be understood that during much of the transition period, the banking sector has been undergoing major reform: bank regulation was established, weak banks were closed, nonperforming portfolios were written-off, and credit facilities and monetary policy instruments were developed. Confidence in the system has been weak, and monetary issue has been concentrated in currency. The policy stance of the NBK since 1994 has been one of tight credit, with high interest rates and a close eye toward the new foreign exchange market. There was special concern that plentiful foreign exchange inflows would lead to excessive monetary growth.

Up to this point, however, the banks could hardly be said to be engaged in the usual business of banking. Household lending is small. Small business lending is in its infancy. As noted, bank lending to the entire private sector has been very small in recent years. Bank foreign borrowing has met with limited success. In May of 1998, Kazkommertsbank launched a successful Eurobond offering: a three-year, 11.25 percent issue. Other banks' plan to issue Eurobonds have been put on hold because of the mid-1998 Russian crisis. The primary business of the commercial banking sector is to buy Kazakh Treasury offerings.

Figure 3.6 surveys banking sector activity during the transition period. It first presents the flows in the three parts of the sector portfolio—claims on the foreign sector, the general government, and the private sector. At the bottom of the figure is the liability flow in broad money. This portfolio and broad money are normally the two equal sides of the banking sector account, but in this case the discrepancy is large in 1995 and 1996. It can be concluded that the charts for broad money and claims on general government are reliable; the errors in foreign claims and private credit relate to uncertainty with regard to the data for deposit money banks.

Figure 3.6 Banking Sector Portfolio Increases (flow data as percent of current GDP)

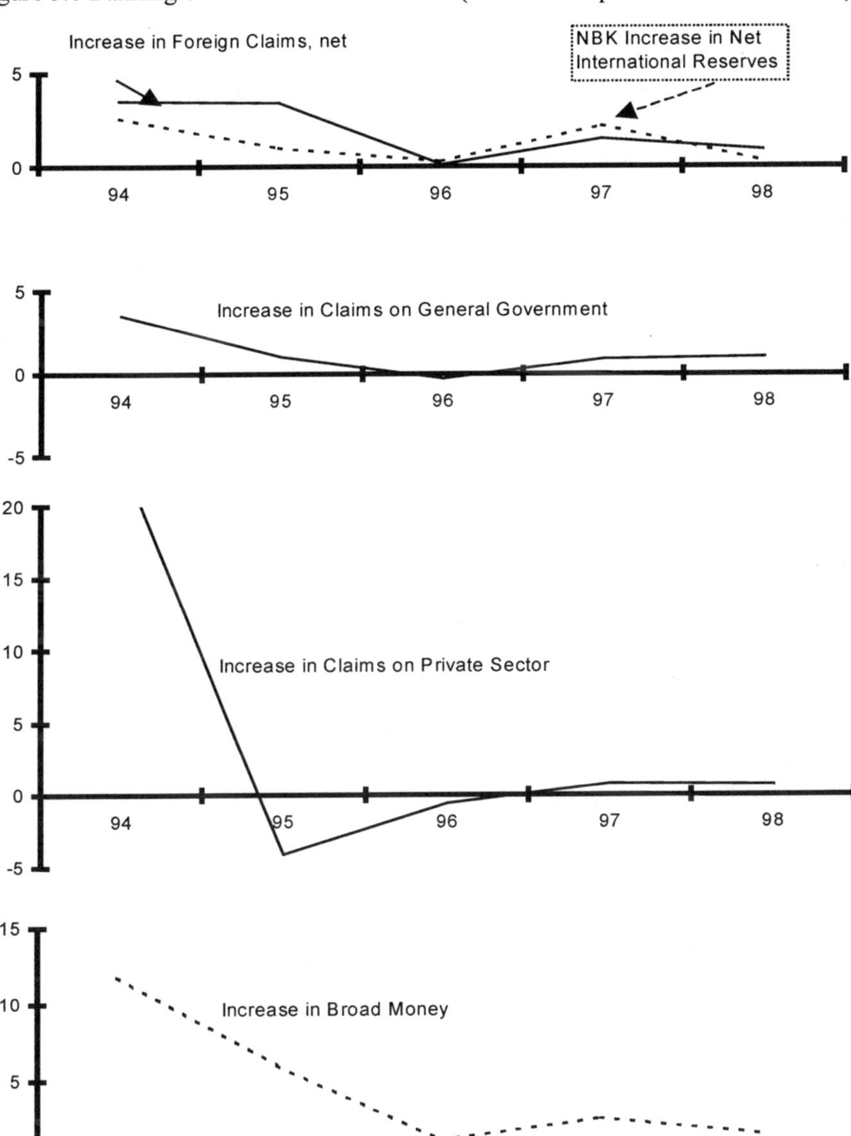

Note: 1998 data are projections

In Figure 3.6 it is possible to see some correlation between international reserve movements in the top curve and the monetary issue. And the portfolio movements in 1996–98 provide a reasonable explanation of the broad money curve. On the whole, the growth in broad money has been modest. With the general economic recovery of 1997, confidence in the banking system seems to have improved, and there is evidence of the beginnings of bank credit demand. As noted, however, the role of the banking system as a commercial lender is barely under way.

Although the flows are not large, the banking sector can be seen in its intermediary role in 1997. In that year, the private sector acquired some 43 billion *tenge* in currency, and deposits thus advanced funds to the banking system. As Figure 3.6 shows, the banking system advanced funds, primarily to the rest-of-world through increased reserves, but also to the general government and private sectors. Thus, one pattern of intermediation was from the private sector to the government through the banking system, and once again back to the private sector through government lending. If private bank credit were to expand, it would reflect intermediation directed back to the private sector.

The sector accounts discussed above can be placed in matrix form for a given year, as in Table 3.1, to show the horizontal balances of the borrowing and lending flows, as well as the vertical sector account balances. With each of the flows expressed as a percent of current GDP, Table 3.1 reveals the simple financial flow structure of the economy that was seen above. The surplus/deficit line shows the rest-of-world surplus of 4.0 percent of GDP financing the government's and private sector deficits of -2.4 percent and -2.5 percent of GDP, respectively. Further down, the government debt issue of 3.6 percent of GDP is seen to be primarily absorbed by the rest-of-world at 2.6 percent. Again, the private sector borrowing of 8.8 percent of GDP is also primarily provided by the rest-of-world at 6.5 percent. The small lending role of the banking sector is noteworthy, with a modest monetary expansion of 2.5 percent of GDP.

Table 3.1. Flow of Funds Matrix for Kazakhstan, 1997 (Actuals as percent of current GDP)[a]

	General government		Banking sector		Private sector		Rest of world		Total	
	U	S	U	S	U	S	U	S	U	S
Investment	2.1		—		10.8				12.9	
Saving		-0.3[b]		0.9		8.3		4.0		12.9
Surplus/deficit (net lending/borrowing)	-2.4		0.9		-2.5		4.0		—	

	General government		Banking sector		Private sector		Rest of world		Total	
	ΔFin. Assets	ΔFin. Liab.	ΔFin. Assets	ΔFin. Liab.	ΔFin. Assets	ΔFin. Liab.	ΔFin. Assets	ΔFin. Liab.	ΔFin. Assets	ΔFin. Liab.
ΔForeign claims, net			1.5					1.5	1.5	1.5
ΔGeneral gov't debt		3.6	0.9		0.0		2.6		3.6	3.6
ΔPrivate credit	1.4		0.8			8.8	6.5		8.8	8.8
ΔMoney + quasi money				2.5	2.5				2.5	2.5
ΔMisc. & Discrep.		0.2		-0.2		-3.6	-3.6		-3.6	-3.6
Total	3.5	3.5	3.2	3.2	13.4	13.4	5.5	5.5	25.7	25.7

Note: GDP = 1,702 billion tenge.

a. Components may not add to totals because of rounding.

b. Includes privatization receipts.

Kazakhstan's Financial System and Economic Policy over the Coming Decade

Kazakhstan faced major macroeconomic hurdles in the autumn of 1998. Close trading links with the fragile Russian economy, a tenuous macroeconomic situation, and growth prospects heavily linked to oil made Kazakhstan highly vulnerable. Domestic financial markets have witnessed increasing volatility. The spread on Kazakh Eurobonds moved from 404 basic points on 17 August, 1998 (the date of the announced devaluation of the Russian ruble) to 1,868 basic points as of 21 September 1998 (for comparison, on that day, Poland's spread stood at 125 bp, Ukraine's at 4,976 basic points, and Russia's at 6,104 basic points). Although the official exchange rate remained at 79–80 to the U.S. dollar, exchange bureaus reported trades approaching 100.

September 1998 could prove to be a watershed month in recent Kazakh economic history. On 16 September, Standard & Poors (S&P) reduced its credit rating to B-plus from BB-minus, and the long-term local currency rating to BB-minus from BB-plus. This can be attributed to the fact that Russia accounts for nearly a third of Kazakhstan's exports and 42 percent of its imports. Not surprisingly, severe ruble problems were acknowledged by Kazakh First Deputy Prime Minister Uraz Jandosov on 7 September, 1998, when he warned, "our enterprises and citizens can face a rather risky situation when accepting rubles as payments…we recommend not accepting rubles as payments for goods exported to Russia, or exchanging tenge for rubles." The NBK announced on 11 September, 1998 that it planned to reduce the limit of currency holdings for commercial banks from 50 percent to 25 percent, and lower the limit for holdings in a single currency from 30 percent to 15 percent. The central bank claimed the move was designed to "reduce currency risks," but it could be argued that the action was aimed at supporting the tenge, and boost demand for tenge-denominated Treasury bills, which had lagged, leading the Ministry of Finance to cancel its three-month Treasury bill auction on 9 September for the second time in as many weeks. The prospects for Eurobond issuance appeared dim as well. Privatization revenues were running at one-third the expected level, and budget revenues were 10–15 percent behind projections.

The key to the economic health of Kazakhstan over the longer term thus revolves around the Kazakh's ability to extract their vast oil resources and transport crude oil across their land-locked borders. Kazakhstan is largely dependent on Russia's pipeline system, allowing it to export no more than 3.5 million tonnes of oil annually to the West, and virtually the same amount to the CIS. Future growth in exports will largely come from the proposed 2,000-mile pipeline linking Kazakhstan to western China. Kazakhstan projects that the pipeline will allow transportation of 20 million tonnes daily (400,000 barrels) when it is fully operational. This compares with total production expected in 1998 of 28 million tonnes (560,000 barrels) per day. Considerable speculation and debate is focused on the pipeline's completion date. Estimates range from 2001 to 2005.

Thus, any comparative longer-term forecasts of the Kazakh economy should consider two scenarios: first, that the effects of the Russian contagion are short-lived, and the Kazakh pipeline comes online as planned, or second, that the region experiences lingering restrictions in access to capital inflows, slower growth, and a delay in pipeline completion and revenues.

To explore the implications of the two contrasting views, this section develops two projection scenarios for Kazakhstan through the year 2006. The first, representing the impact of moderate contagion and no pipeline delays, projects an economy growing in real terms at 2 percent yearly until 2000, and 3 percent thereafter. The second view projects the impact of more vigorous contagion, with slower growth of 1.0 percent until 2000, and only 1.5 percent thereafter. The key factors affecting the growth rates are the intensity of the investment effort, the timing of the delivery of the pipeline, and the availability of capital from abroad. A critical question to be examined is how the Kazakh financial system would react to a rationing of foreign capital inflow.

The two projections are derived from a World Bank RMSM-X type model, applied to Kazakhstan. This model begins with assumed growth rates for major economic variables such as production, investment, and exports. These growth rates are applied to a recent historical base year, carrying the national accounts into the future. Such projections of the government budget, the balance of payments, and the monetary accounts, together with the basic national product accounts, permit the derivation of the private sector and its finances. This, in turn, allows for an examination of the consistency of patterns of saving, investment, and finance over the period of the projection.

A Moderate-Growth Projection (Base Case)

The moderate-growth scenario is summarized in Table 3.2. The GDP growth rate is projected to reach 3 percent yearly by the turn of the century, with inflation projected to decline to 4.5 percent by the end of the forecast period. A key factor in setting the 3 percent growth rate is the similar growth rate of gross domestic investment leading up to pipeline completion, a pace that moves investment from 13 to 15 percent of GDP, then declines after 2002. This moderate investment boom is seen to be closely tied to pipeline activity and mineral development, financed by direct foreign investment. In other areas, investment advances only slowly. Several elements suggest a lagging development of general business confidence: the precarious trade situation with Russia, the delays in privatization and structural reform, and the lack of a well-developed banking sector. In these circumstances the productivity improvements essential for the modernization of Kazakhstan's economy will not appear quickly. This is presented in the projection by a quite gradual decline in the incremental capital output ratio (ICOR) over the forecast period.

The projection assumes a continuation of the vigorous growth in real exports through 1998, tapering off until 2001, when the pipeline is scheduled to come online, then slowly declining over the balance of the forecast period. Modest economic growth, coupled with favorable growth in exports, yields a rise in the ratio of exports to GDP from 32 percent to almost 38 percent over the forecast period. Imports are expected to remain at their current levels of about 36 percent of GDP, a somewhat optimistic projection considering the fall in the Russian ruble and Russia's dominance in the trade of Kazakhstan. The current account deficit remains high, at about 7 percent of GDP, during the investment boom, but moderates to 5 percent as pipeline exports develop.

The fiscal policy expressed in the projection is moderately tight—current expenditures remain near the present level of 21 percent of GDP. The projection assumes slow but steady progress in the establishment of a viable tax regime, with current revenue rising from 18.0 percent to 19.7 percent of GDP, about enough to offset the decline in privatization receipts. Government saving—if we add in the privatization receipts (capital revenues)—remains steadily near zero throughout the projection. The projection has, however, permitted a substantial rise in government investment from the recent 2 percent of GDP up to 5 percent during the boom years, followed by a decline. The result is a government deficit that rises to 8.0 percent of GDP by 2001, but falls thereafter to 5.4 percent.

Table 3.2 Base Case (percent; US$ million)

Indicator	Estimated 1997	1998	1999	2000	2001	Projected 2002	2003	2004	2005	2006
Real annual growth rates										
GDP at market prices	1.5	2.0	2.0	2.0	3.0	3.0	3.0	3.0	3.0	3.0
Consumption per capita	0.4	4.3	-0.1	-0.7	-1.2	1.5	5.3	1.9	2.5	3.8
Debt outstanding and disbursed (DOD)	3290	4456	4835	5451	6490	7023	7385	7732	8235	9122
DOD/GDP	14.3	18.1	18.8	20.4	23.1	23.8	23.6	23.4	23.6	24.8
Debt service (US$ millions)	582	588	980	734	763	884	878	896	945	1051
Debt service/XGS	7.7	7.9	12.0	8.3	7.7	8.3	7.7	7.3	7.1	7.5
Debt service/GDP	2.5	2.4	3.8	2.7	2.7	3.0	2.8	2.7	2.7	2.9
National accounts: percent of GDP										
Gross domestic investment	13.8	13.7	13.7	14.8	14.9	15.0	12.0	12.1	12.2	12.2
Gross domestic fixed investment	12.8	12.7	12.8	13.8	13.9	14.0	11.0	11.1	11.1	11.2
Gross domestic savings	9.9	8.0	9.7	11.7	13.9	14.7	12.8	13.3	13.4	12.9
Gross national savings	13.8	13.7	13.7	14.8	14.9	15.0	12.0	12.1	12.2	12.2
Government investment	2.0	3.9	4.9	5.4	5.0	4.5	3.5	3.5	3.7	3.8
Government savings	-3.5	-2.4	-2.5	-2.5	-3.0	-1.8	-2.0	-1.9	-1.7	-1.6
Private investment[a]	11.8	9.8	8.8	9.4	9.9	10.5	8.5	8.6	8.4	8.4
Private savings	11.9	8.3	9.1	10.5	12.6	11.7	9.7	9.9	9.5	8.7
ICOR[b]	7.3	7.0	7.0	7.0	5.0	5.0	5.0	4.0	4.0	4.0
General govt accounts: percent of GDP										
Total revenues	21.7	18.0	21.0	18.5	20.7	21.0	20.8	20.8	21.0	19.7
Current expenditures	21.6	20.9	21.0	21.1	21.5	20.8	21.0	21.1	21.2	21.3
Capital revenues	3.5	2.7	2.5	2.3	2.1	1.9	1.8	1.7	1.5	1.4
Capital expenditures	3.4	5.0	5.6	5.9	5.3	4.7	3.7	3.7	3.9	3.9
Investment	2.0	3.9	4.9	5.4	5.0	4.5	3.5	3.5	3.7	3.8
Overall balance (- = deficit)	-5.5	-6.3	-7.4	-8.0	-8.0	-6.3	-5.5	-5.5	-5.4	-5.4
External accounts										
Total export volume, annual growth rate (percent)	9.6	7.0	5.3	5.4	10.9	5.8	6.4	6.2	5.6	3.7
Export/GDP (percent)	32.6	30.2	31.5	32.7	34.9	35.7	36.4	37.2	37.8	37.8
Total import volume, annual growth rate	10.5	11.2	0.9	2.6	2.9	3.2	3.1	4.6	5.1	5.2
Import/GDP	36.5	35.9	35.5	35.8	35.9	36.0	35.6	36.0	36.5	37.1
Current account/GDP	-5.4	-7.8	-7.1	-6.9	-5.3	-5.1	-4.3	-4.2	-4.3	-5.1
Inflation rate (period average)	17.8	9.4	7.0	5.0	5.0	5.0	5.0	4.5	4.5	4.5

a. Includes changes in stocks. b. Fixed investment only.

The financing of the private sector will now be analyzed with the help of Table 3.3. It will be convenient to consider the projection in two phases: the modest investment boom (1998–2002) and the aftermath of the pipeline completion (2002–06). In phase one, private investment expands moderately, from 185 to 271 billion tenge, peaking at 10.5 percent of GDP in 2002. Thereafter it rises only very gradually, declining as a percentage of GDP. The two phases present sharply contrasting patterns of finance.

Table 3.3. Moderate Growth Projection (Base Case), Private Sector Finance

	1998	2002	2006
Private investment (billions of tenge)	185	271	294
Financing			
Internal finance[a]	41	151	110
Percent internal	22	56	37
Borrowing from abroad	144	92	136
Direct foreign investment	100	105	114
Medium and long term	44	-13	22
Bank borrowing	-5	23	44
Private investment (percent of current GDP)	9.8	10.5	8.4
Financing			
Internal finance[a]	2.2	5.8	3.2
Borrowing from abroad	7.6	3.6	3.9
Direct foreign investment	5.3	4.1	3.3
Medium and long term	2.3	-0.5	0.6
Bank Borrowing	-0.3	0.9	1.3

a. Net of capital transfers to government. As a result components may not add up to total.

Private saving rises more rapidly than private investment between 1998 and 2002, a consequence of the drop in rest-of-world saving from 7.8 percent of GDP to 5.1 percent. And when private saving is translated into an estimate of private internal finance, the increase over this period is rapid, from 22 percent of investment to 56 percent (see Table 3.3). Internal finance is supplemented heavily by foreign borrowing in this period, with 1998 the peak year. Although foreign borrowing then declines somewhat, it remains the major supplement to internal finance. In short, the investment boom is financed by rising private saving and a heavy foreign capital inflow.

In the years from 2002 to 2006, private investment falls as a share of GDP from 10.5 percent to 8.4 percent. Internal finance falls with the investment, while borrowing from abroad grows enough to maintain its GDP share, primarily in the form of direct foreign investment. As Table 3.3 illustrates, however, there is an additional financing need, and this need is met by a doubling of bank borrowing over these years. The projection assumes that after 2002 the banking sector will be restored to health and will be able to meet growing credit demands.

The banking sector provides little lending in the early years of the projection: the stock of bank credit rises only from 6.0 percent of GDP to 7.7 percent in the years to 2002. Thereafter, the lending flow is about 2 percent of GDP annually, and by 2006 the stock of bank credit has risen to 13.2 percent of GDP. These proportions demonstrate the small role played by the banking sector. The economy's foreign borrowing, of course, raises the stock of foreign debt somewhat more, to a total of about 25 percent of GDP.

Overall, this moderate growth projection pictures the stresses of the "pipeline boom" as under reasonable control by 2006. The balance of payments' current account deficit, which rises to 7 percent of GDP, returns to the 5 percent level. Similarly, the government deficit, which rises to 8 percent is brought back to 5 percent of GDP. What is assumed here is the availability of a reliably large inflow of foreign capital. To question this assumption, one must move to the alternative projection, with slower growth and restrained capital inflow.

A Lower Growth Projection (Alternative Case)

The alternative projection is based on a scenario in which the current economic situation in Russia would have considerable and persistent impact on Kazakhstan. While no attempt has been made to model the present trade and foreign exchange distress, this projection does assume several major contagion effects in the coming years. The first is a dampening in the growth of trade. This is, of course, indicated by the situation in Russia. Second, it is assumed that business confidence will be shaken, and private investment will fall from roughly 9 percent of GDP to 3 to 5 percent. Completion of the pipeline is delayed to 2003. Finally, the current massive capital inflow will be constrained, and will fall steadily to less than half its recent flow. These forces are expected to reduce the GDP growth rate of 3 percent in the base projection to 1.5 percent. Table 3.4 outlines this alternative, lower-growth projection.

Table 3.4 Delayed Pipeline Scenario, Low Investment, Russia continues slide (percent; US$ million)

Indicator	Estimated 1997	Projected 1998	1999	2000	2001	2002	2003	2004	2005	2006
Real annual growth rates										
GDP at market prices	1.5	0.5	1.0	1.0	1.5	1.5	1.5	1.5	1.5	1.5
Consumption per capita	5.8	0.1	-0.3	-2.5	0.6	0.4	-1.5	0.2	1.3	1.4
Debt outstanding and disbursed (DOD)	2330	3546	4116	4614	5595	6122	6298	6219	6175	6156
DOD/GDP	10.1	14.6	16.4	17.8	20.9	22.1	21.8	20.7	19.7	18.9
Debt service (US$ millions)	582	511	908	676	576	699	716	704	697	727
Debt service/XGS	7.7	6.8	11.1	7.7	6.2	7.2	6.6	6.1	5.7	5.7
Debt service/GDP	2.5	2.1	3.6	2.6	2.2	2.5	2.5	2.3	2.2	2.2
National accounts: percent of GDP										
Gross domestic investment	4.9	7.8	6.8	8.9	8.2	8.3	8.3	8.3	8.4	8.4
Gross domestic fixed investment	3.9	6.8	5.9	7.9	7.2	7.3	7.3	7.3	7.4	7.4
Gross domestic savings	3.5	3.7	4.9	7.9	8.5	9.2	11.0	11.7	11.7	11.7
Gross national savings	2.0	1.8	2.4	4.9	5.1	5.5	7.1	7.7	7.6	7.7
Government investment	2.0	3.9	4.9	5.4	5.0	4.5	3.5	3.5	3.8	3.8
Government savings	-3.6	-3.5	-3.6	-3.8	-4.3	-2.6	-2.4	-2.5	-2.4	-2.4
Private investment[a]	2.9	3.9	2.0	3.4	3.2	3.8	4.8	4.8	4.6	4.6
Private savings	5.6	5.3	6.0	8.7	9.4	8.2	9.5	10.2	10.1	10.0
General govt accounts: percent of GDP										
Total revenues	21.5	20.2	20.0	19.9	19.7	19.5	19.9	19.8	19.9	20.1
Current expenditures	21.6	20.9	21.1	21.3	21.7	20.1	20.4	20.5	20.6	20.8
Capital revenues	3.5	2.7	2.5	2.4	2.2	2.1	1.9	1.8	1.7	1.6
Capital expenditures	3.4	5.0	5.6	5.9	5.3	4.7	3.7	3.7	3.9	3.9
Investment	2.0	3.9	4.9	5.4	5.0	4.5	3.5	3.5	3.8	3.8
Overall balance (- = deficit)	-3.5	-5.7	-6.7	-7.3	-7.3	-5.3	-4.2	-4.4	-4.6	-4.7
External accounts										
Total export volume, annual growth rate (percent)	9.6	7.0	5.3	5.4	3.9	3.1	9.9	5.3	3.3	3.3
Export/GDP (percent)	32.6	30.7	32.3	33.8	34.6	35.0	37.2	38.2	38.6	39.0
Total import volume, annual growth rate	3.2	14.1	-0.6	2.2	0.0	0.7	3.8	3.1	3.3	3.4
Import/GDP	34.0	34.8	34.2	34.8	34.3	34.0	34.5	34.9	35.3	35.8
Current account/GDP	-2.9	-6.0	-4.5	-3.9	-3.1	-2.7	-1.2	-0.7	-0.7	-0.8
Inflation rate (period average)	17.8	9.4	7.0	5.0	5.0	5.0	5.0	4.5	4.5	5.0

a. Includes changes in stocks.

In this projection—without the investment boom—the balance of payments current deficit does not rise, but remains at 3 to 4 percent of GDP until 2002, and then declines in the second half of the decade to about 1 percent. In addition to the general slide in imports that accompanies slower growth, the lessened business confidence and reduced availability of foreign finance are assumed to substantially reduce imports of capital goods and services. Although exports suffer in the middle years, they are restored with the completion of the pipeline. The resulting reduction in the current account deficit in the later years is a companion of both reduced capital inflow and—as rest-of-world saving declines—increased domestic saving (these topics will be treated later).

The fiscal picture in the alternative projection is changed in two ways. First, although the authorities maintain the same tight control over current expenditures, at about 21 percent of GDP, the more sluggish economic growth adversely affects revenues. Including capital revenues, they remain at about 20 percent of GDP throughout the decade. Government investment is still permitted to grow, as in the base case. The overall deficit is thus about 1 percent of GDP higher—rising to 9 rather than 8 percent of GDP—in the alternative projection. The second contrast is seen in financing. It has been assumed that the rationing of capital from abroad will apply to government as well as private borrowing. This would mean that government borrowing from abroad, which in 2001 is more than half of government borrowing—4.1 percent out of 7.3 percent of GDP—would fall to 1.2 percent of 4.7 percent of GDP. As a consequence, the government would continue its reliance—about 1.5 percent of GDP—on borrowing from the banking sector.

The financial situation faced by the private sector is outlined in Table 3.5. First, it is seen that private investment has fallen sharply in 1998, both absolutely and as a percentage of GDP, and remains low (despite some growth) to the end of the projection period. At the start, internal finance from business saving is negligible—the crude estimate for 1998 reads negative—and the financing is entirely composed of borrowing from abroad. Over the decade, internal finance becomes substantial, financing 53 percent of the rising investment in 2002 and 43 percent in 2006. Meanwhile, borrowing from abroad drops sharply after 1998 and remains small. The projection assumes that direct foreign investment, having been reduced in 1998 to half its 1997 figure, will be maintained at this level. So the reduction in private foreign borrowing over the projection must be absorbed by medium- and long-term borrowing. The negative figures in this "other" foreign borrowing for 2002 and 2006 indicate a net repayment of such debt to foreigners. Finally, it should be noted that the necessary additional financing between 2002 and 2006 comes from increased bank borrowing, which rises to 2.1 percent of GDP.

Table 3.5. Lower Growth Projection (Alternative Case), Private Sector Finance

	1998	2002	2006
Private investment (billions of tenge)	72	91	143
Financing			
Internal finance[a]	-28	48	61
Percent internal	-39	53	43
Borrowing from abroad	91	19	12
Direct foreign investment	46	44	47
Medium and long term	45	-25	-35
Bank borrowing	-11	19	65
Private investment (percent of current GDP)	3.9	3.8	4.6
Financing			
Internal finance[a]	-1.5	2.0	2.0
Borrowing from abroad	4.9	0.8	0.4
Direct foreign investment	2.5	1.8	1.5
Medium and long term	2.4	-1.0	-1.1
Bank Borrowing	-0.6	0.8	2.1

a. Net of capital transfers to government. As a result, components may not add up to total.

It is useful to offer an interpretation of the pattern of private sector finance described above. First, in 1998 the high rest-of-world saving (6.0 percent of GDP) leads to a low private sector saving rate (5.3 percent of GDP). As foreign saving declines (with the decline in imports) to 1.0 percent of GDP over the projection, the private savings rate increases correspondingly. This is an important cause of the rise in internal finance and can be assumed to take the form of retained business earnings. Nevertheless, the scarcity of such business saving until 2002 must be seen as a cause of the weak investment. Furthermore, in the later years, when foreign debt must be repaid, business saving is the source of funds to do so, and the funds used for debt repayment are not available to finance real investment. Most central, of course, is the impact on investment of the decline in the general availability of capital from abroad, which is portrayed in the alternative projection.

A major restriction in the foreign capital inflow will undoubtedly depress the Kazakh economy. It would also launch a search for domestic financing alternatives. The option presented in the alternative projection is a more rapid expansion of the banking sector. By 2006, the banking sector is growing at 4.0 percent of GDP annually (double that in the base case), with the stock of bank credit at 18 percent of GDP and the quantity of broad money at 28 percent of GDP. The acceleration is seen to be caused partly by government demand for borrowing, which rises to 2.1 percent of GDP as its foreign sources dry up, and partly by private demand, which increases to the 1.9 percent of GDP needed to finance even limited growth in investment (Table 3.5). The projection assumes that the banks would meet each of these needs, envisioning a major new role for the banking sector in the financing of investment.

Conclusions

Two contrasting pictures of investment finance have been presented in the two projection scenarios. If the economy remains buoyant (despite its current difficulties), if the pipeline is brought to completion, and if the foreign capital inflow continues freely over the years to come, a 3 percent annual growth in private investment is projected. In addition to foreign borrowing, more than half of this total would be financed by internal business finance, supplemented by growing bank borrowing (Table 3.3). If depression prevails, however, pipeline completion is deferred, and the inflow of foreign capital is restricted, a much-reduced growth rate for private investment is foreseen, some 1.5 percent annually after a sharp early fall. About 80 percent of this reduced volume of investment would be financed domestically through internal finance, supplemented with growing bank borrowing (Table 3.5). In this alternative case, financing difficulties squeeze investment.

Major elements of private sector financing may not be greatly influenced by Kazakhstan's policies. These elements would probably include the general availability of foreign capital and the volume of internally generated business saving, which depends primarily on the level of enterprise profits. But bank finance is another matter. Both projections show a major need for added private sector bank borrowing after 2002. This is especially critical in the alternative scenario, where reduced foreign borrowing must be replaced domestically. Yet, as noted above, regular bank lending to private business is just beginning in Kazakhstan. A rapid development of the banking sector is needed so that it will be available to meet both long- and short-term business credit needs. The development of this business lending function by the banks may well require policy attention. It is the key policy implication of this analysis.

4.

Romania—Dealing with the Twin Deficit

Stephen J. Peachey

This chapter looks at recent Romanian experience in light of the slow pace of fundamental reform of the state sector, but the remarkable resilience of private sector saving behavior. The chapter concludes that maintaining confidence in the banking system is vital to the retention of Romania's domestic capacity to finance stronger investment-led growth. The recently instituted deposit insurance scheme and continued tight banking supervision are therefore vital to financial and economic stability.

Background

The Romanian economy has had a difficult transition; there has been little political will to push forward with effective reform of the large state enterprise sector. In only two of the past five years has the GDP deflator risen by less than 100 percent, and after a period of positive real growth between 1993 and 1996, there have been two years of sharp retrenchment. Despite all this, the private sector has grown to account for almost 60 percent of GDP. In effect, this represents real stability of private sector activity against a background of real declines in state sector activity averaging roughly 5–6 percent annually since 1990. The nonbank/ nongovernmental sector (NBNGS)—which is broadly equivalent to the private sector—has managed to maintain reasonable savings rates and has generally kept investment at around 15–20 percent of GDP. It has also managed, against a background of generally negative real deposit rates, to slowly rebuild its claims on the banking sector after the hyperinflationary demonetization of the early 1990s. Indeed, in dollar terms, NBNGS deposits are now back at pre-reform levels.

This rebuilding of deposit balances—and the equally significant reduction in reliance on cash—points to a fundamental grasp of the realities of the market economy paradigm by the private sector. The average Romanian household and entrepreneur have maintained real savings to provide some protection against an uncertain macroeconomic environment. Moreover, they also perceive that in a highly inflationary world it is preferable to hold savings as a bank deposit rather than as cash in hand, but this belief rests on the maintenance of confidence in the banking system.

Private sector prudence was demonstrated in 1997 when the shock therapy program severely curtailed the activity of the large state enterprises that serve as the anchor for much private activity. The private sector response was to cut outlays (particularly on durables) and to restore the real value of deposits as quickly as possible. Thus the ratio of deposits to GDP fell only slightly, reaching 15 percent in mid-1997 (from 17 percent in mid-1996), although inflation hit almost 300 percent in 1997 and real deposit rates averaged -60 percent. Tentative estimates for 1998 suggest all the lost ground has been recovered.

The focus of this chapter is to illustrate the importance of the banking sector as a channel for NBNGS savings. A number of questions are addressed. To what degree does the banking sector return deposited funds to the productive economy? To what extent does the government sector absorb funds from the private economy? And how significant is the foreign financing of NBNGS investment?

The Macroeconomic Base Case

The macroeconomic base case underpinning the flow of funds projections in this paper are based on a scenario run on the World Bank's RMSM-X model for Romania during the preparation of the 1998–99 World Bank Country Economic Memorandum. This scenario envisages the policy induced recession that started in 1997 continuing through until 2000 before a return to quite strong positive real growth (+4.5 percent year-on-year) by 2002. The dis-inflationary trend re-established in 1998 is also assumed to continue, with the annual rise in the GDP deflator falling to 10 percent by 2002.

Underpinning stronger growth is a marked rise in public, and later on private, investment, neither fully covered by increased saving and as a result the current account deficit widens from 6–7 percent of GDP in 1996–97 to over 13 percent by 2002. One other feature of this scenario is that Government is assumed to have to start repaying external debt from 2000 onwards, leaving private capital inflows to take up the strain of financing the enlarged current deficit. Other macroeconomic characteristics of this scenario are shown in Table 4.1

Table 4.1. Romania: Key Economic Data

	1995	1996	1997	1998	1999	2000	2001	2002
Real GDP g owth (percent y-on-y)	7.1	4.1	-6.6	-4.0	-3.0	0.0	3.0	4.5
GDP deflator	46.6	33.2	146.7	41.3	45.0	25.0	15.0	10.0
Current deficit (percent of GDP)	-4.0	-6.9	-6.6	-7.9	-7.9	-7.9	-10.0	-13.1
Government current deficit (percent of GDP)	-0.1	n/a	n/a	n/a	n/a	n/a	n/a	n/a
NBNGS financing gap (percent of GDP)	-4.5	-3.1	1.8	-2.9	-3.9	-4.4	-7.3	-11.1
Current savings	13.5	n/a	n/a	n/a	n/a	n/a	n/a	n/a
Investment	-17.0	n/a	n/a	n/a	n/a	n/a	n/a	n/a

Forces Driving the Banking Flow of Funds

An important part of this analysis is to try to put recent and prospective growth of the Romanian banking system into a stock-adjustment context that links bank balance sheets to the size of the economy they support. This is the same approach taken in the Latvian and Estonian cases also presented in this volume. The monetary position of Romania is shown in relation to other transition economies in Figure 4.1.

Figure 4.1 Romania—Comparative Monetary Characteristics (mid 1996)

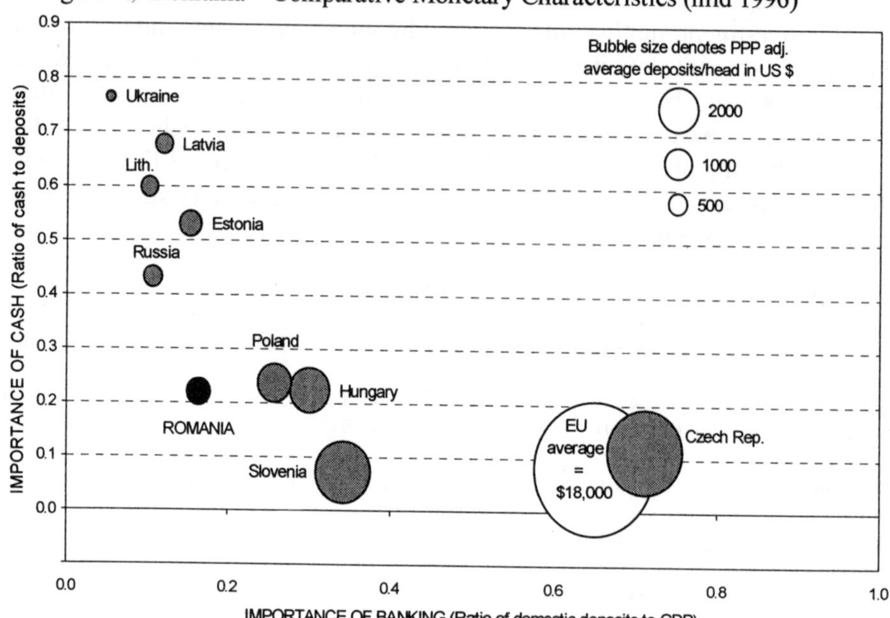

Note: PPP adj = purchasing power parity adjusted
Source: Bank of Romania Quarterly Bulletin.

Romania's monetary development is well behind the main Central European transition economies (particularly those targeted for the first wave of accession to the EU), but generally ahead of even the more advanced former Soviet economies (although by mid-1998, Estonian deposits had reached 21 percent of GDP, compared with 18 percent for Romania). But it understates the degree to which the Romanian banking system has retained its relevance to the wider economy. The recovery in the ratio of deposits to GDP is quite significant—up from a low point of 10 percent in 1993/94 to 18 percent in 1998. Moreover, the Romanian economy is much less cash-oriented than even the most advanced former Soviet economy. As regards the future, the flow of funds projections are based on slow but steady growth in the ratio of deposits to GDP but no further fall in the cash to deposits ratio. This would be sufficient to bring the overall level of monetization up to the sort of levels typical of other Central European Economies once stabilization is secure. Figure 4.2 illustrates these trends over time.

Figure 4.2. Romania—Evolution of Monetary Characteristics

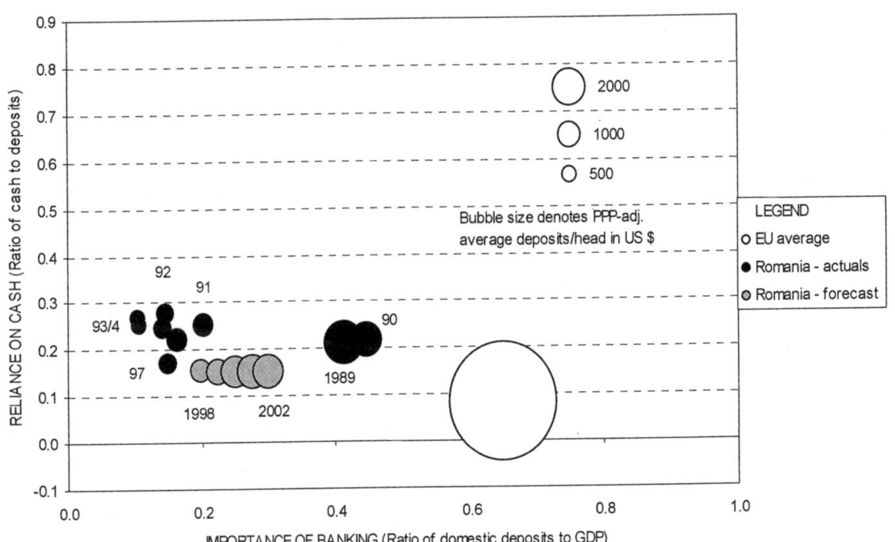

Note: PPP adj = purchasing power parity adjusted
Source: Bank of Romania Quarterly Bulletin.

While this involves none of the rapid remonetization witnessed in Estonia or Latvia, for example (at least since they started to recover from their respective banking crises in 1992/93 and 1995), it does illustrate the robustness of depositors' behavior between 1996 and 1998. The reaction to shock therapy could easily have been to let the real value of deposits sharply erode in the face of the rapid inflation through 1997 (300 percent), especially given nominal deposit rates that averaged 56 percent. In an attempt to preserve the real value of their savings, however, in 1997 Romanian depositors added the equivalent of almost 6 percent of GDP by way of new money on top of an equal amount of interest accrued. Moreover, they reacted rationally to an acute inflation tax on holdings of cash by reducing further the ratio of cash to deposits. Key trends in monetary and banking indicators are shown in Table 4.2.

What makes this behavior particularly interesting is that it came the year after two significant private sector bank failures (Dacia Felix and Creditbank). The "crisis," such as it was, never had the numerical significance of the bank crises in Estonia and Latvia (where 40 percent of the assets of the banking system were lost), but the two banks concerned were part of the new generation of private banks. That depositors retained confidence in banks was in part the result of prompt action by the National Bank of Romania (BNR), which provided liquidity lines to the banks concerned. These were restricted in use; they allowed the failed banks to pay back personal depositors, even as BNR sought liquidation. Weaknesses in bankruptcy procedure led to interminable delays in the liquidation process, but the BNR action prompted depositor confidence to recover quickly.

This would seem the classic recipe for moral hazard, but the authorities moved fast to tighten control. New banking and bank bankruptcy laws were passed in 1997 and a formal Deposit Guarantee Fund was established in 1996. The Fund has since gone on to issue rules that will ultimately mean that high-risk banks will pay more for their coverage than better-capitalized and more prudent banks. In many ways this is probably a more direct and effective constraint on risk-taking behavior than control exerted by small depositors. The level of coverage is generous and indexed semi-annually, but there is some risk-sharing for large depositors. More important, those who might have a contributory role in any bank mismanagement receive no coverage.

Taken together, the tightening legal framework and the risk-oriented, explicit deposit insurance created a climate that did not allow economic turmoil in the first half of 1997 to translate into a banking crisis (as it so easily could have done). New flows in and out of banks did, of course, fall in real terms, but remained significant, even when measured against rapidly inflating   GDP.

Table 4.2. Romania—Monetary and Banking Indicators

	1995	1996	1997	1998	1999	2000	2001	2002
Broad money (leu billion)	18107	30316	62145	96217	141810	190416	243688	300605
Cash outside banks	3764	5383	9200	15240	21237	27828	35238	39209
Deposits (including forex)	14343	24933	52945	80977	120573	162588	208450	261396
Velocity of circulation (mid-year)	5.4	4.5	5.4	4.4	3.9	3.5	3.2	2.9
Deposit:GDP ratio	13	17	15	20	23	25	28	30
Cash:deposit ratio	24	22	17	15	15	15	15	15
Deposits per head (PPP adj. $)	626	770	657	730	1010	1310	1550	1690
Bank lending (Leu billion)	21372	36896	58292	76956	104667	126252	158070	208236
Nominal growth (percent)	70.2	72.6	58.0	32.0	36.0	20.6	25.2	31.7
Real growth (percent)	16.1	29.6	-36.0	-6.5	-6.2	-3.5	8.9	19.8
New loans as percent of GDP	10.1	11.8	4.6	3.8	3.5	2.4	3.4	5.1
New deposits as percent of GDP	-5.7	-11.6	-12.2	-6.7	-5.9	-5.6	-5.1	-5.2
Other new net claims as percent of GDP	1.8	-1.8	-1.0	0.0	0.0	0.0	0.0	0.0
Net supply (+)/take-up of funds to/from NBNGS (as percent of GDP)	4.4	0.2	-7.6	-3.9	-2.4	-3.2	-1.7	-0.1

Note: Forex = Foreign Exchange; PPP adj = purchasing power parity adjusted
Source: Bank of Romania Quarterly Bulletin.

The size of these two-way flows between banks and the NBNGS is another interesting feature of the Romanian flow of funds. New lending relative to GDP ran consistently above 10 percent per year until 1997. For other lower-inflation transition economies this would almost certainly be unsustainable—witness Estonia's experience in 1997 and that of many of the countries hit by the Asian crisis. This is not to say that Romanian banks are somehow superior at handling rapid credit portfolio expansion—65 percent of end-1997 loan balances were graded substandard or worse.[1] Rather, it points to two factors that sustain such lending:

- High inflation is very forgiving of poor credit management.
- Very high new lending relative to GDP is matched by high new deposits, and this avoids the need for excess reliance on net foreign funding of the banking system.

A Methodology for Forecasting Romania's Flow of Funds

At the heart of any flow of funds model are a series of balancing endogenous flows that are designed to highlight emerging strains in the financial system as it seeks to reconcile sector net financing requirements. It is important that these do not involve too many of the cells of the flow of funds matrix—otherwise clarity is lost. Therefore, a number of minor variables can be set exogenously. It is equally important that any "swing" variable that must absorb inconsistencies in financing requirements be highly visible. The approach to complete a flow of funds forecast for Romania should thus be as follows:

- Set the financing gap for each sector from the macroeconomic forecasts for sector savings and investment balances and reasonable assumptions on the gap between these and the identified financing gap (that is, the error line).
- Set a number of minor flow variables exogenously (often at zero, if past values are trivial), the most obvious candidates being BNR finance of government, non-monetary T-bill issue, foreign finance of government, government finance of the NBNS, and both government and NBNGS investment abroad.

---

1. Although BNR credit-risk grading norms *are* quite strict by the standards of transition economies.

- Set NBNGS take-up of cash and new depositing exogenously off the back of a forecast of the re-monetization process discussed earlier.
- Set foreign finance of NBNGS exogenously to a reasonable percentage of GDP.
- Set bank lending to NBNGS as a swing variable to close overall NBNGS net financing.
- Chose one of the two following options:
  - Set government and foreign depositing with banks exogenously, derive total new depositing with banks accordingly (after adding in new NBNGS depositing as set above), and let bank lending to each act as the swing variable to close their respective financing gaps.
  - Set bank lending and let new depositing be the swing variable.
- Adjust forecast foreign finance of the NBNGS as a percentage of GDP to bring about a better balance between inward foreign finance direct to the NBNGS and indirectly through net foreign finance of the banking sector (which should not be allowed to grow too large without constraining new bank lending to the NBNGS).

If this approach is followed, net foreign finance of the banking system effectively becomes a swing variable for the whole flow of funds. If it becomes too positive (consistently above 5 percent of GDP for a number of years, for example), bank lending is probably too high. If foreign finance of the NBNGS cannot be raised to compensate, consideration should be given to cutting back the overall NBNGS net financing requirement. Similarly, if net foreign finance of the banking system becomes too negative (that is, banks are exporting too much capital), consideration should be given to increasing bank lending to the NBNGS by either reducing NBNGS reliance on foreign finance or widening the overall net financing requirement.

Summary Sectoral Financing Patterns

A persistent, and now growing, public deficit, which is generally covered by a moderate (albeit variable) rest-of-the-world surplus together with net saving by banks, allows for modest net financing to flow into the NBNGS. However, the mechanism for this apparent crowding-out is complex, particularly when it involves the Central Bank. Nevertheless, private investment levels in Romania have been held back by a lack of available net financing from banks, and this in turn reflects persistent bank finance of the public sector, either directly or through the Central Bank. It has also reflected relatively low inflows of direct foreign finance. The base case scenario, shown in Figure 4.3, eases the latter constraint on the NBNGS but crowding out by the public sector continues to deprive it of bank finance.

Care has to be taken in analyzing the net financing gap of *government*, which appears to have fallen from over 10 percent of GDP in 1991 to below 3 percent in 1997, but the earlier figures bear no resemblance to published general government saving and investment figures. The gap almost certainly can be attributed to either arrears and/or the changing status of state enterprises. These discrepancies, however, diminish rapidly between 1991 and 1995, and the modest widening of the gap since 1995 is probably a reliable estimate of government's true call on national savings. The counterpart is clearly monetary finance, apart from 1992 when foreign overseas finance was a significant element in covering the overall financing gap. The base case scenario assumes a continuation of these trends but with the reliance on bank finance growing as net repayments are made on past foreign borrowing.

The positions of the *Central Bank* (BNR) and the *banks* need to be taken together. The banks are dominated by two-way flows to and from the NBNGS. The degree to which the widening government financing gap is— or is not—drawing funds away from the NBNGS must be analyzed in the following areas:

- The net inflow of funds to BNR
- Offsetting BNR finance of banks
- Banks' direct net lending to government.

Figure 4.3. Sector Net Financing as a percentage of GDP—Base Case

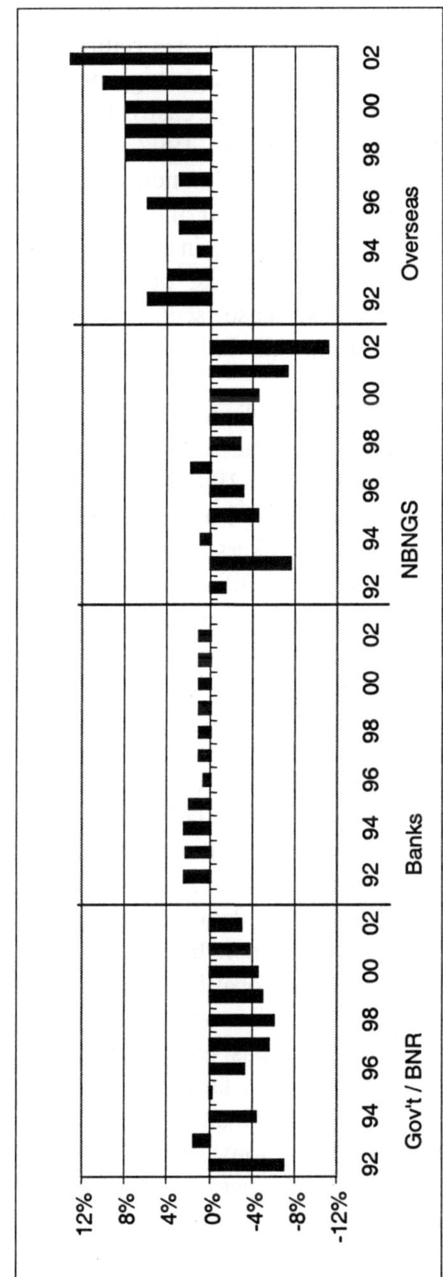

The mix has changed over time, but not necessarily in a systematic way. Apart from 1991/92 and 1997, BNR has returned resources to the banking sector equal to those gathered through high-powered money creation from banks and the NBNGS (as holders of cash). In 1991/92, crowding-out could be considered an issue, whereas in 1997 the build-up of official foreign currency reserves and BNR's own financing gap were the main counterpart of funds drawn in from banks and the NBNGS. This last item can be considered a form of crowding-out, in that BNR is absorbing the strain of paying interest on bankers' balances, but is not charging government for funds on-lent. In the base case scenario monetary sector finance of government switches from this hidden form towards more explicit net borrowing from banks.

As already noted, NBNGS reliance on cash is falling relative to deposits, and this was compatible with the reduction in high-power money (HPM) creation relative to GDP between 1993 and 1996. Direct net bank finance of government was significant in 1991 and started again in 1995. Between these two periods, banks were net takers of funds from government (albeit to a declining degree relative to GDP). Overall, therefore, apart from 1997, crowding out cannot be considered a significant problem. Banks have been both net takers and providers of funds to the NBNGS, and the forces driving this behavior were described in detail in the previous section. Banks are not generally net takers of funds from rest-of-the-world although small net borrowing is a feature of the base case scenario.

There is, of course, more to crowding-out than excessive finance of general government. This is particularly important in Romania, where so much enterprise remains majority state-owned. Identifying flows to and from state rather than private enterprise is beyond the scope of this exercise (and not yet supportable by published data). However, one of the strongest forces in the recovery in NBNGS deposit balances has been household deposits, which have recovered to pre-reform levels as a share of total bank balances (but now on a voluntary—not a forced—basis).

Financing of the NBNGS has historically been largely determined by whether banks are net suppliers or takers of funds. There are, however, signs of growing inward net foreign finance. This was particularly important in 1997, when it compensated for some of the increased net take-up of NBNGS funds by banks. At just over 6 percent of GDP, net foreign finance of the NBNGS would normally be considered easily sustainable, especially for a country that still has so much to do in privatization. The base case scenario assumes a very significant rise in net foreign funding because banks are assumed to continue draw funds away net from the NBNGS (albeit to a smaller degree than in 1997).

Against a background of limited privatization and relatively robust private sector savings behavior, it is not surprising that Romania has not historically relied heavily on foreign finance. In some ways this has protected it from the sort of shock experienced by Estonia and the Czech Republic in 1997. As already noted, government makes relatively little use of foreign finance and the base case scenario assumes repayments of government foreign borrowing; banks tend to be net placers of funds abroad rather than net takers. This brings the focus to direct finance of the NBNGS, which had started to grow strongly and is a trend that will have to continue if the NBNGS financing gap is to be funded while government absorbs available bank finance.

The above analysis suggests that three key variables need to be monitored:

- The net drain on the monetary sector (BNR and banks) represented by government funding needs
- Any tailing-off of direct foreign finance of the NBNGS
- Persistent and significant widening, in either direction, of the gap between new NBNGS deposits with banks and new bank lending to the NBNGS.

An alternative scenario

The most obvious weakness of the base case scenario described above is the assumed widening of the current account deficit. This might prove sustainable if the projected levels of net direct foreign finance of the NBNGS forecast are achieved but this would be unprecedented by past standards and must represent a major vulnerability. The alternative scenario (Figure 4.4) presents a much more sustainable financing picture because of:

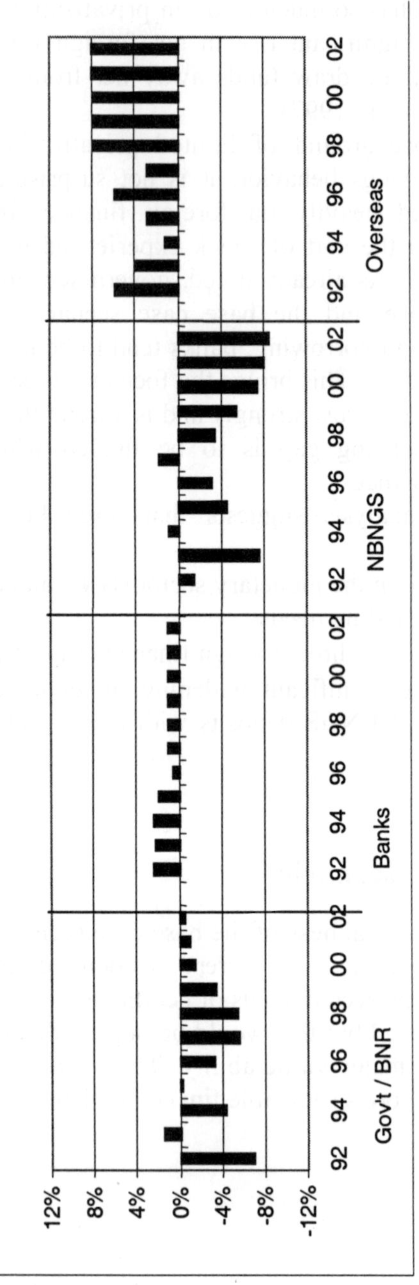

Figure 4.4. Sector Net Financing as a percentage of GDP—Alternative Scenario

- A gradual elimination of the government net financing gap and no net repayment of public foreign debt from 2000 onwards which virtually eliminates the net drain on the monetary sector (BNR and banks) represented by government funding needs; banks are therefore freer to fund the NBNGS.
- The current account deficit and the NBNGS financing gap are capped at 8 percent of GDP (compared to both rising well above 10 percent of GDP in the base case).
- Stronger growth of NBNGS deposit balances such that the ratio to GDP reaches 40 percent by 2002—for example, back to pre-reform levels but, under this scenario, as voluntary not forced saving.

The more interesting result is that although the net NBNGS financing gap in this scenario is lower than in the base case, the gross supply of new finance rises steadily towards 20 percent of GDP in 2002 instead of staying mostly around 11 percent of GDP in the base case (before rising to 18 percent of GDP in 2002). This should support much stronger levels of gross investment than the base case scenario, and providing this is into productive assets, (particularly in the traded-sector) then the projected GDP recovery should prove much more sustainable.

Conclusions

In the case of Romania, transition has been characterized by a gradual rebuilding of NBNGS savings (principally deposits with banks), even against a background of persistent hyperinflation. This is perhaps a surprising result given Romania's slow progress on fundamental restructuring of the state sector, particularly state enterprises. It is very important to preserve a channel for increased domestic savings, because this provides a good platform for faster, domestically financed, investment-led growth, without the "problems of success" witnessed in Estonia and the Czech Republic when they became too reliant on buoyant inflows of foreign finance that disappeared after the 1997 Asian crisis.

Confidence in the banking system is therefore vital, and the recently established Deposit Guarantee Fund has an important role to play in securing and maintaining such confidence. But it is equally important that protection of a sound banking system does not lead to conditions of moral hazard.

Adding a flow of funds dimension to the traditional macroeconomic forecasts can support monetary and fiscal policymakers—it can show the degree to which the financing needs of government are either directly or indirectly crowding out private investment.

To be effective as a monitoring tool, much still needs to be done to improve the model developed here, particularly in six key areas.

- The adjustment of changes in bank balance sheets for currency movements (because data are lacking, no allowance has been made for the revaluation of domestic interbank positions or bank positions in relation to the BNR, although it is known that foreign currency claims and liabilities form a significant element of these positions).

- The ideal model would be developed with separate lines for Leu and foreign currency banking flows, because the high proportion of foreign currency banking activity carries with it special vulnerabilities. This could be combined with detailed analysis of the direction of foreign currency lending to allow better judgements of whether banks are truly laying off the currency risk involved in taking domestic foreign currency deposits.

- Access to more detailed monetary return data would allow the model to address the split of banking flows between the private and majority state-owned elements of the nonbank/nongovernmental sector effectively.

- Finer distinctions need to be drawn within the balance of payments data in relation to the sectors that are involved in both inward and outward capital flows.

- A more explicit model of the link between current budget flows and the overall net financing gap of the government sector also needs to be developed. This would help bring in privatization activities to the workings of the model.

- An appropriate treatment of arrears, particularly between sectors (for example, tax arrears), is needed.

Despite these caveats, the raw base data for financial balance sheet and flow analysis is already available on a sufficiently frequent and timely basis to make a flow of funds model a working tool for policymakers.

Fiscal Imbalance

Hungary
Russia

5.

Hungary—Tapping Resilient Household Savers

Anna Kerekes

Hungary's economic system has undergone comprehensive liberalization since 1990, the beginning of the transition from central planning to a market economy. Subsidies have been cut, trade distortions reduced, most food prices freed, enterprise budget constraints tightened, new bankruptcy and banking laws adopted, and state enterprises privatized. All these measures were intended to correct relative prices. As elsewhere in the region, the reforms were accompanied by a sharp drop in output and a surge in inflation. Although the transition to a market economy continues, the decline in output has ended and recovery has begun (see Table 5.1).

In 1995, GDP in Hungary was 15 percent below its 1989 performance. There are only two transitional countries in the region with more favorable figures, Poland and Slovenia, where the slowdown in output remained well below 10 percent. Poland experienced a lengthy and serious recession before 1989. The neighboring countries—the Czech Republic, Romania, and the Slovak Republic—had slowdowns like that of Hungary, while in the Baltic states—Estonia, Latvia, and Lithuania—the downswing was much more serious, between 40 and 60 percent.

In real terms a slowdown brought on by market reforms occurred in all the countries of the Central European region, but it seems to have taken place independently of the extent of indebtedness. Not only did the recession hit such considerably indebted countries as Hungary and Poland—whose net debt ratios were still above 40 percent in 1994 (more than twice the average in the region) (World Bank 1996)—but also the Czech Republic, Romania, and the Slovak Republic, countries that did not carry the burden of past debts.

Preceding the stabilization of the Hungarian economy was the extreme imbalance that took shape in 1993–94, and which was characterized by the dramatically worsening positions in the balance of payments current account and the budget deficit, as well as in real wages. Government intervention in 1995 brought about a sudden change, with an immediate and spectacular improvement in the economic balance. A gradual upswing followed in a growing number of areas of the economy. In 1995, exports led this rising trend; in 1996, capital expenditures; and in the summer of 1997, consumption contributed to the upturn. Meanwhile, the balance proved to be stable. In 1997, the balance of trade and the balance of payments improved further. It appears that the Hungarian economy finally managed to emerge from the trap where it languished for about a quarter-century: "either growth or equilibrium" (Antal 1998).

Although it precipitated a transitory halt in the upward trend, the economic stabilization of 1995 did not cause an actual fall-back. In addition to tightening aggregate demand, some measures were taken (devaluation, introduction of a larger customs duty, decrease in taxes on investments) that, while increasing inflation (the rate of inflation increased by 7 percentage points from 1994 to 1995), diminished the possibility of fall-back. Holding down wages, decreasing budget expenditures, and implementing a crawling peg for exchange rate devaluation brought about a steady decrease in inflation, toward the level accepted in Western Europe.

Nineteen ninety-eight brought a break-through in the containment of inflation. From 1997 to 1998 the inflation rate decreased by 8 percentage points, which was—apart from an improvement in productivity—mainly caused by suppressed world crop prices and by the global fall in crude oil prices. As a result of a successful disinflationary process in Hungary, the 30 percent inflation rate dropped close to 10 percent within three years.

In this Chapter, the main factors in the development of the Hungarian financial system have been examined deploying the flow of funds approach. To study the role of the financial system in the allocation of resources among economic participants, financial accounts were prepared for the period between 1993 and 1997 for households, the general government, the financial institutions, and the foreign sector, as well as flow of funds timelines. For 1997, a flow of funds matrix of the country was assembled. (Definitions of the sectors, the choice of data sources, and the method of

Table 5.1. Main Features of Economic Stabilization of Hungary, 1991—98 (percent, unless otherwise indicated)

	1991	1992	1993	1994	1995	1996	1997	1998[a]
Real GDP growth	-11.9	-3.1	-0.6	2.9	1.5	1.3	4.4	**5.1**
Final consumption growth	-5.1	0.6	5.4	-2.3	-6.6	-3.4	2.4	**3.4**
Gross capital expenditure growth	-21.1	-20.4	32.3	19.8	8.2	14.4	9.1	**11.8**
Export growth	n.a.	2.1	-10.1	13.7	13.4	7.4	26.8	**20.6**
Import growth[b]	n.a.	0.2	20.2	8.8	-0.7	5.7	25.9	**22.9**
Consumer price index (Dec/Dec)	32.2	21.6	21.1	21.2	28.3	19.8	18.4	**10.6**
Unemployment rate	n.a.	9.8	11.9	10.7	10.2	9.9	8.7	**8.2**
Real earnings growth	-7	-1.4	-3.9	7.2	-12.2	-5	4.9	**5.1**
Current account/GDP	-0.8	-0.9	-9	-9.4	-5.6	-3.8	-2.2	**-3.6**
Budget deficit/GDP	-3.2	-6.9	-6.7	-9.6	-7.3	-4.6	-4.7	**-4.9**
Net external debt/GDP[c]	43.6	35	37.7	43.5	35.3	27.9	20.7	**19.7**
Consolidated gross state debt/GDP	66.9	64.9	83.6	83	86.2	72.3	64.1	**61.8**
Growth rate of M3	35.7	27.6	15.7	13.3	20.1	22.5	19.4	**11.4**
Growth rate of loans	17.7	12.2	20.9	18.1	12.8	6.5	11.7	**5.2**
Nominal interest rate of 3M T-bill	31.9	14.5	24.1	32.0	30.5	22.2	19.3	**16.3**
Nominal interest rate of 12M T-bill	31	18	25	32.4	31.3	21.5	19	**16.2**
Nominal exchange rate growth[d]	-14.1	-7.4	-9.8	-13.5	-21.2	-16	-13.1	**-10.3**
Real exchange rate growth[e]	10.7	7.2	9.7	-1	-3.1	3.3	4.3	**-0.9**
GDP (billions of forints)	2,498.3	2,942.6	3,548.3	4,364.8	5,614	6,845.4	8,395	**9,758.4**

a. Data are estimated.
b. In 1993 and 1994, including Russian arms deliveries received as compensation to amortize debts.
c. Denominated in foreign exchange, net of intercompany loans.
d. Official devaluation against the currency basket.
e. Based on the CPI.
Source: Annual Reports of the National Bank of Hungary, 1993–97.

compiling the financial accounts is included in Annex 2 to this chapter.)

For the basic flow of funds series projections, a 24-equation model was constructed. The model combines the flow of funds framework and behavioral equations that describe state debt, the budget deficit and external debt, the current account, money demand function, and domestic interest rate behavior. (See a more detailed description of the model in Annex 1.)

Period of dichotomy: growth versus equilibrium

In the pre-transition era, Hungary's banking activities were initially restricted to the enterprise sector, and the central bank provided funds to the commercial banks. Within this system, savings were collected and intermediated by the central bank. At the same time, the demand for loans was virtually infinite, because commercial banks and enterprises still operated under soft budget constraints, and heavy losses did not lead to bankruptcy. In an economic environment with an unlimited supply of loans, the interest rate sensitivity of enterprises and the risk aversion of banks were very low. The central bank used direct monetary tools—including setting the level of mandatory reserves, credit quotas, and interest rate ceilings—to control monetary aggregates.

In 1992 new laws on accounting, banking, and bankruptcy were put in place that exerted pressure on banks to enhance their efficiency. New accounting rules revealed the capital adequacy ratio of the major banks to be much lower under international accounting standards than under Hungarian rules. The new banking law, which was introduced with transitional provisions, modeled the risk-weighted capital adequacy rules and provisioning requirements for nonperforming loans on the European Community (EC) banking directives. In addition, the new bankruptcy law initiated many reorganization and liquidation procedures. Although few companies were liquidated in the first year, the banks' nonperforming loan portfolios increased rapidly. Finally, the new banking law required a reduction of government shareholdings in the banks to 25 percent by 1997; the government had intended to find strategic investors for the larger banks much earlier. This necessitated the prompt improvement of the solvency and profitability of these institutions, and the operating environment for banks and firms changed dramatically.

The most visible response of the banks to this new challenge was to sharply curtail their lending to enterprises. Banks could not charge interest rates that were sufficiently high to cover their perceived risk without making loans so expensive that default became more likely. Only the riskiest enterprises—or those that did not expect to service their debt—applied for loans. Direct limits on lending in these circumstances provided a means for banks to manage risk: moderately risky clients could borrow, but generally not as much as they intended. A credit crunch began.

The only economic participant able to accept the high interest rates was the government. To a limited extent, heavy government borrowing may have crowded out other borrowers. At the end of 1993 the increase in nonmarketable government bonds in the financial assets of the banking sector reached 8 percent of GDP (Figure 5.1) and, at the same time, the rise in marketable deficit-financing government bonds was almost 5 percent of GDP (Figure 5.2). Overspending of the budget was close to 10 percent of GDP, which—with relatively low savings in the domestic private sector—pushed net corporate borrowings to under 2 percent of GDP (Figure 5.3).

Figure 5.1 Change of Financial Assets of Financial Institutions

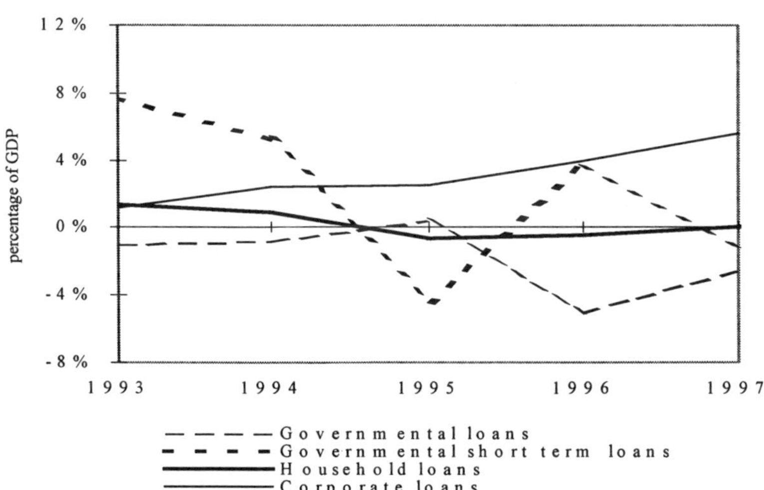

Figure 5.2 Change of Financial Liabilities of General Government

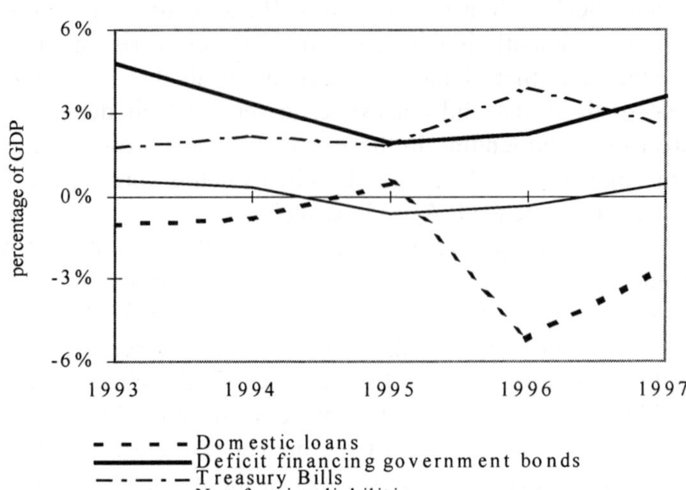

Figure 5.3 Net Lending/Net Borrowing of Institutional Sectors

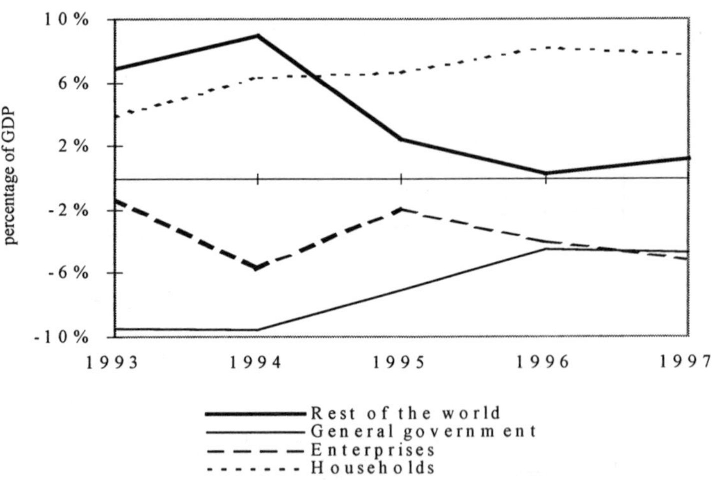

The macroeconomic environment had deteriorated by the end of 1994. With the recovery of demand, the current account deficit widened to nearly 9 percent of GDP. Simultaneously, the ratio of the budget deficit to GDP stood at almost 10 percent (Figure 5.3). The external accounts deteriorated despite

rapid growth in Hungary's export markets, the reversal of several adverse supply shocks, and a substantial tightening of monetary policy. Foreign direct investment and private capital flows were insufficient to finance the current account deficit. Foreign direct investment sharply decreased, from 6 percent to 2 percent of GDP (Figure 5.4), and the Central Bank was forced to increase its net foreign borrowing.

Figure 5.4 Financial Position of the Rest of the World

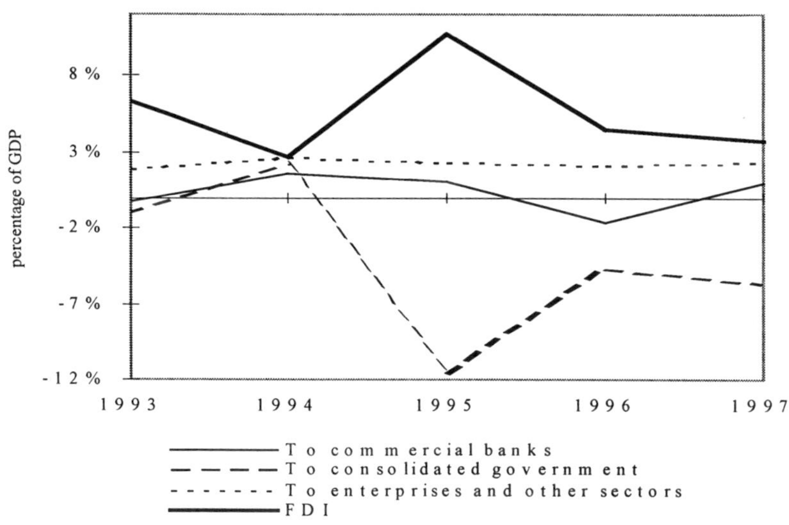

To obtain a clear picture of macroeconomic developments in Hungary, it is necessary to consider the evolution of the consolidated public sector, including the National Bank of Hungary (NBH). The reasons for this include the important fiscal responsibilities of the NBH in servicing sovereign foreign debt and the extensive web of extrabudgetary funds. The foreign borrowing of the consolidated public sector reached 2 percent of GDP in 1994 (Figure 5.4). Consolidated interest payments grew rapidly, driven by the growth of foreign debt service, the increased domestic debt burden produced by bank recapitalization (including the purchase of nonperforming loans), and rising domestic interest rates. The gross debt of the consolidated government rose to nearly 90 percent of GDP in 1994.

Monetary policy was tightened and interest rates rose. With higher interest rates, household savings increased. As can be seen in Figure 5.5, of the financial liabilities of the banking sector, only household deposits grew and strengthened, reaching 3 percent of GDP in 1994. The change in financial assets of households comprised a smaller increase in currency compared with previous years, and by an increase in securities that exceeded forint deposits. Ownership of securities among citizens doubled, approaching 4 percent of GDP in 1994 (Figure 5.6). With the rise in domestic interest rates, however, it became more efficient to reduce the debt-burdened budget deficit. Without major structural changes in fiscal policy, there was a real danger that a vicious circle would develop.

Figure 5.5 Change of Domestic Financial Liabilities of Financial Institutions

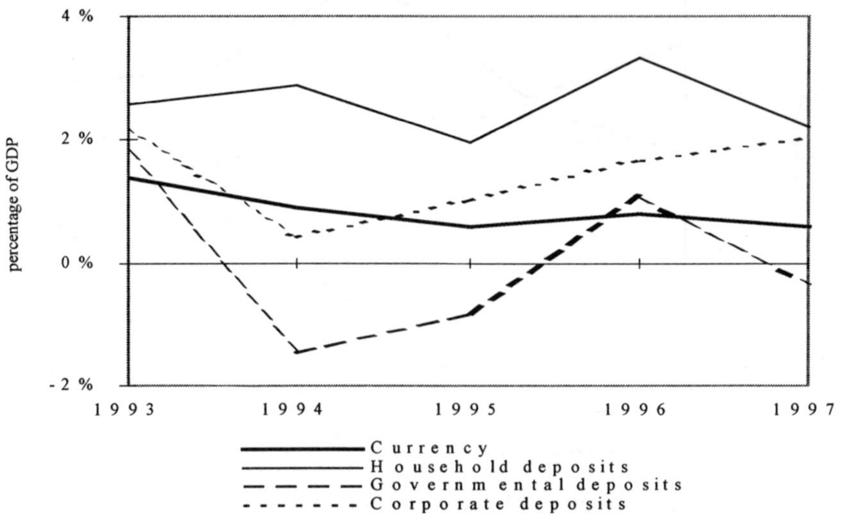

Figure 5.6 Change of Financial Assets of Households

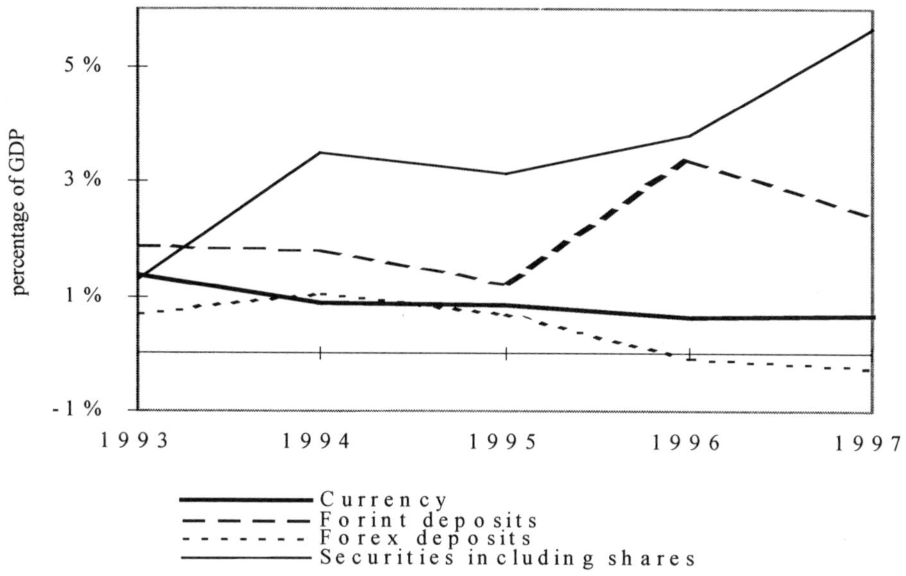

In March 1995 a firm action plan for macroeconomic policy and structural reform was presented. A fundamental element of the strategy was a tight wage policy, which was intended to reduce consumption and imports, while at the same time reducing budget pressures and lowering public consumption. Improved cost competitiveness through reduced real wages was to be supported by further structural reforms. The government announced its intention to accelerate privatization and to end direct and indirect support of enterprises. The principal fiscal measures in the March package to increase budget revenues included an import surcharge of 8 percent on all imports until mid-1997; excise tax increases, particularly on cars; and an expansion in the contribution base of the health and pension funds. The measures to reduce budget expenditures included the withdrawal of family-support allowances such as maternity pay and leave provisions, a cut in wage allocations to central budgetary units, and cost savings in the health system, by introducing better control of medicines, for example.

The fiscal plan was to tighten the budget by around 3 percent of GDP, reducing the general budget deficit to 6 percent. An ambitious target for privatization revenues—mainly from selling the energy utilities, including power generation and gas companies—was fully achieved, which decreased the budget financing requirements by a further 2 percentage points. The result of these budgetary control measures can be seen in Figure 5.2, which shows that the financing requirements of the general government decreased greatly. In 1995, state bond issues dropped to half of those of the previous year, from 4 percent to 2 percent of GDP. The increasing trend toward funding from foreign sources came to a halt; in 1995 the foreign liabilities of the state not only stopped growing, but decreased by 1 percent of GDP. In the same year foreign liabilities of the consolidated public sector decreased by 10 percent of GDP (Figure 5.4). Supporting the 1995 budget and the March 1995 supplementary budget, a number of proposals were put forward to reform the social security system and the state administration, although it is clear that these were only the initial steps in a multiyear reform program.

As a result of stabilization measures, in 1995 a substantial improvement toward equilibrium was seen both within Hungary and in the country's foreign relations. This improvement continued in 1996. The role of the general government in income redistribution declined with the reduction of the budget deficit, while the current account improved. Figure 5.3 illustrates that domestic saving increased, primarily because of greater net household lending and a decrease in the net borrowing of government and enterprises. In 1995 this was brought about by the private sector, which became a net saver; in 1996 it was based on a faster improvement in the budget deficit compared with the preceding year. In 1996 the annual consumer price index decreased to below 20 percent, and with the decrease of inflation, interest rates started to drop as well. The cost of budget financing declined considerably over the year—the DWIX index, calculated from the weighted yields on Treasury bills, declined from 31 percent to 22 percent. The government's gross debt to GDP ratio decreased by 13 percent, which was largely attributable to the use of the proceeds of privatization to repay debt.

With two-digit inflation, the net saver position of economic participants may be distorted by the significant inflation-compensation content of interest expenses, which cannot actually be regarded as revenue. According to calculations prepared for 1995, with an inflation level of 28 percent, the inflation interest income of households reached 4 percent of GDP—that is, the reported net saver position of households was that much better than the actual figure (Huszar and Sandor 1996). The reverse was true for the budget—for debtors, the inflation content of interest expenses worsens this reported position. In 1995 this distortion reached 7 percent of the GDP—while the budget balance showed a 6 percent deficit, the operational balance showed a surplus of 1 percent of GDP.

Economic growth recovered strongly in 1997. This was accompanied by a decline in net household lending to below 8 percent of GDP, while the net borrowing position of the general government remained essentially unchanged, at some 5 percent of GDP. With the economic recovery, the required external financing increased, and was supplied through the continuous indebtedness of commercial banks and the private sector (Figure 5.4). While the foreign borrowings of the consolidated government reached 5 percent of GDP—which appeared on the balance sheet of the central bank as a decrease of foreign resources—the trend of foreign borrowings of commercial banks reversed. In contrast to the decrease of 2 percent of GDP in 1996, it increased by 1 percent of GDP in 1997. The increasing demand for foreign financing sources was largely met by foreign direct investments and by the slightly increased foreign borrowings of the corporate sector.

This upward trend was accompanied by better terms in the government's domestic debt. Through the decrease in inflation, confidence in the economy increased, which made it possible to lengthen the average maturity of securities. The short-term Treasury bill issues were gradually replaced by government bonds of longer maturities. In 1997 government bond issues reached 4 percent of GDP, almost twice the issues of the previous years (Figure 5.2), while the issue of shorter-term Treasury bills decreased by half, to 2 percent of GDP.

There were significant changes in the structure of household savings as well. The traditional form of savings—deposits—decreased, while new, alternative forms of investment became prominent with the flourishing of investment funds, pension funds, insurance companies, and the reopening of the Budapest Stock Exchange after a 40-year pause (within a few years it became the most commonly subscribed stock exchange of the region, surpassing even the Warsaw Stock Exchange). In 1997 the pace of increase in household forint deposits slowed to 2 percent of GDP; at the same time, household investments in shares and other securities experienced spectacular growth. Instead of the 4 percent of GDP seen in 1996, these investments increased to 6 percent of GDP in 1997 (Figure 5.6).

The following phenomena can be read from the flow of funds matrix of 1997, which was compiled on the basis of the financial accounts of four institutional sectors (see Annex 2):

- Owing to the sharp decrease in the foreign liabilities of the Central Bank, the intermediary role of the financial sector narrowed in 1997, and the increase in monetary transactions (some 2 percent of GDP) became smaller than the increase in nonmonetary transactions, which was more than 14 percent of GDP.

- Because of the emerging activity of new funds, such as pension funds, investment funds, and the like that appeared in the financial account of the enterprises sector, the increase in financial savings attracted by the financial sector to 4 percent of GDP represented close to a 50–50 proportion between households and the corporate sector.

- The redistribution of financial savings could be characterized by a modest increase in domestic loans (below 2 percent of GDP) while foreign liabilities decreased by almost 2 percent of GDP. As one of the main features of financial progress, the decrease in government loans continued, to some 3 percent of GDP. At the same time, corporate loans increased markedly, to more than 4 percent of GDP.

- Within nonfinancial transactions, two large items were observed: first, the increase of government bond issues to 4 percent of GDP, which financed almost all the budget deficit, and, second, foreign direct investments of almost 5 percent of GDP, which covered a significant portion of the requirements of enterprises.

Period of Sustainable Growth

The future evolution of the Hungarian financial system was examined with reference to two possible growth projection scenarios, considering European Union membership by 2002–04 (see Box 5.1).

In the high-growth scenario, it is assumed that the 5 percent real growth achieved in 1998 will continue (Monetary Policy Guidelines in 1999). The high-growth scenario enables Hungary to grow at a rate at least twice that of the average EU country. The high-growth scenario was compared with a moderate-growth scenario (with 3 percent real growth). In this scenario, Hungary would not grow at a higher rate than the EU average. The realization of this unfavorable scenario would make Hungary vulnerable to future balance of payments shocks, and it would no doubt complicate and lengthen the wait for EU membership. Assuming that the average real growth rate calculated for the entire projection period will not be influenced by the economic cycle, the projection is calculated under a constant real growth rate.

Box 5.1 EU Membership

Four criteria have been set up for each member state to fullfil the requirement to achieve a high degree of macroeconomic convergence (Maastricht treaty):

1. A member state's price index should not exceed that of the three best-performing member states by more than 1.5 percentage points.
2. The ratio of general government deficit to GDP should not exceed 3 percent, and the ratio of public debt to GDP should not exceed 60 percent.
3. A member state should not devalue its currency bilateral central rate against any other member state for at least two years.
4. A member state's average nominal long-term interest rate should not exceed that of the three best-performing member states by more than 2 percentage points.

In the projection, inflation will gradually slow down. Moreover, an exchange rate devaluation that is smaller than the difference between domestic and foreign price levels is estimated. This indicates a real appreciation of the forint. Although in 1998 a slight real devaluation of the national currency occurred because of an unexpectedly large decrease in the annual inflation index, in the medium term, the increase in productivity achieved through economic development will make a real appreciation of the exchange rate unavoidable. According to model calculations, this could mean a 1–3 percent real appreciation in the next decade. Another consequence of the slowdown of inflation in 1998 is that, under the projections, the real interest rate will grow to 7 percent for a time in 1999, but after the turn of the century it will gradually fall back to its normal 3–4 percent level. The decrease of inflation will probably lead to a slight decrease in the velocity of money circulation, but an increase will follow as the economy grows steadily. The overall plan—which stipulates that the official devaluation rate will be cut semiannually, until it is abolished in 2002, and that inflation will decrease annually—could make it possible to tie the forint to the Euro, and allow Hungary to join the European Monetary Union.

Considering Hungary's favorable macroeconomic performance, the credit rating agencies gradually improved the risk rating of the country's debts during 1997–98. The country risk premium was about 5 percent at the end of 1998. The projections assume that the decrease in risks brought about by economic development would lower the country risk premium to 2 percent by 2007. No significant change is expected in the value of foreign direct investments expressed in U.S. dollars. A stable FDI, expressed as a percentage of a growing GDP, shows a slight decline. On the basis of the 3 percent FDI to GDP ratio in 1998, the estimated FDI for 2007 is set at 2 percent of GDP.

Nonfinancial transactions (such as state guarantees, debtor consolidation, or exchange rate losses on hard currency debts) are not included in the state budget deficit, but influence the state debt figures, and are not expected to disappear. Other governmental expenditures—amounting to 4 percent of GDP in 1998—are expected to shrink to 2 percent of GDP. The forint—hard currency ratio within gross government debt was changed in favor of forint debts, because preventing of the growth of hard currency debts in relation to GDP remains a policy priority. The ratio of forint debts was 61 percent of gross government debts in 1998, while a 10 percentage points higher ratio of 71 percent is expected by the end of the next decade.

A major objective included in both scenarios is the reduction of the debt-to-GDP ratio in the next decade. The financial flows of Hungary have been planned on the basis of a current account and a budget deficit with sustainable debt dynamics.

As a condition for participating in the European Monetary Union, the Maastricht treaty requires the reduction of the general government deficit and the size of the government debt ratio. Hungary, as a candidate for EU membership, must consider these limits. The question is more complicated than simply meeting the numerical requirements, however, because the Hungarian method of calculating gross government debt differs from EU practice. Problems of statistical calculation in the Hungarian method exclude the debts of local municipalities, which have been increasing rapidly in the past few years. Although the Hungarian method places total government debt at 61 percent of GDP in 1998, which is only 1 percent less than the EU convergence criterion, switching over to the EU method will probably require a further reduction in the debt-to-GDP ratio. But the Maastricht treaty includes no requirements regarding the current account deficit or the foreign debt ratio; the reduction of the latter is based only on convention.

Maintenance and improvement of the external balance may not only be important on the basis of fundamental ratios, but also from the point of view of sustainability of the exchange rate system.

Theoretically, the expected deficits in the current account and the general government balance would be sustainable if their financing did not lead to increases in the net foreign debt ratio and the gross government debt ratio. It is easy to see that these two balances are directly connected through the interest payments on foreign government debt. What kind of assumption could be realistic regarding the government and nongovernment proportions of foreign debt? With the completion of the privatization process, the decrease in the government's foreign debt can be covered by increasing domestic debt. Sterilization of the capital inflow has prompted spontaneous government debt conversion since 1995. However, planning additional decreases in foreign government debt could be the correct move if the real interest rate on the government's new domestic debt were more favorable than the rate on foreign debt. As a consequence of relatively high domestic nominal interest rates, interest payments could be increased as a proportion of the budget as a result of debt conversion. Therefore, although it is an economic priority to decrease the ratio of hard currency debt to GDP, the nominal difference in the interest rates on the forint and on hard currency debts makes it advisable to renew the hard currency debt portfolio to the extent possible. According to 1999 agreements, the existing hard currency debts were to be renewed in their entirety.

At the same time, after a decline in 1998, the pace of foreign capital injection into the corporate sector will continue to slow. With the spreading of syndicated lending, companies can now obtain credits within Hungary with increasingly long maturities, and no longer must go abroad. This is why the projection tentatively assumes that the government's proportion of foreign debt could increase, while enterprises' foreign debt could decrease.

Table 5.2 Main Features of Sustainable Growth in Hu*Note*: H = high-growth scenario, M = moderate-growth scenario.

Assumption	1999		2000		2001		2007	
	H	**M**	**H**	**M**	**H**	**M**	**H**	**M**
Real GDP growth	5.0	3.0	5.0	3.0	5.0	3.0	5.0	3.0
Consumer price index[a] (Dec/Dec)	8.6	9.0	7.5	8.0	6.0	7.0	2.0	3.0
Devaluation of exchange rate	6.0	6.0	4.0	5.0	2.0	4.0	0.0	0.0
Risk premium of the country	3.5	3.5	3.5	3.5	3.5	3.5	2.0	2.0
Net foreign debt/GDP	18.0	18.0	16.5	16.5	15.0	15.0	11.0	11.0
Gross governmental debt/GDP	57.0	57.0	51.5	51.5	48.0	48.0	41.0	41.0
M3 / GDP	45.5	45.5	43.5	43.5	45.5	45.5	50.0	50.0
Foreign direct and portf. inv./ GDP	2.0	2.0	2.0	2.0	2.0	2.0	2.5	2.5
Other government expenditures/GDP	2.5	2.5	2.0	2.0	2.0	2.0	2.0	2.0
Government forint debt to gross debt	61.0	61.0	63.0	63.0	65.0	65.0	71.0	71.0
Foreign inflation[b]	1.4	1.4	1.7	1.7	1.7	1.7	1.7	1.7
Foreign interest rate[b]	3.2	3.2	3.6	3.6	3.6	3.6	3.6	3.6
Calculation								
Nominal domestic interest rate	11.1	12.2	9.4	11.5	7.2	10.4	5.7	5.7
Real domestic interest rate	6.3	5.9	3.3	3.8	3.2	4.2	3.6	2.6
Real exchange rate growth	1.0	1.4	1.6	1.1	2.2	1.2	0.3	1.3
Current account/GDP	4.2	3.5	4.1	3.3	3.7	2.9	3.9	3.8
Budget deficit/GDP	-4.7	-3.6	-3.7	-2.7	-3.5	-2.9	-3.4	-2.7
Growth rate of M3	8.8	7.2	7.9	6.4	16.3	15.2	7.1	6.1
Growth rate of loans	6.7	3.6	6.5	2.5	13.9	10.0	8.5	7.0
GDP (billions of forints)	11,127.5	10,955.8	12,560.2	12,187.2	13,979.5	13,431.5	22,692.3	20,285.6

Note: H = high-growth scenario, M = moderate-growth scenario.

a. In the high growth scenario, inflation data of 1998, 1999, and 2000 are Warburg Dillon Read projection, Reuters, 28 December, 1998.

b. Compiled according to the same proportion as the forint's currency basket and on the basis of 1998, 1999, and 2000 Lehman Bothers projection figures, 18 December 1998.

Source: Author's calculations based on the flow of funds model.

The ratio of government debt to GDP is influenced by numerous factors: first, the primary balance of the state budget, which characterizes the actual budget policy; second, the increase in formerly accumulated debts, which is subject to the existing level of debt, long-term real interest, and economic growth; and third, factors not included in the state budget deficit, but that still influence the state debt figure, such as government guarantees, debtor consolidation, and the exchange losses on hard currency debts. It can be shown that the values set as convergence criteria are consistent, considering the growth and inflation rate characteristic of EU member countries—that is, with a 3 percent annual real GDP index and 1 percent annual inflation, a 60 percent gross government debt can co-exist with a 3 percent government deficit. In the high-growth projection it is assumed that a higher rate than Western Europe is experienced, while the moderate-growth scenario assumed a similar growth rate, but with a larger domestic inflation rate. Increasing GDP, allows a larger budget deficit so as to maintain the ratio of government debt to GDP. The decrease in the projected real interest rate and other budget expenditures strengthen this same trend. A 20 percent decrease in government debt within a decade will push the level of sustainable budget deficit to about 3 percent (Figure 5.7) over the period concerned.

Figure 5.7 Gross Governmental Debt and Deficit in the High-Growth Scenario

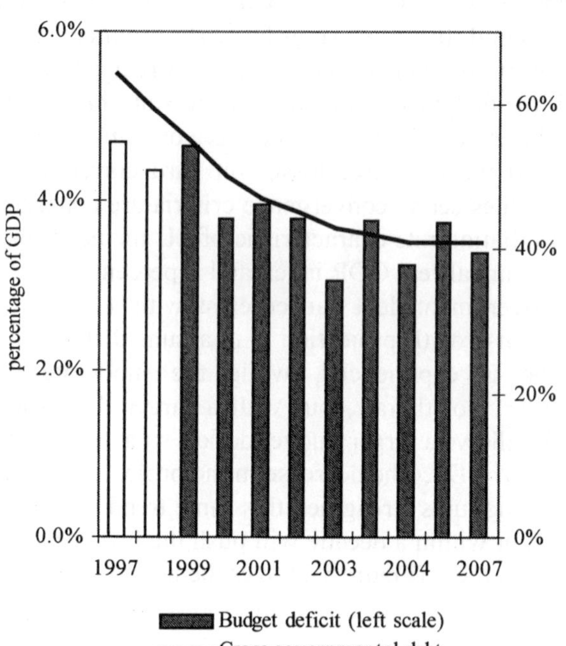

It should be emphasized that, according to the analysis, future fiscal policy will not be constrained by a pre-planned change in the debt ratio and the sustainability of the debt ratio. This doubtlessly represents an important change compared with 1994, when the government position was less than sustainable. Recently, however, the basic fiscal questions have been connected to the adjustment of expenditures. With the decrease in inflation, the total governmental deficit also decreased, but this does not justify increasing primary expenditures. More important, in the following decade there are several elements that will increase expenditures, including the cost of catching up with NATO and the EU, the projected health reform, and pension reform.

The ratio of foreign debt to GDP depends, first, on the current account balance; second, on the change in accumulated debts (which is subject to the existing level of debts, the long-term real exchange rate, and economic growth); and, third, on the value of foreign direct and portfolio investments. The projected economic growth and real exchange rate appreciation allow an increase in the current account deficit to maintain the ratio of foreign debts to GDP. As for the development of the current account, in the two growth projections the deficit is expected to grow from 3 percent of GDP in 1998 to 4 percent of GDP by 2007, paralleling a decrease in the Hungarian net foreign debt from 19 percent in 1998 to 11 percent by 2007 (Figure 5.8). This conclusion follows a cautious FDI inflow forecast of around 2 percent of GDP. It is necessary to note that the resulting size of the sustainable current account deficit can be interpreted in such a way that if in one year the deficit is higher than the estimated figure, during the next year the deficit must be lower. It appears that a sustainable current account deficit, and consequent decrease in the ratio of foreign debt to GDP, will not be difficult to reach during the following decade.

Figure 5.8 Net Foreign Debt and Current Account Deficit in the High-Growth
Scenario

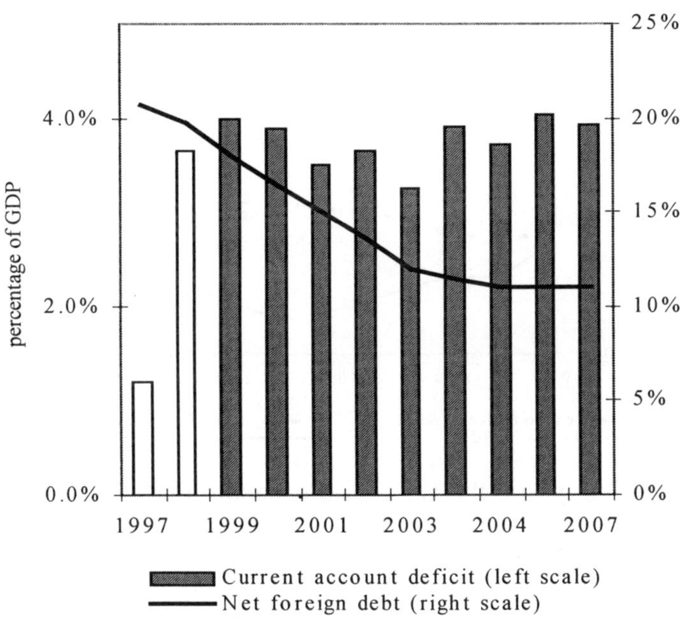

As a consequence of the relatively high sustainable current account deficit, there is a large difference between domestic savings and investments at the national level (Figure 5.9). Fluctuation in household savings (Figure 5.10) and the temporary widening of the net borrowing position of enterprises will lead to occasional increases in the net borrowing position of the total private sector. The direct role of the general government would not be substantial in the prospective growing difference between domestic savings and investments, because its borrowing requirements would rise only slightly over the preceding year, especially in the moderate-growth projection (Figure 5.11). An increase in the primary surplus of the general government should accompany the increase in the net borrowing position of the enterprise sector at a time when household savings will temporarily decrease. That would be the only scenario in which the borrowing requirements of the corporate sector would not lead to a substantial deterioration of the external financial situation.

Figure 5.9 Net Position of Institutional Sectors in the High-Growth Projection

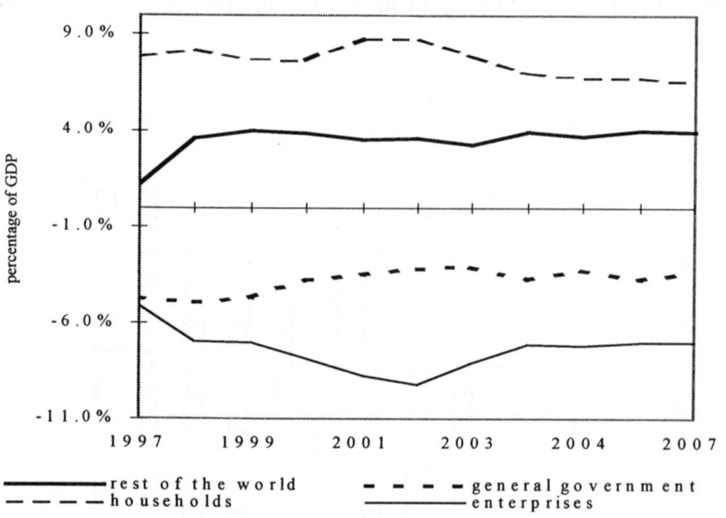

In the coming years, the Hungarian economy is expected to grow in a favorable environment, although there will likely be transitory upsets from significant shocks, mainly through the capital markets. Such shocks have been felt from events such as the Asian currency crisis of October 1997, the Russian political crisis of August 1998, and the Stock Exchange slump. Except for Russia, the economies hit by these shocks are not closely tied to the Hungarian economy, but the shocks strongly influence foreign investors' behavior toward emerging markets, and thus toward Hungary. In a third projection the effect of increasing regional political risk, when FDI inflows significantly decrease to 1 percent of GDP (Figure 5.12). As a result of a narrowing net saving position in the rest of the world, the net borrowing position of the enterprises decreases as well.

Figure 5.10 Net Savings of Households and Real Interest Rates in the High-Growth Scenario

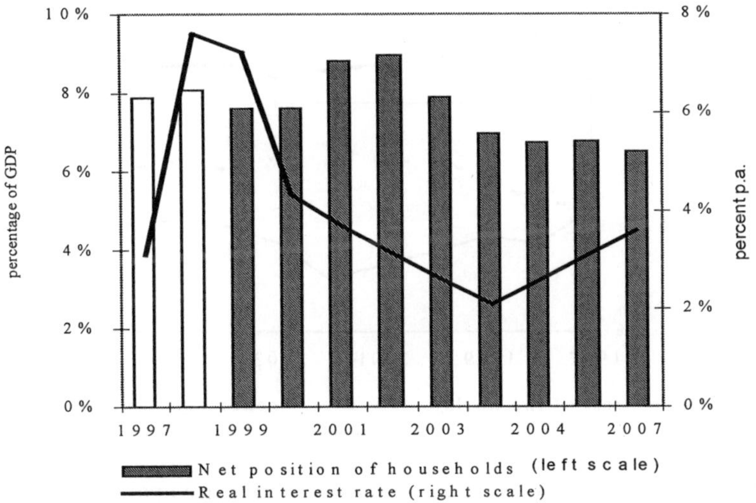

Figure 5.11 Net Position of Institutional Sectors in the Moderate-Growth Projection

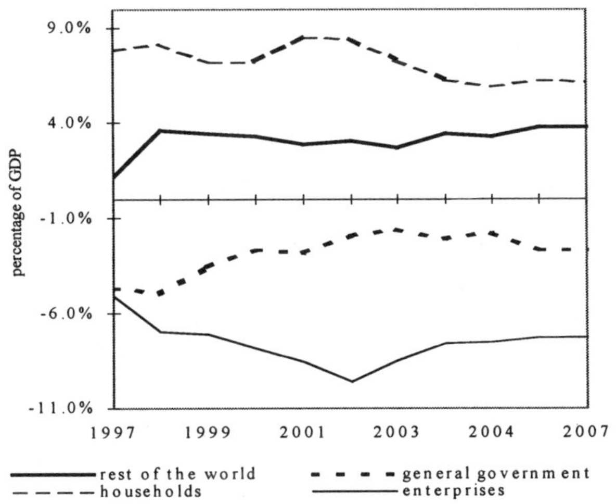

                                                           Financial Systems in Transition

Figure 5.12 Net Positions of Institutional Sectors with Increasing Regional Political Risk

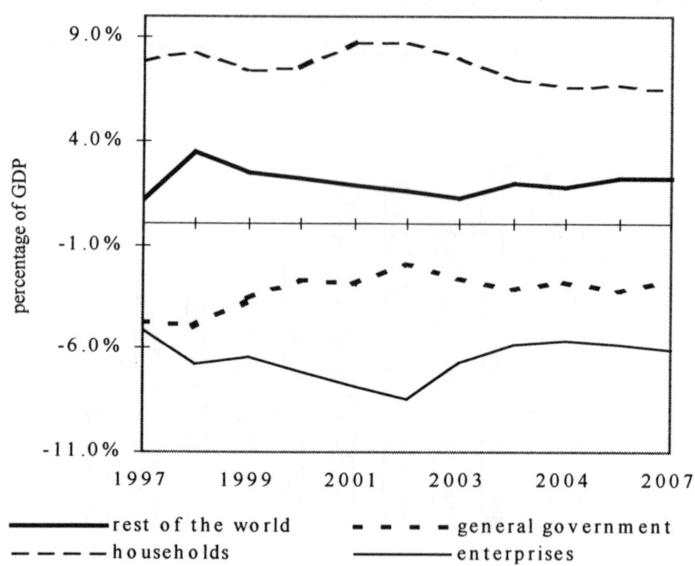

When the two growth scenarios described above are analyzed in terms of flow of funds (and their end-point in 2007 compared with 1997), the following main trends become apparent (see also Annex 2):

- Assuming the high real GDP growth rate, the increase in the overall volume of financial transactions is 19 percent of GDP in 2007. It is higher by 2 percent of GDP than in the moderate projection, and it is also higher by 2 percent than it was in 1997.
- Owing to a slight increase in foreign liabilities of financial institutions, the intermediary role of the financial sector will widen by 2007. The pace of increase in monetary transactions will grow from the 1997 level of 2 percent of GDP to 7 percent in the moderate-growth scenario and to 9 percent in the high-growth scenario.
- According to the projections, the increase in nonmonetary transactions will slightly exceed the dynamics of monetary transactions. Starting from the 11 percent of 1997, this difference tightens to 3 percent in the moderate-growth scenario, while decreasing to below 1 percent in the high-growth scenario.

- The projections suggest that over the next ten years the pace of growth in both currency and deposits will slow. The growth of currency will fall from 1 percent of GDP (in 1997) to below 1 percent by 2007, while the growth in deposits will fall from 4 percent of GDP in 1997 to 3 percent of GDP by 2007. The financial sector would attract financial savings in a greater proportion from households than from enterprises.

- With the weakening increase of domestic savings, the increase of domestic lending projected in the medium-term will be supported by the growing foreign indebtedness of the financial sector. While foreign sources of the banking sector decreased by 2 percent of GDP in 1997, an increase of 1 percent is projected for 2007. In the high-growth projection, the estimated larger sustainable current account deficit could only be financed in one way—by increasing the foreign borrowing of the financial sector.

- With increasing GDP, FDI and the nonfinancial sector's foreign borrowings will show a slight decrease when expressed as a percentage of GDP. FDI will decrease to 4 percent of the GDP in 1997 and to 2 percent of the GDP by 2007, while foreign borrowing by nonfinancial institutions will decrease from 3 percent of GDP in 1997 to 1 percent by 2007. In the high-growth scenario, this decrease is naturally higher when expressed as a percentage of GDP.

- According to the projections, domestic lending will strengthen within the next ten years. It will grow from 2 percent of GDP in 1997 to 3 percent by 2007 in the moderate-growth scenario, while reaching 5 percent of GDP according to the high-growth scenario. The higher domestic lending is driven in both scenarios by corporate lending that remains at the 1997 level and a decreasing government debt repayment.

- A decrease in government debt repayment makes it possible to decrease the government's net bond issue from 5 percent of GDP in 1997 to 3 percent by 2007. In the high-growth projection, the larger sustainable budget deficit would be financed by a greater number of government bond issues than in the moderate-growth projection.

- The increase in household savings in shares and other securities will be steady, at about 4 percent of GDP. In the higher-growth projection, the increase of gross household savings is larger (by 0.5 percent of GDP) than in the relatively unfavorable projection. With unchanged levels of investments in shares and other securities, this is mainly the product of a slightly greater rise in deposits and currency and government bond holdings by each household.

Conclusions

Summarizing the results of the two growth scenarios, it is clear that a higher-growth rate has a favorable influence on the ratios of debt to GDP. If the growth rate is higher than the real interest rate charge on debts, the debt to GDP ratio would decrease, despite the constant nominal debt volume. Consequently, the high-growth scenario allows a higher current account and budget deficit. This does not mean that these deficits would actually be greater, but that the constraints on the current account and the general budget deficit would be less binding. However, during the process of accessing EU membership, the government deficit must comply with the appropriate Maastricht criterion, which limits the general government deficit to a maximum of 3 percent of GDP. In the high-growth scenario, the Maastricht criteria become the effective constraint for the budget.

The sustainable current deficit in the moderate-growth scenario proved to be the real constraint for both the budget and the current account. The moderate real economic growth rate has an unfavorable influence on the debt to GDP ratio—if the growth rate is much closer (but not lower) than the real interest rate, the debt to GDP ratio barely improves compared with the high-growth scenario. Consequently, the moderate-growth scenario results in tighter and more binding current account and general government deficit constraints. To sum up, under the moderate economic growth scenario, there is a real danger that a fiscal policy adjustment would be needed unless the projected significant debt reduction is realized. However, considering that the recent level of gross government debt is close to the corresponding Maastricht criterion (60 percent debt to GDP ratio), during the process of accessing the EU, a significant further reduction of public debt relative to GDP would not be a policy priority. The need for a sustainable level of debt can be satisfied, because the real growth rate would not be less than 1.5–2 percentage points of the projected real interest rate.

Finally, on account of its stronger growth performance, the Hungarian macroeconomic environment has decisively improved over previous years. In Hungary the old dichotomy of growth versus equilibrium will probably not manifest itself as sharply as in the spring of 1995. High GDP growth, significant FDI inflow, and ever-smaller debt-to-GDP ratios, ensure that the Hungarian government will not have to follow a restrictive fiscal policy, at least until a potential increase in import demand leads to a widening of the trade deficit.

Annex 1: The Simple Flow of Funds Model Used in the Projection

This Annex briefly describes the model that was set up for the basic flow of funds time-series projections. The model includes financial constraints for four sectors. These equations are based on a consistency framework that assembles data into a flow of funds matrix structure. The model combines the flow of funds framework and some behavioral equations describing the debt stabilizing budget deficit and current account relations, money demand function, and domestic interest rate behavior characteristic of small, open economies.

Financial constraints

The double-entry accounting framework ensures consistency in the data by requiring that financial constraints for all economic sectors be satisfied simultaneously. All four parts of the model have a financial constraint. The financial constraint for monetary institutions is the following:

$$(5.1) \quad dLOAN = dM3 + NFLF.$$

The change in loans ($dLOAN$) equals the change of the monetary aggregate ($dM3$) and the volume of the net foreign liabilities absorbed by financial institutions ($NFLF$) during the period.

The financial constraint for the rest of the world is:

$$(5.2) \quad NFLF = CA—NFL—FDI.$$

The net foreign liabilities of financial institutions ($NFLF$) increase if the current account deficit (CA) increases, if net foreign liabilities of other sectors (NFL) decrease, or if foreign direct investment (FDI) decreases.

The financial constraint for the general government determines the change in domestic government loans:

$$(5.3) \quad dLOANG = DEFG—NFLG—dBONG.$$

This equation indicates that change in government loans ($dLOANG$) must be equal to the total budget deficit ($DEFG$) minus the government's net foreign borrowing (*NFLG*) and the issue of deficit-financing government bonds (*dBONG*).

Finally, the financial constraint for the private sector is:

$$(5.4) \quad POZH = dCUR + dDEPH + dBONDGH + dINS—dLOANH.$$

Equation 5.4 states that the net lending position of households (*POZH*) equals the change in currency (*dCUR*), the change in household deposits (*dDEP*), the change in governmental bonds (*dBONDGH*) and other securities (*dINS*) held by households, minus the change in household loans (*dLOANH*).

The net lending/net borrowing position of the corporate sector can be calculated on a residual basis:

$$(5.5) \quad POZE = CA—DEFG—POZH.$$

The net position of enterprises (*POZE*) equals the current account deficit, minus the budget deficit, minus the net lending position of households. The disadvantage of this method is that errors made in the estimation of net lending in any of the sectors also cause distortions in the net lending of the corporate sector.

Money Demand Function

The money demand function applied here reflects the monetarist approach (Polak 1997). At the analytical level, simplicity is inevitable because of limitations of statistical data (such as the absence of full-scale consumption, saving, and investment data) and the absence of econometric models that describe the Hungarian economy. Money demand is projected with the basic quantity theory of money:

$$(5.6) \quad dM3 = k*Y—k_{-1}*Y_{-1}—DEV*FOREXDEPT/M3.$$

The change in M3 is higher if the inverse of the velocity (*k*) increases, if nominal GDP (*Y*) increases, if exchange rate devaluation (*DEV*) decreases, or if the forex deposit volume in percentage of M3 (*FOREXDEPT*/M3) decreases. At the same time, M3 can be expressed as:

$$(5.7) \quad M3 = CUR + DEP.$$

The M3 monetary aggregate equals currency (*CUR*) and deposits (*DEP*), where deposits also include financial securities, a special characteristic of Hungarian bank accounting rules.

Interest Rates and Exchange Rate Determination

It may be reasonable to say that in small, open countries such as Hungary, the domestic interest rate is fully dependent on the international level of interest rates; the exchange rate; and, assuming risk-averse investors, on the risk premium (Kerekes 1998).

$$(5.8) \qquad i = (1 + DEV_{+1}) * (1 + i_F) * (1 + PREM) - 1.$$

The domestic nominal interest rate (i) is higher if the expected exchange rate devaluation (*DEV*) is higher, if the foreign nominal interest rate (i_F) is higher, or if the risk premium (*PREM*) increases. In order to eliminate the effect of cross-rates, it is sensible to plan foreign interest on the basis of the composition of the forint currency basket. From 1 January 1997 the currency basket has contained Deutsche marks and U.S. dollars in a 70 percent to 30 percent proportion. From 1 January 1999, instead of Deutsche marks, the Euro will become part of the basket. From 1 January 2000, the currency basket will consist solely of Euros. Because the forint rate is based on a crawling peg declared in advance, the devaluation consists of the official devaluation and the movement within the band. The width of the band ranges from +2.25 percent to -2.25 percent from the official rate. From 1 January 1999, the monthly devaluation rate of the forint crawling peg changed from 0.7 percent to 0.6 percent.

The ex-post real interest rate can be calculated as:

$$(5.9) \qquad r = (1 + i)/(1 + \pi_{+1}) - 1$$

where the real interest rate (r) is higher if the nominal interest rate is higher, or if next year's inflation (π_{+1}) is lower.

In a small, open economy, a similar relation can be written for the domestic price level, because the domestic price level is fully dependent on the world price level and the exchange rate. As a result, the real exchange rate can be calculated as:

$$(5.10) \qquad e = (1 + \pi)/(1 + \pi_F)/(1 + DEV) - 1.$$

The real exchange rate (e) increases if the domestic price level increases (π), if the foreign price level decreases (π_F), or if exchange rate devaluation decreases.

Budget Deficit Stabilizing Total Government Debt

If changes in the debt/GDP ratio are known, the primary surplus of the government can be calculated as:

$$(5.11) \quad p = (i-g)*d_{-1}/(1+g) + a - \Delta d.$$

The primary surplus (p) required to stabilize the debt/GDP ratio is higher if the desired level of debt (Δd) is smaller, if interest rates (i) are higher, if growth (g) is weaker, or if other items (a) are greater. Therefore, the sustainable level of the total budget deficit applied in the simple flow of funds projection model can be expressed as:

$$(5.12) \quad DEFG/GDP = p - i*c*d_{-1} - i_F*(1-c)*d_{-1}$$

where the total budget deficit is higher if the primary surplus is bigger, if domestic and foreign interest rates are lower, or if the debt is smaller. All variables are expressed as a percentage of GDP. The behavioral equation for the government deficit is derived below.

The change in government debt can be expressed in the following form:

$$(5.13) \quad \Delta D = (I-P) + A$$

where I is interest payments, P is the primary surplus, and A is other items outside the budget deficit that affect government indebtedness (privatization revenues, currency devaluation losses, bonds issuance for recapitalizing banks, and the like).[1]

To facilitate the analysis of government debt sustainability, equation 5.13 can be rewritten in ratios to GDP. Dividing both sides of equation 5.11 by Y (nominal GDP) and defining:

$$(5.14) \quad I = i*D_{-1},$$

and

---

1. The original equation form was taken from Moghadam 1997.

$$(5.15) \quad Y = (1 + g)^* Y_{-1}$$

where I is the nominal interest rate and g is the nominal GDP growth, we obtain:

$$(5.16) \quad D/Y - D_{-1}/(1 + g)^* \ Y_{-1} = i^* D_{-1}/(1 + g)^* \ Y_{-1} - P/Y + A/Y.$$

This can be rewritten as:

$$(5.17) \quad \Delta d = (i - g)^* d_{-1}/(1 + g) - p + a$$

where $d = D/Y$, $p = P/Y$, and $a = A/Y$.

It can be proven that the upper relation stands for real interest rates, and real growth rates as well. The primary surplus can be derived from equation 5.17.

Current Account Balance Stabilizing Net Foreign Debt

The last behavioral equation of the flow of funds projection model is the sustainable current account deficit. A sustainable foreign position—one that maintains a stable net foreign debt/GDP ratio—can be derived using the same method. Such deficits are useful benchmarks, because a higher deficit implies that the debt ratio will rise before stabilizing at a higher level. We expressed all variables in domestic currency. Considering that:

$$(5.18) \quad NFL = NFD + NFE, \text{ and}$$

$$(5.19) \quad \Delta NFL = CA.$$

The net foreign liabilities (NFL) equal the sum of the net foreign debt (NFD) and the net foreign equities liabilities (NFE), while the current account deficit (CA) equals the change in the net foreign liabilities. The change in foreign debt can be expressed as the current account deficit, less the net foreign equity inflow:

$$(5.20) \quad \Delta NFD = CA - \Delta NFE$$

where ΔNFE is the net inflow of FDI plus the net inflow of portfolio equity security investment. Dividing both sides of equation 4.18 by Y, the nominal GDP, and defining:

$$(5.21) \quad Y = (1 + g)^* Y_{-1},$$

where g is the growth rate of nominal GDP, we obtain:

$$(5.22) \quad NFD/Y - NFD_{-1}/(1 + g)^* \, Y_{-1} = CA/Y - ECI/Y.$$

Therefore, equation 5.22 can be rewritten as:

$$(5.23) \quad \Delta nfd = -g^* nfd_{-1}/(1 + g) + ca - eci$$

where $nfd = NFD/Y$, $ca = CA/Y$, and $eci = ECI/Y$.

If the change in the net foreign debt/GDP ratio is known, the current account deficit of the balance of payments can be calculated as:

$$(5.24) \quad ca = g^* nfd_{-1}/(1+g) + eci + \Delta nfd.$$

According to equation 5.24, the current account deficit required to stabilize the net foreign debt/GDP ratio is higher if the desired level of net debt/GDP is higher, if growth is stronger, or if foreign equity inflows are greater. The growth rate (g) can be defined in the currency composition of the net foreign debt, and is the sum of real GDP growth, foreign inflation (GDP deflators weighted according to the currency composition of net foreign debt), and real exchange rate appreciation of the Hungarian currency against the same currency basket, calculated on a GDP deflator basis (suggested in Beaumont 1998).

Annex 2: Financial Accounts of the Institutional Sector and the Flow of Funds Matrix of Hungary

In order to examine the role of the financial system in the allocation of financial sources, the balance sheets of four sectors was prepared for the period 1993 to 1997: households, general government, financial institutions, and the rest of the world. The flow of funds matrix was constructed for 1997, and the financial accounts of the four sectors for the period between 1997 and 2007 was projected in a simplified form. Because the projections were based on two kinds of growth scenarios, two flow of funds matrices were prepared for 2007.

Data Sources

When compiling the financial accounts, the balance of payments, the total balance of the banking system, the balance of the National Bank of Hungary, household receivables and liabilities, and the budget financing figures of the State Debt Management Agency were used . There were several contradictions and deficiencies in the data sources. This problem was solved by ranking the sources. Independent of the figures in the financial accounts of the sectors, the figures in the balance of payments were employed to determine the size of foreign sources. If there were contradictions between the financial accounts of the sectors and the credit balance of the banking system, the credit balance of the banking system was always used as a basis.

The specific published sources were:

- Annual Reports of the National Bank of Hungary, 1993–97
- Monthly Reports of the National Bank of Hungary, 1/1998–10/1998.
- National Accounts of Hungary, Hungarian Central Statistical Office, 1996
- Government Securities Markets, State Debt Management Agency, 1997–98

Institutional Sectors

When determining the sectors, the System of National Accounts' (SNA) rules were followed. The institutional units in the case of households, the general government, and the rest of the world are the ones recommended by the SNA. In the financial institution sector, only banks appear, because historical figures are not available for all financial activities. Other financial services such as insurance companies, pension funds, and inventory funds are treated separately, as part of the enterprise sector which was itself derived as a residual.

Financial Instruments

When compiling the financial accounts of the institutional sectors, the main categories of financial instruments determined by the SNA were followed. Before the forint became convertible in 1997 there were substantial household hard-currency deposits because of the quantitative limit of hard-currency exchange. Both assets and liabilities denominated in local currency and assets denominated in foreign currency were treated separately.

The Method of Compiling the Financial Accounts

When preparing the financial accounts of the sectors, a number of assumptions were used. Banks were assumed to confine their activities to financial transactions and intermediate the flow of funds among the other sectors of the economy (and made no investments). The net lending of the financial sector was set at zero. Owing to the noticeable difference between the current account and the financial account resulting from deficiencies in statistical recording, the net position of the rest of the world was estimated based on the financial accounts. In the case of general government, in the absence of exact data, the value of the enterprise property of the state was set at 2,000 billion forints in 1993. It was assumed that its value was decreased by part of the income from privatization. Finally, the net borrowing of the enterprise sector was estimated on a residual basis.

Forecasting Financial Accounts

The projected future financial accounts of the sectors were modeled between 1998 and 2007 under the high-growth and the moderate-growth scenario, based on preliminary macro figures for 1998.

As in the preparation of the past financial accounts of the institutional sectors, the stock figures were used as starting points in the projection of flow data of financial accounts. First, the outstanding financial assets and liabilities were projected, and then the differences in the stocks. Finally, the differences of the stocks denominated in foreign currency were adjusted with the effect of expected devaluation. It was assumed that there will be no other changes of volume. The financial accounts of the foreign sector were projected directly, without forecasting the stocks.

The financial accounts of the institutional sectors was modeled in a simplified form. The assets denominated in local currency and in foreign currency were not treated separately in the case of deposits and loans, but as one group. The financial account of the rest of the world was projected in net form, setting off receivables against liabilities. The size of net foreign sources is shown in the account of each sector according to the financial account of the rest of the world. Netting of the instruments distorts the aggregate balance sheets of the institutional sectors.

Flow of Funds Matrix

The flow of funds matrix of Hungary was made for five sectors. In order to follow the development of the financial system, the instruments were divided into two main groups: monetary transactions and instruments representing nonmonetary transactions. Monetary transactions show the flow of money from financial institutions to the other economic participants in detail, while the flow of money among the other sectors is shown among the nonmonetary transactions. For the sake of this grouping foreign credits were divided into two parts: foreign credits to financial institutions and foreign credits to nonfinancial institutions.

References

Addison, Doug. 1989. *The Word Bank Revised Minimum Standard Model, Concept and Issues.* World Bank Policy Research Working Paper No. 231. Washington, D.C.

Antal, Laslzo. 1998. "Transition and After, Results of the Hungarian Economy." Mozgó Világ 1998/6.

Barabás, Gyula, I. Hamecz, and J. Neményi. 1998. *General Government Deficit, Deficit Financing and Debt.* National Bank of Hungary Research Paper. Budapest.

Beaumont, Craig. 1998. "Sustainability in the Hungarian Balance of Payments." International Monetary Fund, Washington, D.C. Processed.

Cottarelli, Carlo, and others. 1998. *Hungary: Economic Policies for Sustainable Growth.* International Monetary Fund Occasional Paper No. 159. Washington, D.C.

Huszár, G., and Gy. Sándor. 1996. "Alternative Treatment of Interest Flows and Its Impact on the Accumulation Accounts, SNA in Transition Countries."

International Monetary Fund. 1997. *Hungary: Selected Issues.* International Monetary Fund Staff Country Report 97/103. Washington, D.C.

Jakab, M. Z., and Gy. Szapáry. 1998. *Experience of the Crawling Peg Regime in Hungary.* National Bank of Hungary Research Paper. Budapest.

Kerekes, Anna. 1998. *Calculations of Inconsistency.* Budapest: National Bank of Hungary.

Kiss, G. P. 1998. *The Role of General Government in Hungary.* National Bank of Hungary Research Paper, Budapest.

National Bank of Hungary. 1999. *Monetary Policy Guidelines.* Budapest: Monetary Policy Department, Magyar Nemzeti Bank.

Moghadam, Rezai. 1997. "Debt Dynamics in Hungary." In *Hungary: Selected Issues.* International Monetary Fund Staff Country Report 97/103. Washington, D.C.

OECD. 1997. *Hungary, Economic Surveys.* Paris.

Polak, Jacques J. 1997. *The IMF Monetary Model at 40.* International Monetary Fund Working Paper No. 97/46. International Monetary Fund, Washington, D.C.

Siklos, Pierre L., and Istvan Ábel. 1996. *Monetary Policy Strategies in Transition, Macroeconomic Issues of Recovery in Economic Transition.* Budapest

Szalkai, Istvan. 1995. "Monetary Direction, Introduction to Monetary Economics." Bankárképzõ

Tarafás, Imre. 1995. "Monetary Policy, Tools, and Conditions." *Közgazdasági Szemle*: 1024—43.

World Bank. 1995. *Hungary: Structural Reforms for Sustainable Growth.* World Bank Country Study. Washington, D.C.

————. 1996. *World Development Report 1996: From Plan to Market.* New York, New York: Oxford University Press for the World Bank.

6.

Russia—A National Unwillingness to Pay for Government

John A. Holsen

This chapter discusses Russia's financial evolution in 1993–97, with particular focus on the factors that contributed to the financial crisis that began in mid-1998. Together with the uncertain political situation, the crisis led to a sharp reversal in the progress made in 1997 in restoring real output and getting inflation under control (see Table 6.1). In the first ten months of 1998, real output was 3 percent below that of the same period one year earlier. Almost all the decline came from trends during July–October. The increase in the consumer price index (CPI), which had been held to 11 percent during 1997, reached 88 percent in the year ending December 1998. The ruble, which traded at 5.94 Rbs/US$ in December 1997, had fallen to 20.65 Rbs/US$ by the end of 1998. The sharp depreciation in the ruble was a major factor in Russia's inability to meet external debt service obligations, as well as in the renewal of inflation. The banking system was in crisis. In the prevailing circumstances, neither the government nor private borrowers were able to meet their debt obligations. At the close of 1998 the financial and economic outlook was, at best, both uncertain and worrying.

Prior to the mid-1998 crisis, Russia had appeared to be making slow but steady progress in getting the macroeconomy under control. Given the concern regarding external debt, it is perhaps surprising that Russia achieved current account surpluses throughout the 1993–97 period. And, although declines in investment and savings rates accompanied the decline in gross domestic product (GDP), the aggregate national savings rate in 1997 is nonetheless estimated at 22.5 percent of GDP. The central government budget, however, had negative savings, as well as a relatively large deficit throughout the period.

Table 6.1. Russia, 1993–97

Item	1993	1994	1995	1996	1997
Real GDP growth (% change)	…	-12.6	-4.0	-2.8	0.3
GDP deflator (% change)	…	306.4	170.2	42.8	17.9
Current account BOP deficit [-] (% GDP)	2.4	3.3	2.3	2.8	0.7
Central government budget deficit [-] (% GDP)	<u>-6.5</u>	<u>-11.4</u>	<u>-4.5</u>	<u>-6.8</u>	<u>-5.9</u>
Current savings (% GDP)	-2.4	-6.7	-0.6	-2.8	-2.1
Capital expenditures (% GDP)	4.2	4.7	3.9	4.1	3.8
Rest of economy [surplus] (% GDP)	<u>8.9</u>	<u>14.7</u>	<u>6.8</u>	<u>9.7</u>	<u>6.6</u>
Current savings (% GDP)	31.5	35.6	25.4	28.2	24.6
Investment expenditures (% GDP)	22.6	20.8	18.6	18.5	18.0

Note: Budget capital expenditures include capital transfers to the rest of the economy (ROE), while ROE investment excludes the portion financed by these transfers.

This chapter analyzes the factors leading up to the crisis that began in mid-1998 as they are reflected in flow of funds accounts for 1993–97. These accounts include the three basic macroeconomic management accounts—the central government budget, the monetary sector account, and the balance of payments. These are set in the framework of the national income accounts. Using the identities of the flow of funds accounting structure, these four accounts permit one to obtain a fifth account covering the private sector, or, more accurately, since not all public sector activities are included in the central government budget, covering the *rest of the economy* (ROE). The five accounts make up a consistent accounting structure, in which each of the 33 *matrix variables* is a source of funds in one account and a use of funds in another account. These flow of funds accounts are accompanied by an examination of interest rates and exchange rates, both of which are crucial to understanding the developments of the past several years.

The flow of funds approach can by no means provide a complete explanation of the financial and economic developments of the period. Particularly in Russia and other countries of the former Soviet Union (FSU), the legal, institutional, and cultural framework that is largely taken for granted in Western market economies did not exist when the transition began, and they have come into being only slowly. Under the circumstances, the "rational, profit-maximizing entrepreneur" has probably concentrated on collecting additional assets at favorable prices, rather than using existing assets to efficiently produce the goods the market demands. Also, both corruption and the lack of financial discipline continue to be major stumbling blocks in the transition to a market economy. And finally, the breakdown of trade and payments relationships that accompanied the breakup of the FSU was a major contributor to the declines in production. While acknowledging the importance of these factors, however, an analysis of trends in the economy, as reflected in the flow of funds tables, provides both valuable insights into the past and lessons for the future.

Data Sources and Methods

As perhaps should be expected during a period of transition, there are serious problems with the quality and consistency of the macroeconomic data regarding Russia in the 1990s. To the extent possible, the flow of funds tables are based on data published in the International Monetary Fund's (IMF's) *International Financial Statistics* (IFS). This source provides summary data on the central government budget for 1995–97, more detailed data on the balance of payments for 1994–97, and monetary survey data for 1993–97. The *IFS* is also the source of estimates of nominal GDP (which go back to 1992) and of the quarterly data on exchange rates, interest rates, and prices (produce prices and the cost of living, or COL) index. Supplementing the IMF's data with information published by Goskomstat and by the Institute for the Economy in Transition (the Gaidar Institute in Moscow), it was possible to prepare flow of funds tables for the five years from 1993 to 1997. While it would have been desirable to use a broad definition of *government* that included subnational governments and extrabudgetary funds, the limited data have led to restricting the *government* sector to the central government budget; all other public sector activities are included as part of the rest of the economy.

The preparation of consistent flow of funds matrices often requires decisions on the more appropriate data in cases with conflicting estimates of what is, in principle, the same flow (for example, the change in international reserves as shown in the balance of payments (BOP) and in the monetary account). In such cases, we have given priority to the monetary data, using it as the source of information on both changes in monetary authority net foreign assets and net credit from the banking system to finance the central government budget deficit. The capital account of the BOP was prepared using budgetary data on the government's external borrowing, monetary sector data on the net foreign assets of the deposit money banks, and calculating net borrowing by ROE as a residual. Another problem concerns budgetary interest payments. There is no complete and consistent series that breaks down interest payments between those on external debt and those on internal debt. In addition, the very important government debt in the form of ruble-denominated T-bills is treated as domestic financing in the budget, although many of these T-bills were held by foreign investors. In these circumstances, interest payments on all government debt are initially shown as a flow to the ROE sector, while in the BOP, all interest payments to the rest of world (ROW) are shown as coming from the ROE. Government interest payments to foreigners are thus "passed through" the ROE sector.

The appendix tables include the five flow of funds accounts in the form of flow of funds matrices, and the data are shown in rubles at current prices. Because inflation during the period makes flows in current prices difficult to interpret, information in text tables is generally limited to shares of GDP. In interpreting these shares of GDP data, however, one should bear in mind the trends in real GDP. The data indicate that real GDP fell by 12.6 percent in 1994, by 4.0 percent in 1995, and by 2.8 percent in 1996—a cumulative decline between 1993 and 1996 of 18.5 percent.

Central Government Budget

Table 6.2 summarizes the trends in the central government budget during 1993–97. Current revenues seem to have been "stuck" at about 12–13 percent of GDP. Current expenditures have been closer to 15–16 percent of GDP. The result has been negative budgetary saving of approximately 3 percent of GDP. The budget results were significantly "worse" in 1994, and significantly "better" in 1995. But in 1996 and 1997, the figures are not far from those of 1993. Capital expenditures, which include both real investment and capital transfers (net lending), have been around 4 percent of GDP. As a result, the budget deficit averaged 7 percent of GDP. These budget figures are on a cash, rather than accrual, basis; consequently, they do not take into account either the arrears on tax payments to the government or the government's own arrears in paying its obligations.

Why has Russia been unable to reduce its deficit below these comparatively high levels? Former Prime Minister Yegor Gaidar, in a talk given in January 1997 at the Institute for the Economy in Transition in Moscow, gave his audience the benefit of his practical experience in the matter. He said that for reasons of a socioeconomic and political character, rather than technical issues, it has been impossible to significantly improve budgetary tax collections, while expenditures were linked to the social liabilities inherited from socialism. He contrasted this with some countries of Central Europe and Scandinavia, which were more culturally homogeneous, and enjoyed much greater social consensus on matters of economic policy. "Russia is a large country, culturally nonhomogeneous, plus it is a federation. To count on such an abnormally high level of tax payments in GDP [as in these other countries] means to miss the reality. It should be understood that the limits are of a structural, not technical, character." While agreeing with the desirability of trying to improve the existing tax system, he stressed the need to correlate the central government's expenditure liabilities with its realistically estimated potential revenues.

Table 6.2. Summary of Central Government Budget (percent of GDP)

	1993	1994	1995	1996	1997	Average, 1993–97
Current revenues	12.9	10.8	14.1	12.7	12.3	12.6
Current expenditures	15.3	17.5	14.7	15.4	14.4	15.5
Budgetary saving	-2.4	-6.7	-0.6	-2.8	-2.1	-2.9
Capital expenditures	4.2	4.7	3.9	4.1	3.8	4.1
Deficit [-]	-6.5	-11.4	-4.5	-6.8	-5.9	-7.0
Deficit financing [+]	6.5	11.4	4.5	6.8	5.9	7.0
External [excluding T-bills]	-0.1	0.0	1.5	1.5	2.1	1.0
Banking system	4.8	10.5	6.1	6.5	2.4	6.1
Rest of economy	1.7	0.9	-3.1	-1.2	1.5	0.0

The financing of the budget deficit has relied very heavily on borrowing from the banking system. This form of deficit finance, with its potential to create monetary expansion, averaged over 6 percent of GDP during 1993–97. While there was a significant reduction in borrowing from the banking system in 1997, much of the difference was the product of greatly increased purchases of short-term, ruble-denominated T-bills (as well as other Russian debt obligations) by foreigners. Because adequate data are not available on

T-bills held by foreigners, this form of borrowing is included as financing from ROE. The issues and problems associated with this form of finance are discussed below in connection with the balance of payments.

The Monetary System

Table 6.3 summarizes data on both stocks and flows for the monetary system (monetary authorities plus deposit money banks). While it is the flows that are used in the flow of funds tables, for many purposes it is important to look at the stocks in relation to GDP. Because of the sometimes high, and always changing, rates of inflation during the 1993–97 period, it is important that end-of-year stocks be related to the end-of-period annual rate GDP, rather than to the annual average GDP (which may be at a quite different price level). For now, the end-of-period annual rate GDP has been estimated by "inflating" the annual average figure on the basis of the increase in prices (as indicated by the COL index) between the average level for the year in question and the average level in the last quarter of that year and the first quarter of the following year.

In the days of the Soviet Union, money and quasi-money represented relatively large shares of GDP. Thus broad money (currency, demand deposits, and time deposits) on 30 June 1989 amounted to 60 percent of that year's GDP. To some extent this reflected the "monetary overhang" that existed at the end of the 1980s, but data for earlier years indicated a ratio of broad money to GDP that was generally in the neighborhood of 50 percent. These comparatively high ratios reflected, in part, the lack of other financial assets, and the consequent high levels of savings held as deposit money and quasi-money. With the burst of inflation in the early 1990s, this ratio began to fall (income velocity began to increase). The ratio of broad money to GDP had declined to 10.2 percent of GDP by the end of 1993. As progress was made in reestablishing financial stability, the ratio recovered, and had reached 18.1 percent of GDP by the end of 1997.

Even with the decline in velocity, the flow of savings mobilized through increased holdings of money and quasi-money was only about 4 percent of GDP in 1996 and 1997. (The higher percentages in the earlier years reflected, of course, the "forced savings" associated with maintaining a desired level of real cash balances during periods of substantial inflation.) Taken together with the decline in net international reserves, this gradual remonetization of the economy was sufficient to permit the stock of net domestic credit to grow from 11 percent of GDP at the end of 1993 to nearly 25 percent at the end of 1997.

Table 6.3. Summary Monetary System Flows and Stocks

	1993	1994	1995	1996	1997	Average, 1993–97
A. Flows during year as a percentage of GDP						
Net foreign assets	1.7	-2.1	-0.5	-1.5	-1.7	-0.8
Net domestic credit	21.5	24.4	10.7	8.0	5.0	13.9
To budget	4.8	10.5	6.1	6.5	2.4	6.1
To rest of economy	16.7	13.9	4.6	1.5	2.6	7.9
Assets = liabilities	23.2	22.3	10.2	6.5	3.3	13.1
Money and quasi-money	15.8	11.3	9.0	4.0	3.8	8.8
Other liabilities (net)	7.4	11.0	1.2	2.5	-0.5	4.3
B. Stocks at end of year as a percentage of annual rate GDP						
Money and quasi-money	10.2	12.1	13.8	16.4	18.1	14.1
Net domestic credit	11.0	17.6	17.5	22.8	24.7	18.7
Claims on central government	2.3	6.7	8.2	13.2	13.9	8.8
Claims on rest of economy	8.7	10.9	9.3	9.6	10.9	9.9
All other accounts	-0.8	-5.5	-3.7	-6.4	-6.6	-4.6

There have been serious problems, however, regarding the allocation of this credit between financing the deficit in the central government budget and meeting the needs of the rest of the economy. While the stock of credit to the rest of the economy increased from 8.7 percent to 10.9 percent of GDP between 1993 and 1997, that going to finance the budget grew from 2.3 percent to 13.9 percent of GDP. At the end of 1997, credit to the central government budget exceeded that extended to the rest of the economy. This is both unusual and, from the standpoint of economic growth, undesirable. The inability to get the budget deficit under control has been accompanied by the maintenance of tight restrictions on overall expansion of money and credit. This has contributed to a number of the problems that have plagued the Russian economy, including payments arrears, high real interest rates, and limited growth and investment.

Although down from the extreme levels of 1996, during 1997 the real interest rate on representative commercial bank loans was nearly 40 percent in the first quarter, and seemed to stabilize at around 30 percent during the balance of the year. These high real interest rates are not entirely the result of supply and demand, but should be attributed partly to the bank practice of compensating for large loan losses with high interest rates, rather than depending on credit analysis and collateral. The real interest rates on T-bills during 1997 were also down sharply from the previous year, but hovered around 11–12 percent during the first three quarters of the year. Both the more moderate rate in the first three quarters and the increase in the fourth quarter are doubtless attributable in part to the role of foreign buyers, who demonstrated great enthusiasm for Russian debt securities in 1997, but became cautious toward all emerging markets in the last quarter of the year (Table 6.4).

Table 6.4. Trends in Nominal and Real Interest Rates (percent)

	QIV-95	QI-96	Q2-96	Q3-96	Q4-96	Q1-97	Q2-97	Q3-97	Q4-97	Q1-98
Nominal interest rates (annualized quarterly average)										
Treasury bills	141.3	88.4	144.9	67.6	42.2	31.4	27.1	19.0	26.3	29.1
Lending rate	231.9	187.8	176.4	142.8	80.2	63.9	48.6	38.4	33.8	39.3
Inflation rate	66.3	47.8	25.3	14.5	18.3	17.9	14.4	6.4	2.3	9.2
Real interest rates (annualized quarterly average)										
Treasury bills	45.1	27.4	95.5	46.4	20.3	11.5	11.1	11.9	23.5	18.3
Lending rate	99.6	94.7	120.7	112.1	52.4	39.0	29.9	30.1	30.8	27.6

Source: All rates are annualized quarterly averages. Data are from the IMF's *International Financial Statistics*. The annualized quarterly inflation rate is calculated from an average of the quarterly increases in producer prices and in the COL index

The Balance of Payments

Since the traditional flow of funds approach is handled in current prices, it has significant limitations when there are major changes in relative prices. And this is the case in Russia during the 1990s, when relative prices were changing in response to both increasing integration into the world economy and major changes in the real exchange rate. Consequently, our discussion includes analysis of the real exchange rate as well as of the BOP flows expressed as a share of current price GDP. Table 6.5 summarizes trends in the BOP and Table 6.6 shows the derivation of an index of the real exchange rate. Table 6.7 illustrates the reasons for the massive increase in portfolio investment in Russian debt securities in 1997 by providing a comparison of interest rates in Russia with the London interbank offered rate (LIBOR) converted at the prevailing exchange rates.

Looking at Table 6.5, it can be seen that Russia was a net provider of resources—in both real and financial terms—to the rest of the world during 1993–97. During these years, the current account balance was always positive (that is, foreign savings have always been negative), with an average surplus of 2.3 percent of GDP. The resource balance has always been positive, with an average surplus of 3.6 percent of GDP. While both the real and financial surpluses declined in 1997, they remained positive. However, there is a strong suspicion that the BOP figures in Table 6.5 do not tell the complete story. Errors and omissions are quite high, averaging 1.5 percent of GDP during the five-year period. In U.S. dollars, they ran close to $8 billion annually during 1995–97. In the flow of funds tables, the outflow on errors and omissions appears as a flow from the rest of the economy to the rest of the world. While such negative errors and omissions are often assumed to represent unrecorded capital flight, there are three other factors that seem important in the Russian data. One of these, which would reduce the surpluses on both the resource and current account balances, is unreported imports brought in by shuttle traders. Another, which would affect the current account balance, is unreported remittances to their home countries by workers from other FSU republics. The third is a variant of capital flight: the holding of foreign banknotes within the country, where they are a substitute for ruble broad money, to serve as a store of value, and sometimes as a means of payment. Unfortunately, it is not possible to make sufficiently reliable estimates of these three factors to justify making explicit adjustments in the "official" balance of payments data. While they need to be kept in mind when interpreting the numbers, they are not enough to change the resource surplus or the current account surplus into a deficit.

Table 6.5. Trends in the Balance of Payments (percent and US$ millions)

	1993	1994	1995	1996	1997	Average, 1993—97
A. As percentage of GDP (at current prices and X-rates)						
Exports [G&NFS]	33.7	27.3	26.8	24.1	22.7	26.9
Imports [G&NFS]	29.6	23.3	23.6	20.0	20.0	23.3
Resource balance	4.1	4.0	3.2	4.0	2.7	3.6
Net factor income	-3.3	-0.6	-1.0	-1.2	-1.9	-1.6
Net current transfers	1.6	0.0	0.0	0.0	-0.1	0.3
Balance on current account	2.4	3.3	2.3	2.8	0.7	2.3
Direct and portfolio investment	0.2	0.2	0.6	2.9	11.7	3.1
Budget deficit financing	-0.1	0.0	1.5	1.5	2.1	1.0
Deposit money banks NFA	0.2	-0.4	1.9	0.2	2.1	0.8
Rest of economy	0.6	-5.5	-2.6	-6.8	-14.6	-5.8
Errors and omissions	-1.5	-0.2	-2.3	-1.9	-1.6	-1.5
Increase [-] mon. authority NFA	-1.9	2.5	-1.3	1.2	-0.4	0.0
B. As percentage of GDP at constant 1995 prices and X-rates						
Exports [G&NFS]	15.8	22.9	26.8	30.5	31.7	25.6
Imports [G&NFS]	13.9	19.4	23.6	26.6	29.3	22.6
Resource balance	1.9	3.5	3.2	3.9	2.5	3.0
C. US$ millions						
Exports [G&NFS]	58,368	76,220	93,184	103,459	102,196	
Imports [G&NFS]	51,288	65,043	81,917	86,094	90,065	
Resource balance	7,080	11,177	11,267	17,365	12,131	
Net factor income	-5,659	-1,780	-3,369	-5,290	-8,425	
Net current transfers	2,796	-111	38	23	-361	
Balance on current account	4,217	9,286	7,936	12,098	3,345	
Direct and portfolio investment	400	605	2,098	12,395	52,634	
Budget deficit financing	-101	46	5,140	6,494	9,243	
Deposit money banks NFA	429	-1,059	6,468	972	9,462	
Rest of economy	968	-15,446	-9,099	-29,113	-65,842	
Errors and omissions	-2,551	-439	-7,908	-8,136	-7,162	
Increase [-] mon. authority NFA	-3,362	7,007	-4,635	5,289	-1,680	

Table 6.6. National Accounts and Trade Data Used to Calculate
the Index of the Real Exchange Rate

	1993	1994	1995	1996	1997
A. In current prices (million rubles)					
GDP	172,000	611,000	1,585,000	2,200,000	2,602,000
Exports GNFS	57,884	166,983	424,844	529,772	591,183
Imports GNFS	50,862	142,496	373,476	440,853	521,008
Expenditures	164,979	586,513	1,533,631	2,111,081	2,531,825
B. In constant 1995 prices (million rubles)					
GDP	1,889,064	1,651,042	1,585,000	1,540,620	1,545,242
Exports GNFS	298,379	378,791	424,844	470,455	490,546
Imports GNFS	262,209	320,763	373,476	410,424	452,370
Expenditures	1,852,894	1,593,014	1,533,631	1,480,590	1,507,066
C. Deflators (1995 = 1.0)					
GDP	0.091	0.370	1.000	1.428	1.684
Exports GNFS	0.194	0.441	1.000	1.126	1.205
Imports GNFS	0.194	0.444	1.000	1.074	1.152
Expenditures	0.089	0.368	1.000	1.426	1.680
D. Domestic GDP (GDP exports; million rubles)					
In current prices	114,116	444,017	1,160,156	1,670,228	2,010,817
In constant prices	1,590,685	1,272,251	1,160,156	1,070,165	1,054,696
Price index, "domestic GDP"	0.072	0.349	1.000	1.561	1.907
E. Domestic expenditures (total expenditures—imports; million rubles)					
In current prices	114,116	444,017	1,160,156	1,670,228	2,010,817
In constant prices	1,590,685	1,272,251	1,160,156	1,070,165	1,054,696
Price index domestic expenditures	0.072	0.349	1.000	1.561	1.907
F. Internationally traded goods (exports imports; million rubles)					
In current prices	108,746	309,479	798,320	970,625	1,112,191
In constant prices	560,588	699,554	798,320	880,879	942,916
Price index, internationally traded goods	0.1940	0.4424	1.0000	1.1019	1.1795
Index of real exchange rate (1995 = 1.0)					
Ratio, price index domestic GDP / price index internationally traded goods $(X + M)$	0.370	0.789	1.000	1.416	1.616

Note: The identity of the export and import indices of unit value in 1993 is an accident of the data.

Table 6.7. Interest Rates in Russia Compared with LIBOR Cost in Rubles (percent)

	QIV-95	QI-96	Q2-96	Q3-96	Q4-96	Q1-97	Q2-97	Q3-97	Q4-97	Q1-98
LIBOR (3 months US$; annualized quarterly average)										
Interest in US$	5.9	5.4	5.5	5.6	5.5	5.6	5.8	5.7	5.9	5.7
Cost in rubles	7.8	10.2	10.4	11.7	9.9	8.9	7.9	6.6	7.6	8.2
Spreads over LIBOR cost in rubles										
For T-bills	133.5	78.2	134.5	55.9	32.3	22.5	19.2	12.4	18.7	20.9
For lending	224.1	177.6	166.0	131.1	70.3	55.0	40.7	31.8	26.2	31.1
Percent change from prior quarter										
X-rate [Rbs/US$]	1.8	4.5	4.6	5.8	4.1	3.1	2.0	0.8	1.6	2.4
Inflation rate	13.6	10.3	5.8	3.4	4.3	4.2	3.4	1.6	0.6	2.2

Source: All data are from IMF's *International Financial Statistics* (various monthly issues).

When expressed as shares of GDP, the most striking feature of the current account of the BOP is the apparent decline in exports and imports. Between 1993 and 1997, exports seem to have fallen from 34 percent to 23 percent of GDP, while imports have dropped from 30 percent to 20 percent. This, however, is the result of the appreciation of the real exchange rate. The effect is seen when the coefficients are calculated using data in constant 1995 prices and exchange rates (see part B of Table 6.5). When this is done, instead of declining by one-third, both exports and imports double as a share of GDP.

The 1990s have been a period of large and relatively rapid changes in the real exchange rate in Russia. The decade began with a large depreciation. But by 1994 the exchange rate was appreciating in real terms, and this process continued until mid-1998. Measuring trends in the real exchange rate presents numerous problems, but the issues involved are too important to ignore. There is general acceptance of the proposition that the real exchange rate is indicated by the ratio of the prices of nontradeables to the prices of tradeable goods. In practice, however, these indices are not available. The commonly used alternative approach is to use the ratio of an index of national prices to an index of world prices. This approach, however, suffers from the significant effect of the nominal exchange rate on the "national" price level because of the role of tradable goods in the economy.

To minimize this problem, and to more closely approach the concept of the ratio of nontradable to tradable prices, we have used an approach that looks at the ratio of the prices of *domestic GDP* (that is, total GDP less exports) to the prices of internationally traded goods (exports plus imports). The process is illustrated in Table 6.6. Once one has established GDP, exports and imports in both current and constant prices, it is simple to calculate price indices for domestic GDP and for exports plus imports. As seen in the example in Table 6.6, it makes no difference whether one uses an index of domestic GDP or of domestic expenditures (total expenditures less imports).

When this approach is applied to the data for Russia, one finds that there was a 170 percent appreciation in the real exchange rate between 1993 and 1995. Although the rate of appreciation has slowed, there was still an additional 62 percent appreciation between 1995 and 1997. Recognizing the extent of this appreciation is fundamental to understanding financial and economic developments in Russia, including the "success" in slowing inflation; why such an exceedingly high proportion of the consumer goods sold in Moscow are imported; why some domestic economic activities have suffered because of their inability to compete with imported similars; and the large spread between national interest rates and the interest rates, measured in rubles, that prevailed in 1996 and 1997.

When one looks at trends in the capital account of the balance of payments, two things stand out. The first is the rapid increase in direct and portfolio investment—from US$2 billion in 1995 to US$12 billion in 1996 and US$53 billion in 1997. The second is less rapid, but still very substantial, increase in the net outflow in the rest-of-economy account. The increase in direct and portfolio investment was partly the result of direct and portfolio equity investments, but by far the larger share was made up of investments in T-bills and other Russian debt securities. The capital inflow for these purposes grew from an insignificant US$36 million in 1995 to US$7.8 billion in 1996, and to US$46.4 billion in 1997. Russian interest rates were already relatively high (see Table 6.4) in comparison with international rates. The appreciating ruble added to the spread between the ruble cost of capital on international markets and the rates being paid on T-bills (not to mention for commercial bank lending) in Russia. For example, in the fourth quarter of 1996, the annualized ruble equivalent of a three-month US$ LIBOR was 9.9 percent, while the going rate on T-bills was 42.2 percent (see Table 6.7). The resulting 32.3 percentage point spread, which could be earned on short-term government paper, was clearly attractive to international lenders. The increasing inflow of foreign capital from purchasers of ruble debt securities did several things that, at least initially, appeared to be desirable. First, by adding to the supply of foreign exchange in the auction market, the capital inflows made possible and confirmed the "strong" ruble. Second, the resulting appreciation helped hold down the cost of imports, and hence the cost of living index. Third, it helped the budget by lowering the real cost of borrowing to finance the budget deficit (see Table 6.4). But, in addition to the high risks associated with large short-term capital inflows, this contributed to the Dutch Disease—like problems faced by some domestic producers of tradable goods.

It may be noted that the deposit money banks also borrowed large amounts abroad ($9.5 billion in 1997) that they could use to maintain a larger portfolio of profitable T-bills or to on-lend to borrowers who were paying interest rates that were well above those on T-bills. The spread made external borrowing attractive to borrowers as well as to lenders.

The nature of the increased capital outflow from the rest of the economy (which rose from almost 7 percent of GDP in 1996 to nearly 15 percent of GDP in 1997) is not entirely clear. Part of the problem is that the figures are calculated as residuals in the flow of funds. They are established by taking what in the IMF *IFS* BOP is labeled "Other Investments"—which represent the consolidated international investment position, including both assets and liabilities, but excluding direct and portfolio investments—and then deducting external borrowing to finance the budget deficit as reported in the budget, and also deducting net external borrowing by the deposit money banks as reported in the monetary sector accounts. There is, however, a large difference between the government's external finance as reported in the budget (which shows an *inflow* of US$9.2 billion in 1997), and as reported in the balance of payments published in *IFS* (which shows an *outflow* of US$10.2 billion). The difference presumably reflects the government's large extra-budgetary activities, especially, perhaps, those related to debt relief agreements, in which Russia is involved both as a creditor and as a debtor. There is clearly a need for greater clarification in this area. One contribution of the flow of funds approach in this instance is to identify a large inconsistency between commonly used macroeconomic accounts.

The largest part of the net outflow from the rest of the economy, however, appears to represent purchase of external assets by Russians. As reported in the *IFS* BOP tables, the outflow from the rest of the economy to purchase assets abroad rose from US$28.0 billion in 1996 to US$34.7 billion in 1997. Russian investors seem to have been moving money out of the country at the same time that foreign investors were bringing in their capital in search of very high short-term profits.

The National Accounts

Table 6.8 shows the trends in the major magnitudes in the national accounts, expressed as percentages of GDP. Given the budget and the BOP data, for the flow of funds, the only additional inputs required to complete the national accounts table are total GDP and total investment. All of the other values are either taken from the economic management accounts already discussed (for example, the resource balance and foreign saving; budgetary consumption, investment, and saving) or are calculated from the identities of the accounting structure (consumption, investment, and saving by the rest of the economy).

Table 6.8. National Accounts: Major Magnitudes as a Share of GDP (percent)

	1993	1994	1995	1996	1997	Average 1993–97
Gross domestic product	100.0	100.0	100.0	100.0	100.0	100.0
Net real resources from ROW	-4.1	-4.0	-3.2	-4.0	-2.7	-3.6
Resource availabilities = uses	95.9	96.0	96.8	96.0	97.3	96.4
Consumption	69.2	70.5	74.2	73.4	75.5	72.5
Budgetary	8.3	9.6	8.2	8.5	8.0	8.5
Rest of economy	60.9	60.8	66.0	64.9	67.5	64.0
Investment	26.7	25.5	22.5	22.6	21.8	23.8
Budgetary	1.8	1.9	1.7	1.8	1.7	1.8
Rest of economy	24.9	23.6	20.8	20.8	20.1	22.1
Saving = Investment	26.7	25.5	22.5	22.6	21.8	23.8
Foreign saving	-2.4	-3.3	-2.3	-2.8	-0.7	-2.3
National saving	29.2	28.9	24.8	25.4	22.5	26.2
Budgetary saving	-2.4	-6.7	-0.6	-2.8	-2.1	-2.9
Rest of economy saving	31.5	35.6	25.4	28.2	24.6	29.1

Source: See accompanying flow of funds tables.

Other than the already discussed negative net inflow of resources from the rest of the world and negative foreign savings, the key trends to be noted in Table 6.8 are the declining levels of savings and investment (even when measured as a share of a declining real GDP) and the declining level of ROE consumption when the decline in real GDP is taken into account. Although ROE consumption as a share of GDP rose by 10.8 percent (from 60.9 to 67.5 percent), between 1993 and 1997, this was more than offset by the 18.2 percent cumulative decline in GDP in constant prices (see Table 6.6).

Rest of the Economy

While in a more perfect flow of funds, this ROE account would cover only the private sector, and perhaps be divided into "business" and "household" subsectors, the data available for Russia do not permit a very detailed breakdown. Particularly important are the public sector activities that are outside the central government budget and that are, as a matter of necessity rather than choice, included in the "ROE" in this flow of funds analysis. This clearly reduces the usefulness of the ROE account to show the implications for the private sector of the trends in the economic management accounts.

The ROE savings rate may be measured by calculating saving as a share of disposable income. When this is done (see Table 6.9), it is noted that this rate drops from 34.1 percent (31.5/92.4) in 1993 to 26.7 percent (24.6/92.2) in 1997. This represents a comparatively high marginal saving rate—40 percent. However, in this case it is measured using the declines in saving and disposable income rather than the usual increases. These declines in savings and investment can, in part, be linked to the dearth of reasonably safe and profitable investment opportunities during a period when total output was declining and payments arrears were growing. The observed declines in the investment and savings ratios are also probably at least partially the result of a decline in the relative price of investment goods during the 1993–97 period. As relative prices converged to world levels because of reductions in subsidies and the opening of the economy, the relative prices of investment goods would fall because these prices were already closer to world levels at the prevailing exchange rates. To this reason must be added the relatively higher import content of investment compared with consumption; in this circumstance, the appreciation of the real exchange rate would tend to lower savings and investment ratios calculated using data in current prices.

Table 6.9. Rest of the Economy Account as a Share of GDP (percent)

	1993	1994	1995	1996	1997	Average, 1993–97
GDP at factor cost	93.3	93.6	95.3	96.2	96.5	95.0
Net current receipts from budget	0.7	3.4	-2.9	-1.9	-2.4	-0.6
Net current receipts from ROW	<u>-1.7</u>	<u>-0.7</u>	<u>-1.0</u>	<u>-1.2</u>	<u>-2.0</u>	<u>-1.3</u>
Disposable inco0me	92.4	96.4	91.4	93.0	92.2	93.1
Consumption by ROE	<u>60.9</u>	<u>60.8</u>	<u>66.0</u>	<u>64.9</u>	<u>67.5</u>	<u>64.0</u>
Saving by ROE	31.5	35.6	25.4	28.2	24.6	29.1
Total capital sources	<u>49.8</u>	<u>46.8</u>	<u>28.0</u>	<u>26.2</u>	<u>24.9</u>	<u>35.1</u>
Saving by ROE	31.5	35.6	25.4	28.2	24.6	29.1
Capital transfers from budget	2.3	2.7	2.2	2.3	2:2	2.4
Credit from banking system	16.7	13.9	4.6	1.5	2.6	7.9
Net loans from ROW	-0.7	-5.5	-4.3	-5.8	-4.5	-4.2
Total capital uses	<u>49.8</u>	<u>46.8</u>	<u>28.0</u>	<u>26.2</u>	<u>24.9</u>	<u>35.1</u>
Real investment by ROE	24.9	23.6	20.8	20.8	20.1	22.1
Money and quasi-money	15.8	11.3	9.0	4.0	3.8	8.8
Capital, reserves, etc., of banks	7.4	11.0	1.2	2.5	-0.5	4.3
Loans to finance budget deficit	1.7	0.9	-3.1	-1.2	1.5	0.0

Source: See accompanying flows of funds tables.

The decline in ROE capital sources and uses from nearly 50 percent of GDP in 1993 to less than 25 percent of GDP in 1997 is substantially the result of the decline in inflation, and consequently in "forced saving" in the form of money and quasi-money (MQM) holdings. The increases in MQM dropped by 12 percentage points, from 15.8 percent of GDP in 1993 to 3.8 percent of GDP in 1997. It may also be noted that transactions between the ROE and the banking system represented a substantial net outflow of ROE resources. For the period as a whole, the flows of credit from the banking system to the ROE averaged 7.9 percent of GDP. This should be compared with the flows from ROE to the banks in the form of both MQM and increases in bank capital and reserves; combined, these flows averaged 13.1 percent of GDP during 1993–97.

Main Conclusions

Perhaps the most disturbing trend brought out by the analysis of the flow of funds accounts for 1993–97 is the stagnation of central government revenues as a share of GDP. This, along with the apparent inability to sufficiently constrain expenditures, has led to a budget deficit of 6–7 percent of GDP. The consequences of financing this deficit largely by borrowing from the banking system, in combination with the overall restraints on money and credit, have resulted in very limited credit availabilities for the rest of the economy. Absorption by the central government budget of a progressively larger share of total net domestic credit has contributed to a number of problems in the rest of the economy, including high real interest rates, payments arrears, and shortages of working capital, as well as financing for investments. The explosive growth in short-term external capital inflows in 1996 and 1997 is related to the use of T-bills to finance the budget deficit, to the comparatively high ruble interest rates, and to the appreciation of the real exchange rate. The latter added to the spread between internal and external interest rates (when both are expressed in rubles) and, at least for a while, made investing in short-term ruble debt securities seem very profitable to foreign investors. The risk became obvious in the summer of 1998. Going beyond the usual flow of funds analysis, measures of the appreciation in the real exchange rate suggest that this may have contributed to "Dutch Disease"—like problems, which slowed the recovery of output in Russia, as well as acting as a brake on inflation.

Russia: Flow-of-Funds Tables [1993-1997]

List of 33 Matrix Variables in Flow-of-Funds Tables

Cg	Consumption of central government (per budget)
Cp	Consumption of private sector
CTfp	Current transfers, foreign to private
CTgp	Current transfers, government to private
CTpf	Current transfers, private to foreign
D&PFI	Direct & portfolio foreign investment
E&O	Errors and omissions [in BOP]
FPfp	Factor income paymnents, foreign to private
FPpf	Factor income paymnents, private to foreign
GDPfc	Gross domestic product at factor cost
Ig	Investment of central government [per budget]
Ip	Investment of private sector
Lfg	Loans [net], foreign to government
Lfp	Loans [net], foreign to private
Lgp	Loans [net], government to private
Lmg	Loans [net], monetary to government
Lmp	Loans [net], foreign to private
Lpg	Loans [net], private to government
M	Imports [goods and non-factor services]
MQM	Money and quasi-money
NFAma	Net foreign assets of monetary authorities
NFAdmb	Net foreign assets of deposit money banks
Ngf	Interest, government to foreign
Ngp	Interest, government to private
NOL	Net other liabilities [in monetary survey]

"Government" refers to flows included in the federal government budget.

What is called the"private" sector is really the "rest of the economy", i.e., that which is not part of the federal government budget, or in the case of the capital account, not part of part of the monetary sector. [The current account of the monetary sector is consolidated with the "private" sector.]

For the budget, monetary, rest of economy [private] and rest of world [BOP] sectors, sources of resources are shown horizontally while uses are listed vertically. For the national accounts this relationship is reversed.

NTRev	Non-tax revenues
Sf	Savings of foreign sector [equals -Curbal]
Sg	Savings of government
Sp	Savings of private sector
Sub	Subsidies
Td	Taxes, direct
TTi	Taxes, indirect
X	Exports [goods and non-factor services]

Flow-of-Funds Matrix
Russia - 1993

Current Account	Budget	Monetary	Rest of Economy	Rest of World	National Accounts	Totals
Budget			Td 5,500 NTRev 2,500		Ti 14,200 -Sub -2,700	19,500
Monetary						0
Rest of Economy	Ngp 900 Ngf 2,500 CTgp 5,840			FPfp 0 CTfp 2,774	GDPfc 160,500	172,514
Rest of World			FPpf 5,614 CTpf 0		M 50,878 -X -57,901	-1,410
National Accounts	Cg 14,310 Sg -4,050		Cp 104667 Sp 54233	Sf -4,183		164,977
Totals	19,500	0	172,514	-1,410	164,977	

Capital Account	Budget	Monetary	Rest of Economy	Rest of World	National Accounts	Totals
Budget		Lmg 8,294	Lpg 3,006	Lfg -100	Sg -4,050	7,150
Monetary			MQM 27,120 NOL 12,754			39,874
Rest of Economy	Lgp 4,000	Lmp 28,671		Lfp 960 D&PFI 397 E&O -2,531	Sp 54233	85,730
Rest of World		NFAma 3,335 NFAdmb -426			Sf -4,183	-1,274
Natinal Accounts	Ig 3,150		Ip 42,850			46,000
Totals	7,150	39,874	85,730	-1,274	46,000	

Flow-of-Funds Matrix
Russia - 1994

Current Account	Budget		Monetary	Rest of Economy		Rest of World		National Accounts		Totals
Budget				Td	17,200			Ti	49,000	56,120
				NTRev	0			-Sub	-10,080	
Monetary										0
Rest of Economy	Ngp	8,900				FPfp	7,672	GDPfc	572,080	618,896
	Ngf	3,100				CTfp	984			
	CTgp	26,160								
Rest of World				FPpf	11,572			M	142,496	-11,688
				CTpf	1,227			-X	-166,983	
National Accounts	Cg	58,960		Cp	371,553					586,513
	Sg	-41,000		Sp	217344	Sf	-20,344			
Totals	56,120		0	618,896		-11,688		586,513		

Capital Account	Budget		Monetary		Rest of Economy		Rest of World		National Accounts		Totals
Budget			Lmg	63,996	Lpg	5,604	Lfg	100	Sg	-41,000	28,700
Monetary					MQM	68,950					136,160
					NOL	67,210					
Rest of Economy	Lgp	16,800	Lmp	85,195			Lfp	-33,839	Sp	217344	285,864
							D&PFI	1,325			
							E&O	-962			
Rest of World			NFAma	-15,352					Sf	-20,344	-33,375
			NFAdmb	2,321							
National Accounts	Ig	11,900			Ip	144,100					156,000
Totals	28,700		136,160		285,864		-33,375		156,000		

Flow-of-Funds Matrix
Russia - 1995

Current Account	Budget	Monetary	Rest of Economy	Rest of World	National Accounts	Totals
Budget			Td 117,557 NTRev 6,782		Ti 99,471 -Sub -24,362	199,448
Monetary						0
Rest of Economy	Ngp 24,885 CTgp 54,139			FPfp 19,504 CTfp 3,661	GDPfc 1,509,891	1,612,080
Rest of World			FPpf 34,864 CTpf 3,488		M 373,476 -X -424,844	-13,017
National Accounts	Cg 129,933 Sg -9,509		Cp 1,046,698 Sp 402691	Sf -36,182		1,533,631
Totals	199,448	0	1,612,080	-13,017	1,533,631	

Capital Account	Budget	Monetary	Rest of Economy	Rest of World	National Accounts	Totals
Budget		Lmg 96,735	Lpg -48,400	Lfg 23,434	Sg -9,509	62,260
Monetary			MQM 142,139 NOL 19,535			161,674
Rest of Economy	Lgp 35,190	Lmp 73,296		Lfp -41,484 D&PFI 9,565 E&O -36,054	Sp 402691	443,204
Rest of World		NFAma 21,132 NFAdmb -29,489			Sf -36,182	-44,539
Natinal Accounts	Ig 27,069		Ip 329,931			357,000
Totals	62,260	161,674	443,204	-44,539	357,000	

Flow-of-Funds Matrix
Russia - 1996

Current Account	Budget	Monetary	Rest of Economy	Rest of World	National Accounts	Totals
Budget			Td 152,156 NTRev 8,453		Ti 118,343 -Sub -35,050	243,902
Monetary						0
Rest of Economy	Ngp 39,931 CTgp 77,889			FPfp 22,188 CTfp 3,897	GDPfc 2,116,707	2,260,612
Rest of World			FPpf 49,277 CTpf 3,779		M 440,870 -X -529,793	-35,866
National Accounts	Cg 186,934 Sg -60,852		Cp 1,427,143 Sp 619804	Sf -61,951		2,111,077
Totals	243,902	0	2,260,612	-35,866	2,111,077	

Capital Account	Budget	Monetary	Rest of Economy	Rest of World	National Accounts	Totals
Budget		Lmg 142,780	Lpg -25,611	Lfg 33,256	Sg -60,852	89,573
Monetary			MQM 88,845 NOL 54,717			143,562
Rest of Economy	Lgp 50,628	Lmp 32,846		Lfp -149,081 D&PFI 63,472 E&O -41,663	Sp 619804	576,006
Rest of World		NFAma -27,086 NFAdmb -4,978			Sf -61,951	-94,015
Natinal Accounts	Ig 38,945		Ip 458,055			497,000
Totals	89,573	143,562	576,006	-94,015	497,000	

Flow-of-Funds Matrix
Russia - 1997

Current Account	Budget	Monetary	Rest of Economy	Rest of World	National Accounts	Totals
Budget			Td 180,706 NTRev 9,681		Ti 129,076 -Sub -38,848	280,615
Monetary						0
Rest of Economy	Ngp 41,463 CTgp 86,329			FPfp 24,782 CTfp 2,013	GDPfc 2,511,772	2,666,358
Rest of World			FPpf 73,519 CTpf 4,101		M 521,008 -X -591,183	7,445
National Accounts	Cg 207,188 Sg -54,364		Cp 1,757,636 Sp 640714	Sf -19,350		2,531,825
Totals	280,615	0	2,666,358	7,445	2,531,825	

Capital Account	Budget	Monetary	Rest of Economy	Rest of World	National Accounts	Totals
Budget		Lmg 61,971	Lpg 38,202	Lfg 53,469	Sg -54,364	99,278
Monetary			MQM 97,713 NOL -12,585			85,128
Rest of Economy	Lgp 56,114	Lmp 68,176		Lfp -380,884 D&PFI 304,477 E&O -41,432	Sp 640714	647,165
Rest of World		NFAma 9,717 NFAdmb -54,736			Sf -19,350	-64,369
Natinal Accounts	Ig 43,164		Ip 523,836			567,000
Totals	99,278	85,128	647,166	-64,370	567,000	

Private Sector Imbalance

Estonia

7.

Estonia—When the Problem is the Private Sector

Stephen J. Peachy

This chapter looks at recent Estonian experience in the wake of the volatility in financial markets of 1997 and tries to identify the key financing issues likely to be faced by the authorities if the economy is to secure the rapid investment-led growth envisaged for the run-up to European Union (EU) accession. It is concluded that annual investment-led real growth of 6 percent can only be financed through a combination of strong foreign capital inflows directly to the nonbank/nongovernment sector (NBNGS)—broadly equivalent to the private sector—and continued heavy foreign finance of what would otherwise be unsustainable growth in bank lending. Even for a country in the first wave of accession to the EU, it is not clear that the current world environment will be so accommodating. The chapter therefore goes on to test how much investment and growth would have to be curtailed to achieve a more sustainable financing pattern.

Background

In 1992–93 the Estonian banking system suffered one of the earliest severe banking crises of any of country in the former Soviet bloc. But in many ways, the crisis came before it could really do much material damage to the economy. The banking system had yet to start gathering significant new savings flows, and balances were quickly rebuilt. Moreover, the banks that emerged from the crisis had learned a lesson about sound credit management

129

and were generally well run (at least up until 1997). A strong recovery started in 1994, and was maintained through 1995 and into 1996.

At this point Estonia started to attract considerable inflows of foreign capital, priming the pump for a significant domestic credit and asset price boom. New lending surged, and by 1997 new funds equivalent to 19 percent of GDP were being injected into the NBNGS. Estonian banks, which had started the recovery with relatively strong positive net asset positions abroad, began instead to draw funds in, and net foreign finance of the banking sector reached the equivalent of almost 9 percent of GDP in 1997. Together with accelerating foreign inflows directly into the NBNGS (17 percent of GDP in 1997), this created the conditions for a stock market and investment boom, just as private savings started to slip from about 15 percent of GDP in 1994–95 to below 10 percent by 1997. Real growth surged above 10 percent, and the current account deficit reached 12 percent of GDP.

Fall-out from the Asian crisis late in 1997 triggered a loss of confidence in the stock market, and concerns spread to the interbank markets. Liquidity dried up and Estonian banks found themselves unable to raise new finance from abroad. New lending slowed, as did the inflow of new deposits from the NBNGS. Eventually, one bank that was particularly exposed to the stock market failed, and the government stepped in to protect depositors. This was followed by the Bank of Estonia having to support two medium-size banks engaged in a difficult merger in the wake of the Russian crisis and the failure of at least one other, smaller bank.

This sequence of events has already bought about a marked slowdown in new bank lending to the NBNGS (down to the equivalent of 7 percent of GDP in the first half of 1998) and the virtual end of net foreign funding of the banking system. The only way investment will be sustained is if foreign funding of the NBNGS continues unabated.

This summary of events clarifies the questions asked in this chapter. What happens if foreign finance of the NBNGS tails off? To what extent can NBNGS investment be sustained at 25 percent of GDP without putting unsustainable pressure on the banking system? What special features emerge from having a government sector that is in significant surplus and issues no domestic debt? How are the workings of the Currency Board system manifested within the flow of funds?

The Macroeconomic Base Case

The flow of funds forecasts undertaken here have been built around the macroeconomic projections contained in the recent *Country Economic Memorandum* prepared by the World Bank to support the Estonian authorities in their negotiations for accession to the European Union.[1] Accession is deemed to require maintenance of annual real growth of 6 percent, and the *Memorandum* focuses on the necessary conditions for this to be achieved. The picture presented includes a continued government surplus and a steady recovery in private savings, although not to a particularly high level (reaching just over 13 percent by 2002, compared with private investment of 25 percent of GDP throughout). Because of this, continued high current account deficits are forecast (only falling to 9 percent of GDP by 2002). Other key macroecnomic data in the scenario are listed in Table 7.1.

Table 7.1 The Macroeconomic Base Case: Key Variables (percent)

	1996	1997	1998	1999	2000	2001	2002
Real GDP growth (% y-on-y)	4.0	11.4	8.0	6.0	6.0	6.0	6.0
GDP deflator	23.9	11.4	11.0	9.0	7.0	6.0	5.0
Current deficit (% GDP)	-9.2	-12.0	-10.4	-10.2	-10.0	-9.5	-9.0
Government current surplus (% GDP)	5.0	6.0	6.4	5.5	5.0	4.8	4.6
NBNGS financing gap (% GDP)	-10.3	-17.3	-14.6	-13.3	-12.4	-11.7	-11.0
Current savings (% GDP)	11.4	9.0	10.2	11.5	12.2	12.9	13.6
Investment (% GDP)	-21.7	-26.3	-24.8	-24.8	-24.6	-24.6	-24.6

The Methodology Used in the Flow of Funds Forecast

The *Country Economic Memorandum* contains few explicit forecasts of key financial flows. Therefore, this chapter seeks to look at how different flows might balance out to cover the considerable net NBNGS financing gap,

---

1. "Estonia—Meeting the Challenges of EU Accession, 1998." The projections are interpolations of longer-term forecasts run on the World Bank's RMSM-X model.

which, although declining, remains above 10 percent of GDP throughout the period. The model also incorporates two special features of the Estonian monetary and fiscal framework:

- Running a Currency Board implies that any flow of funds forecast that includes growth in either NBNGS holdings of cash or domestic bank deposits must also include a corresponding outflow into foreign reserves. For increased holdings of cash, this must be on a one-to-one basis, but for extra deposits it need only be proportionate to reflect the ratio between total deposits and bankers' balances at the Bank of Estonia (EB).

- A Currency Board mechanism also limits scope for interest rate management as a tool of active monetary policy. The Estonian government has therefore agreed with the IMF to draw-off some surplus liquidity by running a current budget surplus and investing the proceeds abroad in deutsche mark (DM) bonds (through a mechanism known as the Stabilization Reserve Fund).

The model has been built to include five sectors, with the central bank separated out from the rest of the monetary sector. It works by iterating toward a mix of domestic and foreign flows that can cover the sectoral financing gaps implicit in the macroeconomic forecast for savings and investment. Some flows were set exogenously, and these include:

- A number of flows that had, by 1997, fallen to trivial levels relative to GDP. These were set to zero and include foreign finance of government, central bank finance of both banks and government, and government lending to the NBNGS.

- Net credit flows from banks to government were also set to zero (because the repayment in 1997 virtually cleared the outstanding stock of credit).

- Foreign investment in the NBNGS was set to repeat the 17 percent of GDP recorded in 1997 again in 1998, before falling steadily to 10 percent of GDP by 2002 (still high, but no longer extraordinary).

- NBNGS investment abroad was cut back sharply in 1998 to 2 percent of GDP (compared with 7 percent in 1997). The high 1997 figure almost certainly reflected, in part, an outflow of domestic funds displaced by inward foreign investment. Nevertheless, many of the larger Estonian corporations find their home market too small and have pan-Baltic ambitions, so the share of GDP invested abroad was projected to rebuild slowly through the forecast period (reaching 3.5 percent by 2001).

- Government investment abroad (through the Stabilization Reserve Fund) was set at the nearest half-percentage point below the size of the overall net public financial surplus expressed as a percentage of GDP.
- The build-up of bank's gross claims abroad was held to 3 percent of GDP, roughly the average over the four years to 1997.
- Increases in NBNGS holdings of cash and deposits were set to achieve the recovery path for the remonetization of the Estonian economy described in the next section.
- Increases in bank holdings of cash and reserves at the central bank were set to broadly maintain the ratio of vault cash and reserves to domestic deposits.

The flow of funds was then reconciled by the following endogenous processes, using quasi-behavioral linkages that were built into the model as follows:

- Bank flows to the EB (vault cash and reserves) are matched one-for-one by an increase in official reserves, reflecting the workings of the Currency Board mechanism.
- Any surplus government funds after investment abroad through the Stabilization Reserve Fund were placed with banks.
- Bank lending fills the NBNGS financing gap *after* taking account of declining foreign inflows into NBNGS (see above) and other exogenously set outflows (cash, deposits, and investment abroad) from the sector.
- Bank lending and the necessary build-up of vault cash and balances at the EB drives bank funding requirements. After taking into account deposit inflows from the NBNGS and government, these needs end up being met by borrowing from abroad.

In effect, constraining foreign finance of the NBNGS—even at a substantial 10 percent of GDP annually—means that banks must continue to borrow from abroad to finance what continues to be very rapid expansion of credit to the NBNGS.

Forces Driving the Banking Flow of Funds

An important part of this analysis is the effort to put recent and prospective growth of the Estonian banking system into a stock-adjustment context that links bank balance sheets to the size of the economy they support. This is the same approach taken in the Latvian and Romanian chapters in this volume. The position of Estonia in the run-up to the credit boom of 1996–97 is shown relative to other transition economies in Figures 7.1 and 7.2

Figure 7.1. Estonia—Comparative Monetary Characteristics (mid-1996)

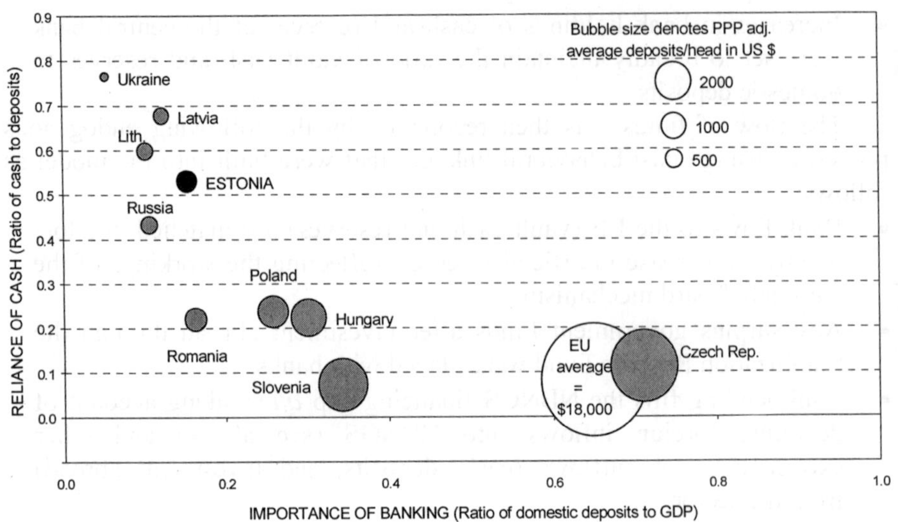

Note: PPP adj = purchasing power parity adjusted.

Figure 7.2. Estonia—Evolution of Monetary Characteristics

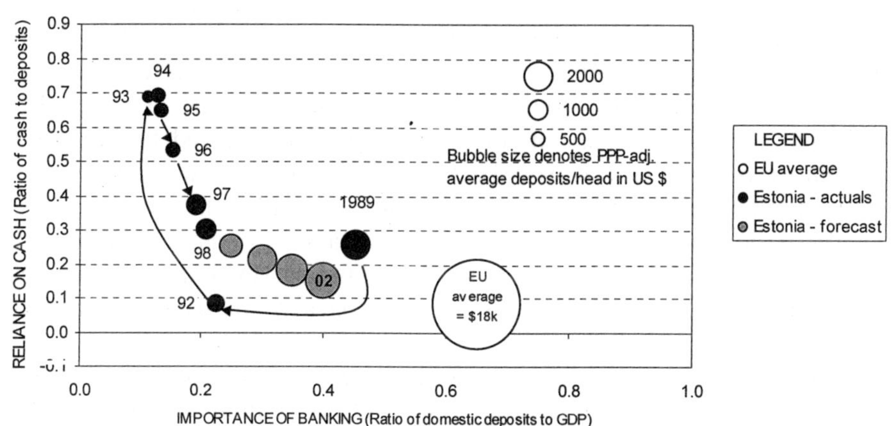

Note: PPP adj = purchasing power parity adjusted.

This puts Estonia toward the front of the former Soviet bloc, but nowhere near the level of monetization of the other (Central European) countries targeted for the first wave of accession to the EU. This understates the situation, however, because the expansion of the Estonian banking system through 1996 and into 1997 has almost certainly resulted in a marked closing of the gap. By mid-1998, deposits had reached 21 percent of GDP (compared with 15 percent in the figures above), and cash had fallen dramatically relative to deposits (down to 30 percent, compared with over 50 percent in the figures above). The rapid remonetization of the economy since the banking crisis of 1992–93 is clear in Figure 7.2.

A reasonably strong link can be demonstrated between the ratio of domestic deposits to GDP and GDP per person—in effect, higher-income economies have proportionately larger banking systems than poorer ones—and Estonian per capita GDP lags behind other first-wave EU aspirants. Given that causality is almost certainly a two-way process—bigger banking systems provide more investment funds to support higher growth—continued remonetization is important to Estonia's ability to achieve real convergence with the EU.

The projections of the banking flow of funds in this chapter are built around the assumption that this process of recovery will continue, although the balance shifts from reducing reliance on cash to increased deposits as a result of higher saving. By the year 2002, the assumption is that the stock of NBNGS deposits will have reached 40 percent of GDP, and NBNGS holdings of cash will equal 15 percent of outstanding NBNGS deposit balances. This would put Estonia slightly ahead of most other first-wave EU aspirants (although by that time they too should have moved further down the remonetization path). It would also return Estonia almost to pre-reform levels of monetization, but this time on a voluntary, rather than forced, basis.

These do not seem to be unreasonable assumptions to make, and, together with the flow of funds mechanisms described in the previous section, they lead to the projections for key monetary and banking variables in Table 7.2.

The profile of the recovery includes a sharp slowdown in 1998 to reflect the impact on the Estonian banking system of last autumn's funding crisis. This had already become evident in second quarter banking statistics, which show a sharp cut in net foreign funding (from the equivalent of 9 percent of GDP down to 1 percent). The second-round effect of this has been to cut new bank lending to the NBNGS from 19 percent of GDP to just 7 percent.

Table 7.2. Projections of Key Monetary and Banking Variables

	1996	1997	1998	1999	2000	2001	2002
Broad money (EEK million)	14,154	19,457	25,205	33,255	42,881	53,897	66,229
Cash outside banks (o/w)	4,271	4,589	5,799	6,651	7,442	8,222	8,639
Deposits (including forex)	9,884	14,869	19,406	26,604	35,439	45,675	57,590
Velocity of circulation (mid-year)	4.3	3.9	3.5	3.1	2.7	2.4	2.1
Deposit:GDP ratio	15	19	21	25	30	35	40
Cash:deposit ratio	53	37	30	25	21	18	15
Deposits per capita(PPP adjusted $)	674	982	1,186	1,534	1,965	2,459	3,040
Vault cash/bankers' reserves (% of deposits)	19	25	25	25	25	25	25
Bank lending (Ls m)	12,935	25,434	30,902	39,642	51,718	67,574	85,706
Nominal growth	74.1	96.6	21.5	28.3	30.5	30.7	26.8
Real growth	40.5	76.5	9.5	17.7	21.9	23.3	20.8
New loans (% GDP)	10.5	19.2	7.0	9.7	11.8	13.8	14.2
New deposits (% GDP)	-6.4	-7.7	-5.8	-8.0	-8.6	-8.9	-9.3
Net funds to NBNGS (% GDP)	4.1	11.5	1.2	1.7	3.2	4.9	4.9

Summary Sectoral Financing Patterns

At its simplest, the Estonian economy is characterized by a very large NBNGS financing gap, covered by declining government and monetary sector surpluses and a persistent current account deficit. This is amply illustrated by Figure 7.3.

Figure 7.3 Summary Chart—Net Sectoral Surpluses/Deficits (Percent GDP)

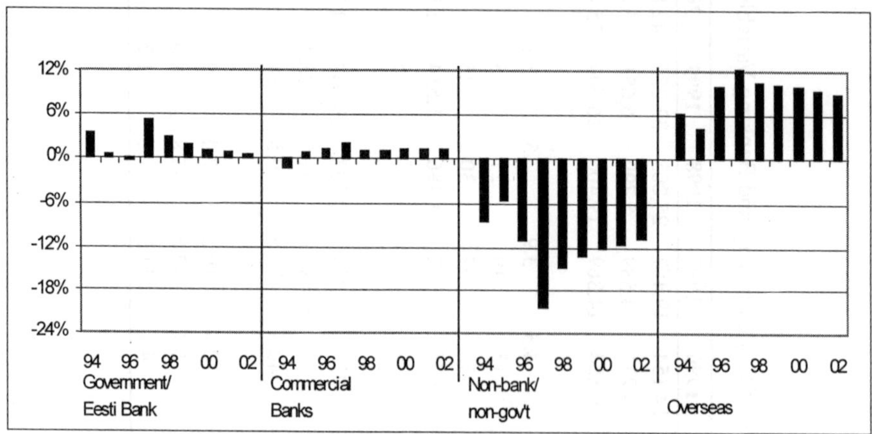

For *government*, financing flows are quite limited from 1998 onward. The financing gap falls from 4 percent of GDP to virtually nothing by 2002. This is a consequence of a modest decline in the current surplus (from 6 percent to 4.5 percent of GDP), a slightly rising investment rate, and the elimination of a strongly positive error. This last point is not as arbitrary as it may seem. The projected surplus for 1998 is higher than for 1997 (although economic circumstances are tightening), and the government is having to draw against the Stabilization Reserve Fund (SRF) to fund its bailout of Maapank. As the surplus declines, so does the projected outflow into foreign assets that represents an accumulating balance in the SRF. Any modest financial surplus above this outflow is deposited with banks, and with virtually no outstanding or new domestic borrowing, the net domestic public debt turns negative. Combining this with an absence of new foreign borrowing, total public debt falls from 6 percent of GDP at end-1997 to 2 percent by end-2002. Taking account of the accumulating balance on the SRF, Estonia would have no net public debt by the year 2000.

The position of the EB is, as described earlier, driven by the growth in cash in circulation, bankers' vault cash, and bankers' and balances with it. These, in turn, are driven by the chosen assumptions on the remonetization of the Estonian economy described above. The offset to this reserve money creation is essentially an equal outflow abroad.

The forces driving the *bank's* position are essentially twofold. Remonetization drives domestic liabilities, and therefore claims on the EB. The NBNGS borrowing requirement drives net funding from abroad. After a pause this year, net new lending to the NBNGS must pick up sharply if investment is to be financed, and this is reflected in an increased net take-up of funds from abroad, which reaches the equivalent of 6 percent of GDP by 2002. This is not as high as in 1997, but it does require confidence in Estonian banks to recover quickly from world perceptions of generalized emerging market risk. Increased emerging-market risk premiums are likely to keep kroon lending rates high. The rise in new lending is a consequence of the assumed fall in direct foreign financing of the NBNGS. By the end of the forecast period, the ratio of new credits to GDP is moving toward 15 percent. This is not quite as high as in 1997 (19 percent), but, in general, sustained new lending equal to more than 10 percent of GDP was a characteristic of many of the economies that experienced financial problems in 1997.

The financing of the NBNGS shows how reliant Estonia is on net inward foreign capital flows. This is particularly true of 1998, when banks appeared to be unable to raise funding abroad to keep covering a significant part of the NBNGS net financing gap. Indeed, the net inflow will have to grow significantly (to about 15 percent of GDP) if the projected 1998 financing gap is to be covered. This is unlikely to be sustainable, and the projections assume that inflows must slow (and outflows pick up again), thereby bringing the net inflow rapidly down to the 6–8 percent that was typical in the past. This is predicated on the NBNGS being able to restart significant net borrowing from banks, who must, in turn, be able to raise the necessary funding abroad.

The continued heavy reliance of Estonia on overseas financing is noteworthy. Taken together, direct and indirect (bank-intermediated) net foreign finance of the NBNGS will amount to 16 percent of GDP in 1998, and over 10 percent in 2002. The gross inflows are, of course, larger. It is very difficult to see this as a sustainable pattern.

Based on this analysis, and the banking flow of funds work in the previous section, four key variables need to be monitored:

- Any move toward a significant net financing requirement by government (although it would take time for this to compete for foreign capital, it could start to draw funds from the banks in competition with their lending to the NBNGS).
- An even faster than projected decline in net foreign finance of the nonbank/nongovernment sector.
- Any failure of the projected recovery in net foreign finance of banks to emerge.
- New bank lending to the NBNGS running ahead of the already high levels shown here.

An Alternative Scenario

The scenario recounted here assumes that the projected decline in direct net foreign finance of the NBNGS does occur, but that banks are unable to cover the remaining NBNGS financing gap because increased foreign finance is unavailable. The second-round effects of this would be the following:

- Growth will be reduced (down by 1 percent annually) by lower private consumption as private saving rises by the equivalent to 2.5 percentage points when expressed as a share of GDP (from only 12 percent in 1998).
- Reduced growth brings the elimination of government's overall financial surplus forward to 2000 (which only happens by 2003 in the higher-growth base case).
- The government draws on the SRF to fund a troubled banking sector, and after this is over, borrows from abroad (probably as much multilaterally as through the capital markets).
- By repatriating/raising foreign currency, government cannot only provide funding for banks, but also create the inflow into foreign reserves that must back the growth in high-powered money needed to support growing bank balance sheets.

- Higher savings drives slightly faster remonetization of the economy. The ratio of deposits to GDP will reach 45 percent (almost exactly where it was before the reform effort).

The overall effect is that gross new bank lending to the NBNGS stays high, but is much more closely matched by new deposits, and for three years Estonian banks actually place more funds abroad than they borrow. This only reverses itself in 2001 and 2002, and by this time foreign confidence in the Estonian banking system should have recovered as the country moves even closer to EU accession. Draw-down of the SRF and increased foreign borrowing still leave the ratio of external public debt to GDP below 8 percent.

Conclusions

Transition is essentially a stock-adjustment process as the economies of the former Soviet bloc return to an economic capacity more compatible with their human and social capital. In the case of Estonia, this process is reinforced by the prospect of accession to the EU, and it is bound to heighten expectations about the success of potential investment projects. The flow regulator that ultimately constrains these expectations is the capacity of the financial system to provide funds to the right projects at the right stage in the transition process. This is bound to be an unstable process, progressing unevenly, and often brought to a sharp halt by crises of confidence of the sort seen in 1997. This chapter suggests that it is possible to build a flow of funds model that can clearly illustrate where tensions are likely to emerge in the intermediation of available investment funds to domestic end-users. The analysis here suggests that these tensions are likely to remain acute over the next five years, and could undermine the Estonian economy's capacity to deliver the strong investment-led growth required for real convergence with the EU. The most likely area of weakness is banks—not just that they might secure the necessary funds from abroad to on-lend to a nonbank/ nongovernmental sector that is almost certainly going to have to face a reduction in direct foreign finance—but also because repeated shocks undermine the institutional aspects of financial intermediation.

There is a great deal that could still be done to improve the projection model, particularly in three key areas:

- The adjustment of changes in bank balance sheets for currency movements (where the assumption has been made that all domestic foreign currency business is deutsche mark denominated, and therefore requires no valuation adjustment).
- Draw finer distinctions within the balance of payments data on which sectors are involved in both inward- and outward-direct and portfolio investment flows.
- Develop a more explicit model of the link between current budget flows and the overall net financing gap of the government sector.

This last point is probably relevant to most transition economies. The position of privatization agencies and related property or compensation funds is not well covered by general government data, and in the case of Estonia, this is complicated by the workings of the Stabilization Reserve Fund.

Finally, as with all transition economies, at some point the nonbank financial sector becomes large enough to merit modeling separately. Estonia is probably beyond this point now, particularly regarding leasing and other nonbank credit grantors, but also investment fund business. Ultimately a new row needs to be introduced into the flow of funds matrices to capture funds raised through capital markets. Resolving this might help narrow some of the wedge that has emerged between calculated net sectoral financing and estimated sectoral savings and investment gaps over the last few years.

Broad Financial Equilibrium

Latvia
Poland

8.

Latvia—Finely Balanced for Growth

Stephen J. Peachey

This chapter chronicles Latvia's financial experience in the wake of its severe banking crisis of 1995. Key financing issues that are likely to be faced by the Latvian authorities if the economy is to secure the rapid, investment-led growth envisaged for the run-up to EU accession are identified. The chapter concludes that investment-led real growth of 5–6 percent annually can be financed by a combination of strong foreign capital inflows and rapid, but not unsustainable, growth in bank lending, provided private sector saving rates also rise. Such a configuration, however, represents a fine balance. The Latvian economy and banking system are very internationalized and could suffer significantly in the wake of the 1998 Russian crisis. If this were to result in the movement of the government sector back into deficit, stagnation of private savings, and the tailing-off of inward foreign direct investment, then the banking sector is unlikely to be able to close the financing gap, and private investment will be curtailed. Nevertheless, the scenario discussed at the end of this chapter suggests that the economy can withstand even a relatively prolonged (2–3 year) slowdown in inward foreign direct investment without any material lowering of growth or investment. In this respect, Latvia can be described as a country with no acute external financing constraint, and any slowdown in growth is likely to come from the direct impact of the Russian crisis on the traded sectors of the economy, particularly its internationalized banking system.

Background

In 1995 the Latvian banking system suffered probably the most acute banking crisis experienced by any of the three Baltic states. The crisis was concentrated in a period of barely a year, and hit new savings as well as old. The banks involved were new private institutions, competing aggressively to gather domestic deposits. The hyperinflation that might have swamped its impact was already over, so that nominal declines in bank balances represented significant real losses to the stock of savings and credit.

Since then, banking regulation has been tightened sharply, so much so that it is now widely considered among the best in the former Soviet Union. Confidence, although badly damaged, eventually returned, and after a year of stagnation immediately following the crisis (1996), strong growth in bank balance sheets was seen in 1997 and the first half of 1998. Domestic nonbank/nongovernmental (NBNGS)[1] deposits grew 46 percent and foreign deposits by 89 percent in 1997. Against a background of the reversal of the earlier heavy net financing of government, credit to the NBNGS expanded by 69 percent over the same period. This rapid growth represented an injection of funds into the private sector equivalent to 6 percent of GDP. This was augmented by continued heavy, and indeed accelerating, inflows of foreign finance (equal to 10 percent of GDP in 1997, up from 8.5 percent in 1996). Together, these two flows supported a rise in NBNGS investment to just over 20 percent of GDP, despite a flat gross savings rate (14 percent of GDP).

It is characteristic of the Latvian banking system that banks do as much if not more business with foreign counterparts as with domestic clients. Fully 60 percent of aggregate bank assets are deployed overseas, and just over 50 percent of liabilities are drawn from abroad. Much of this two-way business is with customers from Commonwealth of Independent States (CIS) countries who are attracted by good service, relatively sound management, and strong regulation. But another factor is the highly internationalized nature of the Latvian economy in general—in effect, large two-way transit trade underpins significant two-way transit banking. It also explains the relatively high dollarization of domestic banking business—52 percent of NBNGS deposits and 54 percent of credits are foreign exchange—denominated. Given that NBNGS deposits outweigh credits by a ratio of 14:10, banks have established a persistent net export of funds as they seek to

---

1. The NBNGS is broadly equivalent to the private sector.

find a home for surplus domestic foreign exchange deposits. By end-1997, Latvian banks had amassed a net claim on nonresidents equal to 5.1 percent of GDP, and the net export of new funds in 1997 alone exceeded 2 percent of GDP.

These factors shape this chapter's analysis. A number of questions are addressed. To what extent can NBNGS investment be sustained above 20 percent, while keeping the current deficit under control? What sort of credit growth is compatible with external—internal balance? How long can the NBNGS continue to rely so heavily on foreign finance, while maintaining effective export of capital through the banking system? What does all this mean for state finances?

The Macroeconomic Base Case

The flow of funds forecasts detailed here are built around the macroeconomic forecasts of the medium-term macroeconomic framework that underpins the Latvian negotiations for accession to the European Union.[2] These forecasts present the prospect of maintained real growth of 5–6 percent, supported by continued fiscal balance and growing private sector savings (rising from the equivalent of nearly 14 percent of GDP in 1996 to over 18 percent by 2002). Taken together, this allows the current deficit to be capped in nominal terms and to decline from the current 6 percent of GDP to 4.5 percent by 2002. Other key variables in this macroeconomic scenario are shown in Table 8.1.

The forecast for the current account deficit as a percentage of GDP has been modified to reflect data revisions following completion of the framework projections. These cut the 1997 deficit from 8 percent to 6 percent of GDP. The medium-term macroeconomic framework left the deficit unchanged as a percentage of GDP between 1997 and 1998, before a steady fall by the equivalent of 2 percentage points over the next four years.

---

2. Ministry of Finance of the Republic of Latvia/Ministry of Economy of the Republic of Latvia/Bank of Latvia April 1998—"Medium Term Economic Strategy in the Context of Accession to the European Union." The model underpinning this macroeconomic framework is similar in nature to the World Bank's RMSM-X model, in that it essentially provides a consistent accounting framework for scenario projections rather than behavioral forecasts.

This path has been kept in the above forecast, but now starting from the lower base of 6 percent of GDP in 1997.

Table 8.1 Latvia: Key Forecast Variables (percent)

	1996	1997	1998	1999	2000	2001	2002
Real GDP growth (y-on-y)	3.3	6.5	5.8	5.7	5.8	5.6	5.3
GDP deflator	16.5	6.5	6.7	4.6	4.4	4.4	4.1
Current deficit (GDP)	-5.5	-6.0	-6.0	-5.5	-5.0	-4.5	-4.0
Government financing gap (GDP)	-1.8	1.9	0.0	0.0	0.0	-0.1	-0.1
Current savings	0.7	4.3	2.9	3.1	3.5	3.5	3.5
Investment	-2.1	-2.5	-3.0	-3.2	-3.5	-3.6	-3.6
NBNGS financing gap (GDP)	4.5	6.1	6.0	5.5	5.0	4.4	4.0
Current savings	13.8	14.1	14.7	15.5	16.2	17.3	18.4
Investment	-18.3	-20.2	-20.7	-21.0	-21.2	-21.7	-22.4

The Methodology Used in the Flow of Funds Forecast

The Latvian medium-term economic framework includes forecasts of key financial flows, but these were not done within an explicit flow of funds framework. This chapter looks more at the behavioral factors driving banking sector recovery. Nevertheless, the forecasts here have been constrained to match certain key elements of the Latvian authorities' financial forecasts, as described below.

The model has been built on five sectors with the central bank (BoL) separated out from the rest of the monetary sector. It works by iterating toward a mix of domestic and foreign flows that can cover the sectoral financing gaps that are implicit in the macroeconomic forecast for savings and investment. Some flows are set exogenously, include:

- Net outflow into official reserves, net monetary finance of government, nonmonetary Treasury bill issue (essentially all to NBNGS), foreign finance of government, and government lending to NBNGS were all set to values taken from the medium-term macroeconomic framework.

- NBNGS investment abroad was set at 2 percent of GDP (slightly above the level reached in 1997).

- Increases in foreign claims on Latvian banks were set equivalent to 10 percent of GDP, slightly below the 1997 levels but above the levels of 1996 (these funds essentially all return abroad under an assumption, taken from the macroeconomic framework, that banks continue to export net funds).

- Increases in NBNGS holdings of cash and deposits were set to achieve the recovery path for the "remonetization" of the Latvian economy described in the next section.
- Increases in bank holdings of cash were set to broadly maintain the ratio of vault cash and reserves at BoL to domestic deposits.

The flow of funds was then reconciled by the following endogenous process, using quasi-behavioral linkages that were built into the model:

- Bank flows to BoL (vault cash and reserves) ultimately return by way of increased government deposits with banks (a consequence of the macroeconomic framework assumption that total net monetary finance of government should be held to zero).
- Together with exogenously set inflows from NBNGS and the foreign sector (see above), this sets the total liability base of banks.
- The liability base of banks drives available funds for lending.
- Bank lending to NBNGS is set to fill the remaining financing gap *after* taking account of foreign inflows into NBNGS (see below) and other exogenously set variables (cash, deposits, T-bills, and investment abroad).
- Remaining bank lending goes abroad and determines net export of funds by the banking sector, but this is constrained to levels forecast in the medium-term macroeconomic framework by adjusting the foreign finance of NBNGS.

In effect, foreign finance of the NBNGS has been juggled with net bank finance of the NBNGS to achieve the required, modest net export of funds abroad by banks that is part of the medium-term macroeconomic framework projections. The picture that emerges is described in more detail below, but essentially revolves around continued heavy foreign finance of the NBNGS (equivalent to about 10 percent of GDP) and rapid growth—but not so rapid as to be unsustainable—of bank lending to the NBNGS.

Forces Driving the Banking Flow of Funds

An important part of this analysis is to try to put the recent and prospective growth of the Latvian banking system into a stock-adjustment context that links bank balance sheets to the size of the economy they support. This is the same approach taken in the Estonian and Romanian chapters also presented in this book. The position of Latvia in the immediate aftermath of the 1995 banking crisis is shown relative to other transition economies in Figure 8.1.

Figure 8.1 Latvia Following the 1995 Banking Crisis

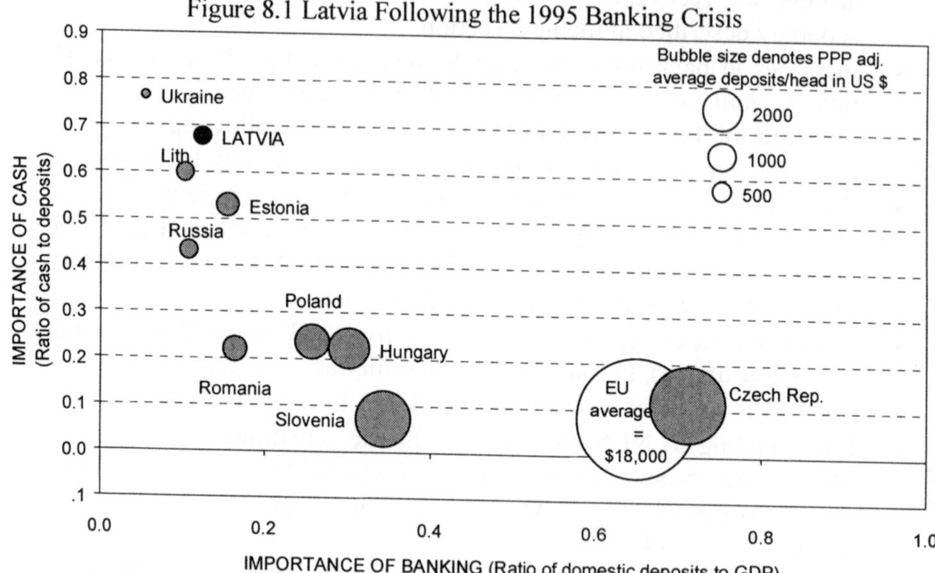

Note: PPP adj. = purchasing power parity adjusted.

The severity of the Latvian banking crisis places the very rapid growth of 1997 in a much more balanced perspective. The banking crisis of 1995 came at a worse time for the Latvian economy than, for example, the Estonian crisis for that economy, which also eliminated a similar proportion (40 percent) of the banking sector. The Latvian crisis did not take place against a background of very high inflation, so its damage could not be inflated away. Moreover, the Latvian banking system had started to grow strongly in real terms before the crisis broke. Between mid-1993 and mid-1994, the domestic deposit base more than doubled as a percentage of GDP—almost all of this gain was lost between mid-1995 and mid-1996. The effect on lending to the nonbank private sector (NBPS) was marked—net credits (after deducting provisions) fell by 45 percent in nominal terms (and was more than halved in real terms).

The reversal of the earlier progress can be seen in Figure 8.2, which maps two key measures (deposits to GDP and cash to deposits) over time. It can be seen that the banking system was already beginning to remonetize before the crisis hit, partly in response to the successful introduction of the national currency (the Lat), but also to strongly positive real deposit rates. This process was thrown into a sharp reversal by the crisis, but after marking time in 1996, the recovery of 1997 was very strong. Cash became less important, and the ratio of domestic deposits relative to GDP had, by mid-1998, recovered almost three-quarters of the ground lost during the crisis.

Figure 8.2 Latvia—Evolution of Monetary Characteristics

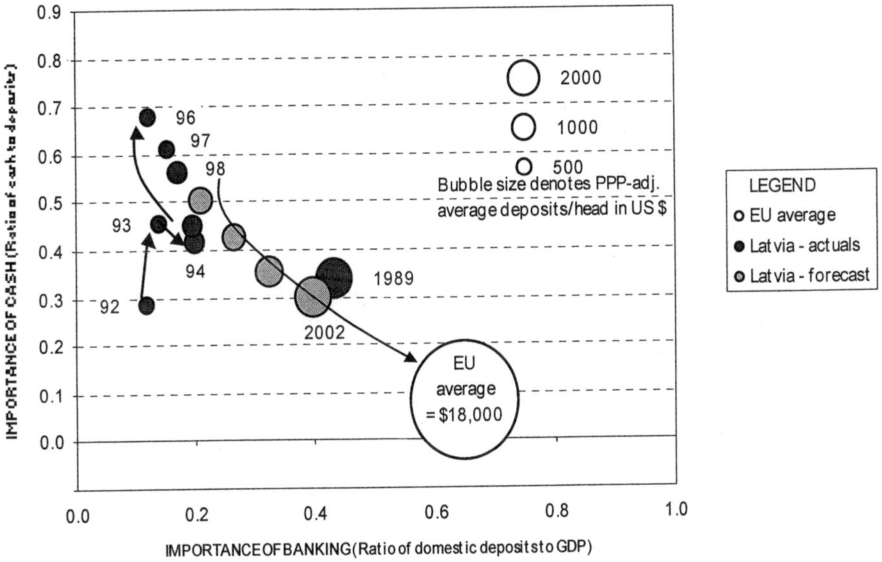

Note: PPP adj. = purchasing power parity adjusted.

The projections of the banking flow of funds in this chapter are built around the assumption that the process of recovery will continue. By the year 2002, it is assumed that the stock of NBNGS deposits will have reached the equivalent to 40 percent of GDP, and NBNGS holdings of cash will equal 30 percent of outstanding NBNGS deposit balances. This would put Latvia slightly ahead of where most leading transition economies are now (although by that time they too should have moved further down the remonetization path). It would also virtually return Latvia to pre-reform levels of monetization, but this time on a voluntary, rather than forced, basis. These seem reasonable assumptions and, together with the flow of funds mechanisms described in the previous section, lead to the projections shown for key monetary and banking variables (Table 8.2).

Table 8.2 Key Monetary and Banking Variables

Variable	1996	1997	1998	1999	2000	2001	2002
Broad money (M2X Ls million)	651	897	1,143	1,511	1,965	2,514	3,199
Cash outside banks	264	333	411	504	586	652	738
Deposits (including forex)	387	564	732	1,007	1,379	1,862	2,461
Velocity of circulation (mid-year)	4.7	4.1	3.6	3.0	2.5	2.2	1.9
Deposit:GDP ratio	12	15	17	21	27	33	40
Cash:deposit ratio	68	61	56	50	43	35	30
Deposits per head (PPP adj. $)	418	547	675	900	1,197	1,571	2,022
Bank lending (Ls m)	235	411	523	771	1,083	1,487	2,053
Nominal growth (percent)	-0.1	74.5	27.4	47.4	40.5	37.3	38.1
Real growth (percent)	-14.2	63.8	19.4	40.9	34.5	31.5	32.6
New loans as percent of GDP	0.3	5.9	3.1	6.2	7.0	8.3	10.6
New deposits as percent of GDP	-1.7	-5.5	-4.6	-6.9	-8.4	-9.9	-11.2
Net absorption of NBNGS funds (as percent of GDP)	1.4	0.4	-1.5	-0.7	-1.4	-1.6	-0.6

Note: It should be noted that the rate of monetary growth is faster here than in the Latvian authorities' medium-term macroeconomic framework, and therefore velocity falls rather quickly (to 1.7 on a year-end basis, compared with 2.2 in the Latvian projections).

The profile of the recovery includes a temporary slowdown in 1998 to reflect the impact of that year's Russian crisis on the Latvian banking system. This has begun to become evident from 1998 second-quarter banking statistics. Uncertainty about possible sanctions on key export sectors earlier in 1998 may lie behind the slight fall in new deposits relative to GDP, and in the wake of the crisis there is likely to be a sharp slowdown in new lending. This pause will take place irrespective of any long-run impact of problems in such an important trading partner on the Latvian economy.

Summary Sectoral Financing Patterns

The current saving of the overseas sector in Latvia's flow of funds structure is more than sufficient to cover the net financing gap of the NBNGS and government, and the two elements of the monetary sector are now—and should remain—in broad balance. To this basic pattern of flows, however, are added more complex two-way flows; the net result is the effective export of funds abroad. To get the full picture, it is best to look at the main financing patterns of each sector in turn (see Figure 8.3).

For *government*, financing flows are quite limited from 1998 onward as the Latvian authorities' medium-term macroeconomic framework assumes overall fiscal balance, with no net monetary funding. What little government lending there is to the NBNGS is offset by very modest NBNGS investment in T-bills and foreign borrowing. Before 1998, the situation is more complex. Fiscal policy had started to loosen before the banking crisis, and in 1995 it was very loose, with heavy borrowing from BoL and significant bank take-up of T-bills. Unfortunately this cannot be shown, because the data are not available to take the full flow of funds analysis back before 1996. By 1996, however, the deficit was coming back under control. The government, although still borrowing from banks, repaid debts to BoL, canceling the monetary stimulus. By 1997 it had moved into significant surplus and both repaid bank debt and redeemed T-bills held by banks. This shows up in the relatively large outflow to the monetary sector, which would have been even larger had the government not increased its liabilities to BoL. This is projected to continue in 1998 and beyond, with BoL deploying funds gathered from banks into growing claims on government, but this is offset by growing bank liabilities to government (see below for a further explanation).

Figure 8.3. Summary Chart—Net Sectoral Surpluses/Deficits, Percent of GDP

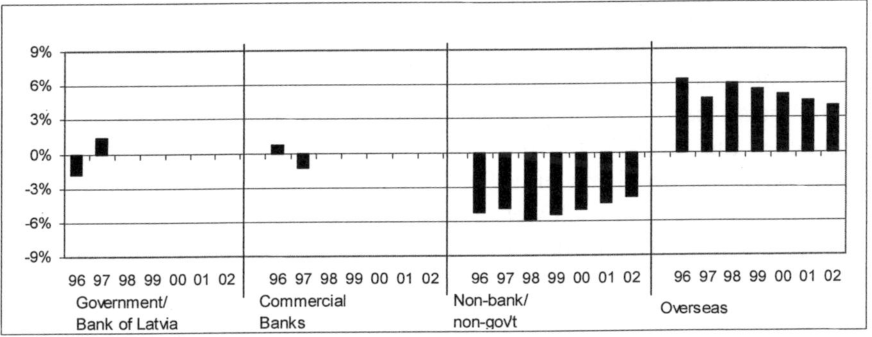

The position of the *central bank* (BoL) and other banks should be taken together. In essence, BoL has relatively few options in this model. The liability side of the balance sheet is driven by accumulation of cash and reserves by both banks and the NBNGS. On the asset side, reserve accumulation is taken exogenously from the medium-term macroeconomic framework; after a brief rise in 1998, it continues at approximately the level seen in 1997, albeit declining slightly relative to GDP. This leaves central bank finance of government to take up the slack, but as already noted, the medium-term economic framework assumes no net monetary finance of government. As a result, funds provided by the BoL to government are assumed to return to the banking sector as increased public deposits. In effect, BoL recycles the accumulation of bankers' reserve balances to the banking sector indirectly, through government, instead of directly, through lending to banks. This was what happened to some degree in 1997, mostly through repurchase of bank holdings of government securities. Given the impact of the Russian crisis, it may be that the BoL will recycle more of the accumulated bankers' reserve balances directly through liquidity support for banks, but thus far there is no record of this behavior, so it has not been modeled.

The forces driving the *banks'* position have been discussed in detail above. In the absence of any need to fund government (indeed, in the face of increased government deposits), banks continue to draw slightly more in deposits from the NBNGS than they return through new lending. The counterpart to this is continued net export of funds abroad. The critical issue to be addressed is whether the gross flows of new credit provided to the NBNGS are sustainable. Here the picture is mixed. Net new lending relative to GDP gets close to the 10 percent threshold, above which credit expansion approaches the levels witnessed in the run-up to the Asian, Estonian, and Czech financing problems of 1997. Few other warning signs are apparent. Growth rates are much slower than in 1997. New NBNGS crediting is matched by new NBNGS deposits, and banks do not need to rely on heavy foreign finance (instead, there is a continued net export of funds).

The financing of the *NBNGS* is particularly interesting—significant net foreign financing is partially offset by net outflows to banks and the state (the latter through increased holdings of cash). The net foreign inflow eases slowly as a percentage of GDP as NBNGS savings rise to cover more of the needed investment financing. This would be a continuation of the pattern established in 1996 and 1997, and is probably not an unreasonable assumption. A number of major privatizations remain to be completed. Moreover, many past privatizations included programs of committed investment by foreign strategic partners. These should still be bringing funds into Latvia. Beyond this, the Riga Stock Exchange should act as a conduit for incoming longer-term portfolio investment through new stock issues.

In the longer term, however, it may not be possible to continue relying on such substantial inflows of foreign capital. If there were to be a tailing-off of inward investment, the model is set to replace these funds with increased borrowing from banks. This, in turn, would eventually lead to a reversal of their current net export of funds. The sustainability of credit growth, and ultimately the willingness of the Euromarket to fund Latvian banks, is covered in more detail in the alternative scenario described in the next section.

The financing pattern of the *overseas* sector is essentially the mirror image of the pattern of the NBNGS. A large outflow from Latvia through the current deficit is augmented by funds drawn from Latvian banks (which are exporting surplus NBNGS deposits) and the build-up of official reserves (where the BoL, in effect, exports growing NBNGS cash holdings). These funds return by way of foreign finance of NBNGS investment. Whether this is entirely appropriate for a rapidly developing country is an open question. Certainly the flow out through the banks and back by inward foreign investment is unusual. It does, however, act as a useful brake on overheating in an economy that already has a reasonably large current account deficit, despite only one to two years of strong growth.

Based on this analysis, and the banking flow of funds work in the previous section, four key variables emerge that need to be monitored:

- Any resumption of significant net monetary (that is, BoL plus banks) finance of government.
- Reduced net foreign finance of the nonbank/nongovernment sector.
- A turnaround to significant negative values for the net flow of banking funds abroad.
- New bank lending to the NBNGS running at the equivalent of more than 10 percent of GDP for more than a year or two (above this threshold, concern should mount regarding the sustainability of credit growth, especially if the current account deficit starts to move much above 5 percent of GDP).

An Alternative Scenario

The most obvious scenario to test is whether—under existing macroeconomic assumptions—the banking sector could compensate for reduced foreign financing of the NBNGS. The assumptions made about continued heavy inflows seem acceptable. A great deal of inward foreign direct investment (FDI) relates to privatization, which still has some way to go in Latvia. Moreover, as already noted, past privatization activity has built up a significant pipeline of commitments to invest by strategic investors. Nevertheless, other transition economies have seen such inflows tail off quite quickly—for example, the Czech economy experienced a fall in gross inward investment in the NBNGS from 11 to 7 percent of GDP between 1995 and 1997. Moreover, some past inward direct investment was targeted on transit trade flows into Russia (which may no longer attract such interest); other flows, particularly into banking, were driven by Estonian capital (which has since become much scarcer). Therefore, a sensible scenario to test is a halving in direct foreign finance of the NBNGS, from around 10 percent of GDP in the base case to only 5 percent in the variant. This will not be immediate (given the pipeline of strategic investment commitments mentioned above), and it is unlikely to be sustained indefinitely.

The assumption made is a fall to 8 percent of GDP in 1998, 6 percent in 1999, and 5 percent in 2000, before picking up slowly to 6 percent in 2001 and 7 percent in 2002 (by this time Latvia will be much closer to EU accession). The key result of this sequence is that government and the banking system could fill the gap *without any need for growth and investment to slow*:

- Government's assumed role is to exploit one of the best transition country debt ratings and to act as a conduit for foreign borrowing (much of it probably multilateral), which would be passed on to the banking system for on-lending to Latvian businesses. The amounts needed are not large—1–1.5 percent of GDP annually for no more than two years, before tailing off to zero by the year 2001. The main consequence would be to stop the fall in external public debt relative to GDP (as in the base case). Indeed, the ratio rises slightly, but remains well below 10 percent of GDP.

- With government borrowing at the levels assumed, banks can then close the remaining uncovered NBNGS financing gap by re-importing previously exported funds. In other words, banks would start to take funds from, rather than place funds with, the Euromarkets, but would not need to become net borrowers (as is already the case with Estonian banks). This should limit the transmission of the current high general transition economy risk premium that applies to most Euromarket business to domestic lending rates. The main consequence would be that on a flow basis, banks would briefly become net takers of funds from abroad, and net suppliers to the NBNGS—in effect, reversing current financing patterns. This effect would last until 2002, when two-way flows between the banks and both sectors would generally be back in balance.

The one area of significant concern is the speed of growth in bank lending implied by this scenario. Net new lending to the NBNGS settles down to the equivalent of a steady 11–12 percent of GDP by the end of the forecast period. This approaches the level seen in many of the economies that experienced financing difficulties in 1997 (Asia, Estonia, and so forth). The scenario also assumes—against some current evidence—that Latvian banks will have sufficient capital and liquidity (even after the Russian crisis) to support the balance sheet expansion implicit in financing NBNGS investment needs.

This alternative scenario also illustrates the importance of a balanced budget to the flexibility Latvian authorities need to respond effectively to private sector financing crises. If government were running a significant deficit, its foreign borrowing capacity would almost certainly already be committed to public financial needs, and banks would also be diverted from funding the NBNGS.

Conclusions

This chapter has shown that it is possible to build a basic flow of funds model from available banking, public finance, and balance of payments data in Latvia. The model, despite its basic nature, illustrates the potential stress points in the financial system, while reconciling competing sectoral financing requirements under different macroeconomic scenarios. Like all flow of funds modeling, this involves a balancing exercise to find the most plausible financing pattern that does not push reliance on one particular flow to unsustainable levels. In setting up the base case and testing a plausible alternative scenario, it has become clear that sustained strong investment-led growth is possible in Latvia, and any tailing-off of current strong foreign capital inflows to the nonbank/nongovernment sector need not result in a material diminution in growth and investment. This comparatively sanguine outlook would not, however, apply if government slipped into significant current deficit. It also takes no account of any institutional damage sustained as a result of the recent Russian crisis. If Latvian banks do not have the capital or liquidity to support balance sheet expansion, there is no way that they could make up for a shortfall in direct foreign financing of NBNGS investment needs.

There is a great deal that could be done to improve the model. First and foremost, there would be merit in pushing the analysis back before 1996, but this requires removing the balances of the failed banks. Quicker progress might be possible on some of the crude working assumptions behind the data platform for the model as it stands, particularly:

- Adjust changes in bank balance sheets for currency movements (an assumption has been made that all domestic foreign currency business is US$-denominated).

- Include more explicit modeling of privatization flows (currently all inward foreign investment is treated as going to the privatized NBNGS entity, not the Privatization Agency).

This last point is probably relevant to most transition economies. The position of privatization agencies and related property or compensation funds is not covered well by general government data. There are philosophical issues to be addressed as to how to treat the use of funds raised through privatization to cover the financial restructuring of state enterprises.

Finally, as with all transition economies, at some point the nonbank financial sector becomes large enough to be worth modeling separately. Latvia is probably just at this point now, and available public data would allow some approximation of flows in and out of nonbank financial institutions to be calculated.

9.

Poland—Toward a Sustainable Financing Structure

Witold M.Orlowski

This chapter examines development of the financial system in Poland during the transition, using the flow of funds methodology. Flow of funds matrices, constructed for all the years from 1992 to 1997, allow the financial flows among various institutional sectors of the economy, and between the economy and the rest of the world, to be traced. The matrices show which sectors financed the economic growth of Poland in 1992–97, or more generally, who financed whom during the transition.

Poland is generally considered one of the most advanced transition economies in liberalization and development of the market institutions (EBRD 1997). Considerable progress has been registered in the development of financial markets recorded since the transition began. Nevertheless, the task of creating an efficient, competitive, predominantly private financial sector has not yet been achieved. Acceleration of this process is taking place, with several critical privatization deals scheduled for the next three years, and a significant liberalization of the access to the market in 1999, the product of commitments to the European Union and the Organization for Economic Cooperation and Development, (OECD).

This chapter will trace the financial flows to and from the financial sector during the transition. Questions about the role played by the financial sector in financing growth cannot be answered, however, without looking at the general picture of the flow of resources in the economy. The relative stability of the financial sector was accompanied by quite dramatic shifts in the saving/investment behavior of the other domestic institutional sectors, particularly general government and nonfinancial enterprises. The position of the total national economy was also changing significantly over time in relation to the rest of the world. All these changes influenced the development of the financial sector.

The development of the financial system in Poland should be seen in the context of the macroeconomic performance of the country during the transition (the main indicators are presented in Table 9.1). Poland considerably outperformed other transition economies in economic growth. The transitory recession was relatively short and shallow. GDP growth had already started in 1992, fueled by the sharp productivity increase. By 1997, GDP was already 11 percent higher than in the peak pre-transition year. As it is generally perceived, the main factor responsible for the early success of the Polish transition was a vibrant private sector, particularly the newly created small and medium-size enterprises (EC 1997). This success placed the Polish financial system in a much more favorable development condition than the systems in the other transition economies. By contrast, the relatively slow privatization of state-owned enterprises and banks, slow and gradual disinflation, and the initial lack of significant foreign direct investment inflows into Poland (until 1995) created serious obstacles to progress in financial area.

As this chapter shows, an efficient financial system, able to allocate domestic and foreign saving into profitable investment projects, is one of the key factors in the future development of Poland, particularly the process of joining the European Union (EU) and hopes for nominal and real convergence with its Western European neighbors. It is frequently pointed out that real convergence requires a significant surge in the investment to GDP ratio, which can only partly be financed by EU development funds (Orlowski 1998). The remaining part of the savings required to finance growth must be mobilized domestically. Once savings are mobilized, the role of the financial sector will be to channel them toward efficient investment.

Special attention should be paid to the influence of the government's behavior on the development of financial markets in Poland. As in the past, this may constitute a crucial factor in determining Poland's growth prospects and the shape of the Polish financial sector.

Table 9.1. Polish Macroeconomic Performance, 1990–97: Growth over Previous Year (percent)

	1990	1991	1992	1993	1994	1995	1996	1997
GDP growth rate	-11.6	-7.6	2.6	3.8	5.2	7.0	6.1	6.9
Industrial productivity	-19.5	1.3	12.6	8.8	13.1	6.5	9.1	11.4
CPI inflation (e-o-p)	585.0	70.3	40.3	35.3	32.2	27.8	19.9	14.9
PPI inflation (e-o-p)	622.4	40.9	34.5	31.9	25.3	25.4	12.4	12.2
Current account deficit (percent of GDP)	1.2	-1.8	1.1	-0.7	2.4	4.6	-1.0	-3.1
FDI & portfolio investment (percent of GDP)	0.0	0.2	0.3	0.7	-0.1	1.9	2.2	3.8

Note: e-o-p = end of period.
Source: Central Statistical Office, National Bank of Poland.

Financial Evolution of Poland since the Beginning of Transition: A Flow of Funds View

The financial sector in Poland suffered from serious underdevelopment under the communist economy. Not only was the scale of the sector very small, but its role in economic life was also reduced because financial intermediation did not play a role in the allocation of resources. The banking system, although not formally organized on a monobank basis (there were specialized banks, and commercial banks from the mid-1980s), was dominated by the State. The stock exchange did not exist, insurance companies played only a marginal role in the economy, and other financial institutions were lacking.

The beginning of the transition—initiated in Poland by the big-bang of 1990—marked a new period in the development of the financial sector. General liberalization of the economy and dismantling of the previous, partly centralized, system of allocation of resources created dynamic, growing demand for financial services. But, shortcomings of the financial institutions—both established and newly created—as well as in financial markets prevented their fully satisfying demand. The major shortcomings were:

- The economy had too few banks, and transactions were largely based on cash.
- Banks were undercapitalized, and did not conform with prudential regulations.
- Most of the banking sector was in the hands of the State and required restructuring.
- The banks inherited serious portfolio problems.
- The competitive pressure on the market was low, very high spreads were covering inefficiencies of the sector, and access of foreigners to the market was severely restricted.
- Banking supervision was almost nonexistent.

Initially, the problems were aggravated by the deepening of the transitional recession. The financial situation of state-owned enterprises (SOE) sharply deteriorated during 1991–92, which led to the radical deepening of portfolio problems for the banks. Inflation and economic instability, although reduced by the stabilization program of 1990, remained very high. A serious problem was created by the large foreign sovereign debt of Poland (foreign debt went into default in the early 1980s). Although the Paris Club decided to reduce Poland's official debt by 50 percent in 1991, the negotiations with the private creditors gathered at the London Club were not concluded before 1994. Because of the unresolved dispute with private creditors—and contrary to common belief—Poland did not obtain any significant capital inflows from abroad until 1995.[1]

The situation started to change slowly in 1992. The economy started to grow again, reaching a path of rapid GDP growth (between 6 and 7 percent) and falling inflation (probably to one-digit levels by the end of 1998) during 1994–98. Political and social stability were considerably enhanced, and Poland's external image improved, particularly when it became one of the frontrunners for early European Union (EU) membership. Despite some slippage in several areas (a conspicuous example was relatively slow privatization), Poland managed to create "a functioning market economy" (EC 1997) that grew quickly, attracting large amounts of FDI, and based on strong fundamentals.

These favorable developments were also reflected in the pattern of evolution of the financial markets. The flow of funds picture of the market, at the beginning of the transition and at present, is presented in Figure 9.1.

---

1. Despite some modest inflow of FDI, the aggregate capital and financial account of the balance of payments corrected for the exceptional financing (that did not reflect any real inflows of capital, but debt rescheduling) and the balance of nonregistered trade (until 1994, added to the capital account), was oscillating around zero during the period 1990–94 (Orlowski and Szczepanska-Maciejuk 1998). Beginning in 1995, Poland started to become a net importer of foreign capital.

Figure 9.1 Changing Structure of the Financial Markets

(value of the stocks of financial assets as percent of GDP)

1991

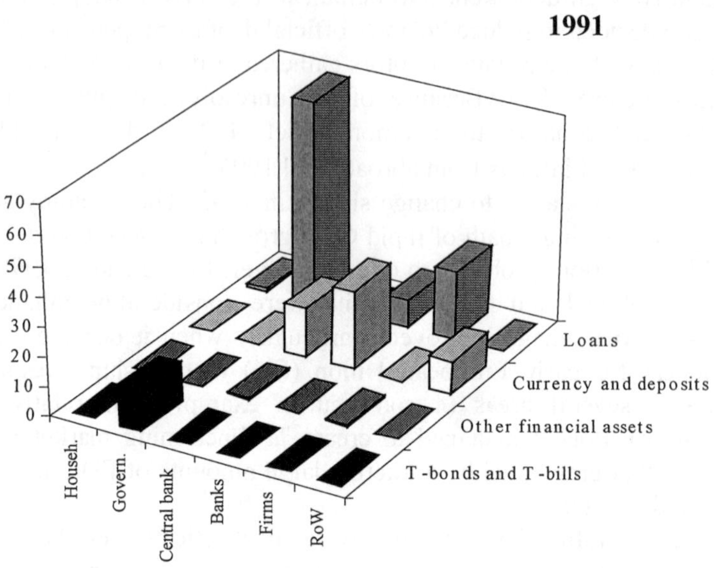

1997

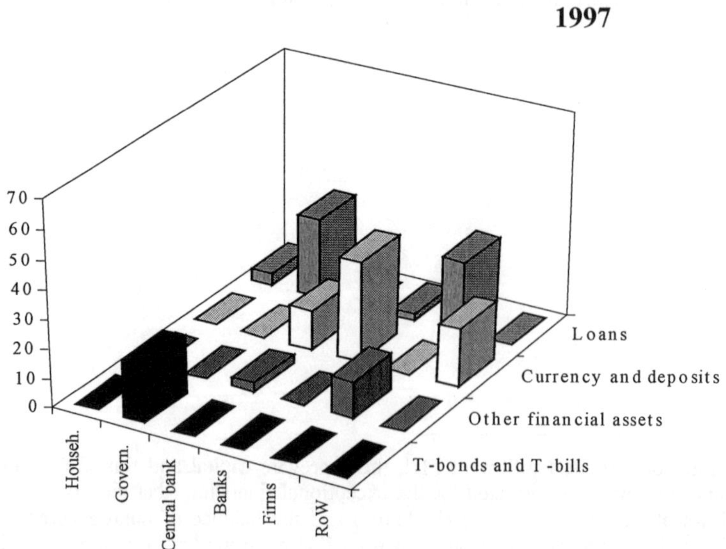

Figure 9.1 shows the stocks of financial assets in the Polish economy, both zloty and foreign-exchange-denominated, in 1991 and 1997, expressed in relation to GDP. The two panels point out the significant change that took place during the transition. The most meaningful aspects of this change are:

- *Contraction in foreign sovereign debt.* In 1991 the financial markets were dominated by huge liabilities of the government. Out of these liabilities, which represented 70 percent of GDP, the foreign debt of the government represented almost 65 percent. Six years later, the foreign debt of the government was equal to only 26 percent of GDP. The fall in the debt was partly the product of the London and Paris Club agreements, but a greater degree of responsibility must go to limited borrowing abroad, combined with GDP growth and the strong real appreciation of the zloty.
- *Increase in bank deposits.* The stock of bank deposits increased from 27 to 35 percent of GDP, and the process was accompanied by a fall of the share of foreign deposits about 33 percent in 1991 to 21 percent in 1997. This trend was mainly caused by the growing strength of the zloty, lessening inflationary uncertainty, and a policy of positive real zloty interest rates.
- *Increase in foreign reserves.* The total amount of net foreign assets in the banking sector (treated in the flow of funds as currency and deposits, although a significant portion is kept in foreign T-bonds) increased from 11 to 20 percent of GDP.
- *Fast development of the capital market.* The stock of capital market instruments (securities and equities) increased between 1991 and 1997 from below 15 percent to more than 35 percent of GDP. A third of this increase was brought about by the growing stock of government securities, but the major share was the product of the increase in the stock of shares, equities, and nongovernment bonds.

One of the major problems that influenced the development of the financial markets in Poland was the behavior of the government. After an initial surplus was obtained in 1990, because of the increase in revenue and the reduction of subsidies, public finance shifted into large deficits in 1991–92 because of the recessionary fall of revenue connected with some relaxation on the expenditure side (see Barbone and Marchetti 1995). The aggravating fiscal crisis was overcome in 1993–94, when the combination of expenditure control and increasing revenue generated by the growing economy allowed the consolidated deficit to be pushed below the 3 percent threshold. In 1993–94 the consolidated general government started generating primary surpluses and the positive gross saving. Reduction of the borrowing needs of the government to the relatively low level of 1992—94 clearly divides the picture of the financing patterns in the Polish economy during the transition into two subperiods: the years dominated by the need to finance the government (1992–94), and the years dominated by the use of saving to finance economic growth (1995–97).

The flow of funds picture of the borrowing requirements of various sectors is presented in Figure 9.2. Net financial flows from the sectors are defined as the difference between the increase in assets and the increase in liabilities held by a sector. A clear picture can be obtained only if the effects of two important off-budget operations (both concerning the government) are eliminated from the data. These are:

- *Foreign debt reduction brought about by the Paris and London Club agreements*. The final agreement was reached in 1994. A complex scheme to reduce Poland's foreign public debt by 50 percent was implemented using various financial instruments, applied to both the principal and interest. The immediate effect of this agreement was to reduce the debt by the equivalent of 7.5 percent of GDP in 1994.

- *Bank recapitalization*. The government worked out and implemented a skillful scheme for bank recapitalization over the period 1993–95. The operation was aimed at improving the quality of bank portfolios by creating incentives for the partial write-off of nonperforming loans. Two main advantages of the operation were minimization of the moral hazard problem arising from the maximum use of market instruments (market-based negotiations of the scale of the debt rescheduling between creditors and debtors, secondary market for nonperforming loans, and the like) and a relatively low fiscal cost. The capital injections into the banking sector were equal to 1.3 percent of GDP in 1993, 1.2 percent in 1994, and 0.4 percent in 1995. The operation is perceived as a success: the majority of the banks used the opportunity to clean up their debt portfolio and to start operating as fully market-oriented institutions.

Figure 9.2. Financing Patterns in Poland: Who Financed Growth? (percent of GDP)

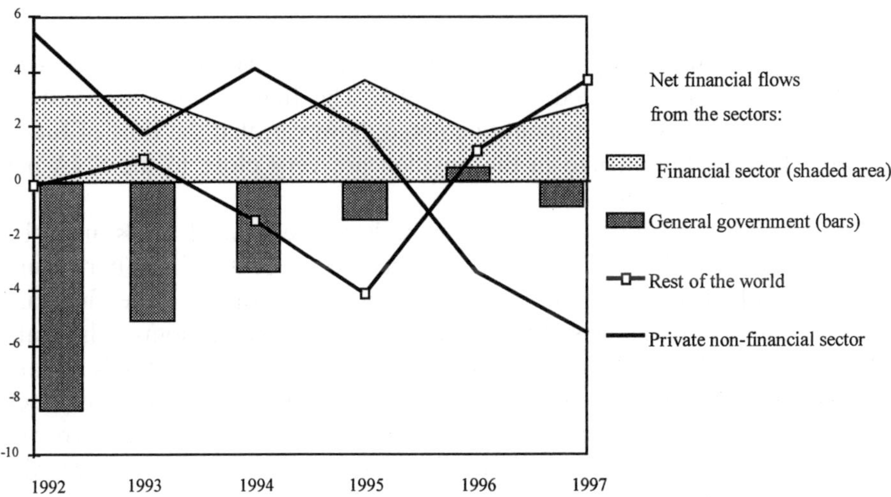

Note: Flow of funds data cleaned for the effects of the foreign public debt
reduction and domestic bank recapitalization.

Another important factor influencing financing patterns in Poland during
the transition was the behavior of the private nonfinancial sector. It should
be noted that the sector is composed of two parts: *households*, which
exhibited stable behavior of lending to other sectors of about 5 percent of
GDP a year (mainly in the form of the growth of deposits), and *nonfinancial
enterprises*. In the case of enterprises, the rapidly growing investment
demand caused the marked increase in financing needs. The flows to the
sector gradually increased from 1 percent of GDP in 1992 to more than 10
percent in 1997. As a result, the private nonfinancial sector shifted from the
position of the net lender, financing other sectors during the first subperiod
(1992–94), to the position of major net borrower in the second subperiod.
With the relatively stable lending behavior of the financial sector (net
flows to the other sectors were between 2 and 4 percent of GDP yearly), the

gap that appeared in the second subperiod between the financing needs of the economy and disposable domestic saving could have been filled only by foreigners. After the Paris and London Club agreements, such activity was possible, and in 1996 the rest of the world started to be a net lender to the economy.

The change in the saving-investment balance of various sectors between 1992 and 1997 is presented in Figure 9.3. The figure shows the system national accounts (SNA). It should be noted, however, that the flow of funds figures showing the change in the position are very close to the SNA net lending/borrowing figures.

Figure 9.3 confirms the conclusions built on the flow of funds analysis. Between 1991 and 1997, the government greatly reduced its borrowing needs, mainly because of the increase in its gross saving. The financial sector shows a remarkable stability as a net lender to the economy. The scale of net lending of households was somewhat reduced, but households remain the largest supplier of domestic saving. The nonfinancial enterprises radically increased their investment, making the sector the largest borrower in the economy. Finally, with the reduced net lending of households, increased net borrowing of enterprises, and the financing requirements of the government reduced to a smaller degree than the increase of the financial requirements of the nonfinancial private sector, the rest-of-the-world became the net lender to the economy, filling the gap between the domestic saving and investment.

Figure 9.3 Saving-Investment Balance in 1992 (percent of GDP)

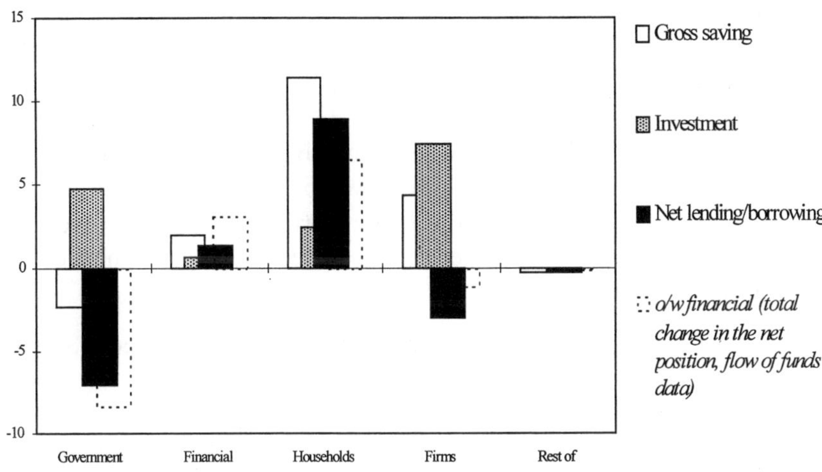

Figure 9.3 Saving-Investment Balance by Sectors in 1996 (percent of GDP) (continued)

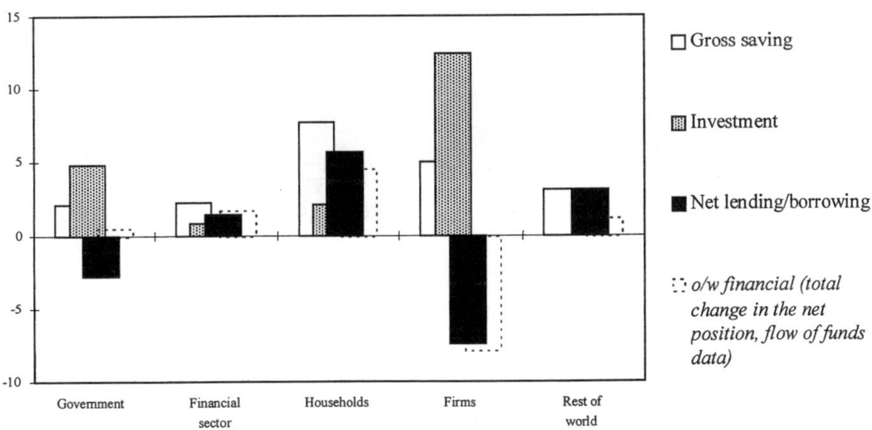

Note: National accounts data.

Figure 9.4 shows the net flows from the financial sector to various sectors of the economy. The only flow that is relatively constant over the period of the transition is the net flow from the household sector to the financial sector. The other flows changed over time:

- During the first subperiod, the most important flows from the financial sector went to the government. The sector helped finance the fiscal deficit and received capital transfers connected with bank recapitalization.
- During the years 1994–95 (between two subperiods), the sectors built up foreign exchange reserves (large flows to the rest of the world).
- During the second subperiod the major portion of the flows went to the nonfinancial enterprise sector. This sector helped finance the economic growth of Poland.

Figure 9.4. Financing Patterns in Poland: Net Flows from the Financial Sector, 1992–97 (Percent of GDP)

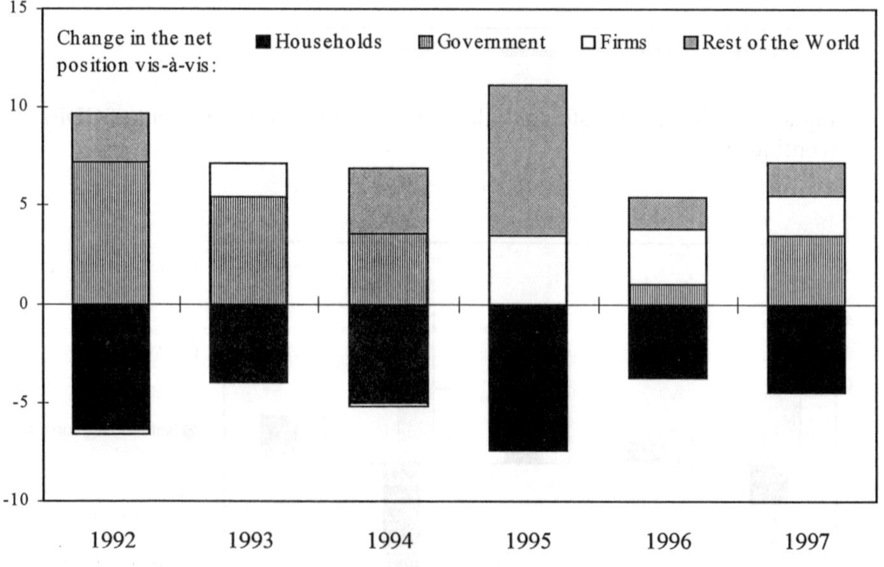

To what extent was the financial sector forced to finance the State during both subperiods? Figure 9.5 shows that the role of the sector was predominant during the overall period.

Figure 9.5. Financing Patterns in Poland: Who Financed the State? (Net flows to the Government as percent of GDP)

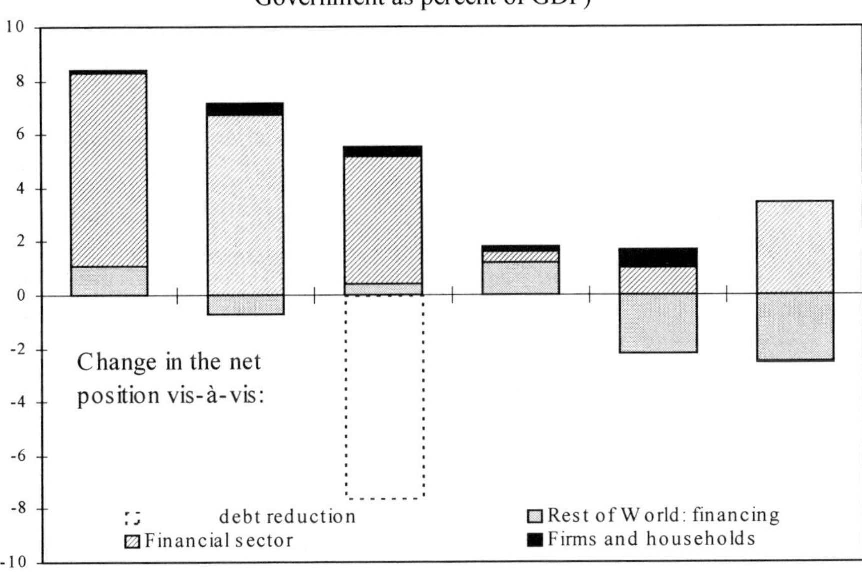

During the whole period 1992–97, the government was very careful not to use foreign financing (despite the temptation created by a cheap, easily available external resources). During the first subperiod, the domestic financial sector had to be the principal provider of financing for the government, because no other financing was available. During the second subperiod the role of the sector, although not as crucial as it had been, remained important because of the government's policy of gradual reduction of its foreign debt. The major change in the net position of the government in relation to the rest of the world was recorded in 1994, when a significant part of Poland's foreign debt was cancelled.

In all, the general assessment of the financing patterns of Poland during the transition points to the following factors:

- The most important element in shaping the financing patterns in the Polish economy was the behavior of the government. During the first subperiod of the transition, 1991–94, the government had huge financing needs that must have been covered—in a time marked by a lack of access to foreign financing—mainly by the domestic financial sector. During this subperiod, the stock of T-bills and T-bonds held by the financial sector increased from 11 to 21 percent of GDP. During the second subperiod, 1995–97, the financing needs of the government were considerably reduced. Although the government tried to diminish the foreign debt burden, and was still relying on the financial sector as the main provider of financing, the stock of T-bills and T-bonds held by the financial sector had fallen to 16 percent of GDP by the end of 1997.

- The financial sector and the household sector played a stable role as providers of funds for the economy.

- By contrast, the nonfinancial enterprise sector was gradually increasing its financing requirements. The supply of domestic saving was large enough to cover the needs of the government and the enterprise sector during the first subperiod, when investment activity was very low. In the second subperiod, however, the dynamics of investment caused a basic disequilibrium between the financing needs of the economy and the supply of domestic saving. The gap was filled by increasing foreign saving (deterioration of the current account).[2]

- Foreign financing began to be available after the foreign debt problem was solved by the Paris and London Club agreements. After 1995 the scale of capital inflows to Poland, including FDI, portfolio investment, and commercial loans, started to be significant. The role of foreign saving in financing the economic growth of Poland became crucial in 1997–98.

Therefore, the government managed to gradually restrict its access to financing, leaving room for the development of a financial market oriented mainly toward financing economic growth. Nevertheless, in a situation of a structurally low saving rate in the economy, that was not enough to secure an equilibrium between the rapidly growing investment needs and available saving. Domestic saving should still be promoted by increasing the gross saving of the government, improving the profitability of the financial and nonfinancial firms, and increasing the saving rates of households if the economy is to avoid excessive exposure to foreign financing (that is, dangerously high current account deficits).

---

2. The problem of the growing current account deficit gained notice in 1996–97. In late 1997, the government adopted a policy of cooling down domestic absorption (through a mix of fiscal and monetary tightening) in an effort to promote domestic saving and to adjust the rate of growth of the economy to the available saving.

Tables 9.2 and 9.3 provide more detailed information on the financial flows recorded in Poland during the transition, including aggregated flow of funds matrices for the years 1992–97 and a matrix of saving/uses in 1996.

The Polish Financial System and Economic Policy over the Coming Decade

The possible paths of development of the Polish financial system and financial markets over the coming decade were examined with the use of a computable general equilibrium (CGE) model of the economy.[3] The model was used to create two development scenarios and to generate the flow of funds matrices connected with each of them.

Both scenarios assume that by the year 2002–03, Poland will become a member of the EU. Membership in the EU would carry with it the following:

- Poland will become part of a large market of more than 400 million consumers. If the country takes advantage of its relatively cheap labor, enhances productivity, and retools export-oriented industries, its relatively fast path of economic growth can be maintained over the next decade (Baldwin, Francois, and Portes 1996).

- As an EU member, Poland can count on generous development transfers. According to current EU plans, the transfers should reach 3–4 percent of Poland's GDP, increasing the inflow of foreign financing without deteriorating the current account (EC 1997).

- Accession to the EU will present some serious challenges for the financial sector that can be grouped into three areas. First, the financial sector will have to comply with the *acquis communitaire*, which means full liberalization of access to the market; harmonization of laws; and effective implementation of prudential regulations, accounting rules, and other market regulations. Second, supervision will have to be strengthened. Third, accession will lead to the creation of a more competitive environment, which may lead to serious problems for nonrestructured domestic banks.

---

3. The model is very close to the CGE model of the Hungarian economy described in Dethier and Orlowski 1998.

Table 9.2 Flow-of-Funds Matrices, 1992–97 (percent of GDP)

	Change in liabilities (flows to)					
	Households	Government	Central bank	Commercial banks	Nonfinancial enterprises	Rest of the world
Change in assets (flows from) **1992**						
Households		0.14	1.29	5.51	0.03	
General government			0.05	1.37	0.02	
Central bank	0.01	6.35		-2.32	-0.01	1.03
Commercial banks	0.41	2.25	0.95		4.04	1.53
Nonfinancial enterprises			0.93	3.32		
Rest of the world		1.07	0.06		1.33	
Change in assets (flows from) **1993**						
Households		0.42	-0.13	4.74	0.04	
General government			0.56	-1.21	0.02	
Central bank	0.00	1.44		0.96	0.00	2.34
Commercial banks	0.67	4.65	0.37		4.17	-0.42
Nonfinancial enterprises			0.54	1.98		
Rest of the world		-0.72	1.91		1.83	
Change in assets (flows from) **1994**						
Households		0.43	1.28	4.24	0.16	
General government			0.24	0.46	0.08	
Central bank		1.59		0.32	0.00	2.95

Commercial banks	0.52	3.86	1.26		3.29	1.97
Nonfinancial enterprises			-0.20	3.67		
Rest of the world		-7.18	1.61		1.44	
Change in assets (flows from)	**1995**					
Households		0.44	2.63	5.59	0.51	
General government			0.23	0.63	0.21	
Central bank		-2.86		0.27		6.61
Commercial banks	0.79	4.08	2.35		4.38	-1.06
Nonfinancial enterprises			-0.11	0.98		
Rest of the world		1.22	-2.05		2.31	
Change in assets (flows from)	**1996**					
Households		0.71	0.91	4.45	0.13	
General government			0.74	0.66	0.06	
Central bank	0.00	-0.01		0.84	0.01	2.83
Commercial banks	1.67	2.44	2.29		5.01	-1.26
Nonfinancial enterprises			0.20	2.04		
Rest of the world		-2.18	-0.05		4.93	
Chang in assets (flows from)	**1997 (estimate)**					
Households		0.11	1.61	4.36	0.28	
General government			-0.41	0.18	0.12	
Central bank	0.00	0.38		-0.27	0.00	2.27
Commercial banks	1.52	2.85	1.44		4.18	-0.21
Nonfinancial enterprises			0.15	2.02		
Rest of the world		-2.52	0.29		7.97	

Table 9.3. Uses/Sources Matrix and Flow of Funds, 1996 (percent of GDP)[a]

	General government		Banking sector		Households		Enterprises		Rest of the World		Total	
	U	S	U	S	U	S	U	S	U	S	U	S
Gross capital formation	4.9		0.8		2.1		12.4		—		20.2	
Gross saving		2.1		2.2		7.7		5.1		3.1		20.2
Surplus/ deficit	*-2.8*		*1.4*		*5.7*		*-7.4*		*3.1*		*—*	
	Financial		Financial		Financial		Financial		Financial		Financial	
Changes	Assets	Liab.	Assets	Liab.	Assets	Liab.	Assets	Liab.	Assets	Liab.	Assets	Liab.
Foreign claims, net			1.6							1.6	1.6	1.6
General gov't. debt		1.0	2.4		0.7		0.0		-2.2		1.0	1.0
Private credit	0.1		6.7			1.7		10.0	4.9		11.7	11.7
Money and quasi-money	1.4			9.0	5.4		2.2				9.0	9.0
Misc. and discrepancy		3.2		0.3		-1.3		-0.4		-1.9	0.0	-0.1
Total	6.3	6.3	11.5	11.5	8.1	8.1	14.7	14.7	2.8	2.8	43.4	43.3

Note: [a]Components may not add up to total because of rounding.

For illustrative purposes, two scenarios of the alternative economic policies were formulated.

(1) MODERATE-GROWTH SCENARIO. This is based on the assumption that the current saving rates will prevail over the next decade. The policy mix that can lead to such an outcome includes (1) lack of fiscal discipline, leading to an average fiscal deficit of almost 4 percent of GDP; (2) accompanying slow disinflation and lack of confidence in the country's overall economic policy; (3) unfinished structural reforms, leaving a large, nonrestructured, and loss-making sector of state-owned enterprises; and (4) great dependence on EU transfers, used partly to finance ineffective public investment projects, and partly transferred for consumption.

(2) HIGH-GROWTH SCENARIO. This is based on the assumption that growth-promoting economic policy will create incentives for saving and investing. A policy mix connected with this scenario includes: (1) enhanced government saving through a balanced budget; (2) gradual reduction of the level of taxation and redistribution of income; (3) rapid disinflation, which will allow the country to join the EU and its Monetary Union; (4) full privatization of the economy and radical restructuring of ailing industries; and (5) careful use of the relatively small EU transfers, and greater dependence on FDI.

The first scenario resembles the EU experience of Greece to some extent, while the second is closer to the experience of The Republic of Ireland in the late 1980s and 1990s. The outcome of both scenarios is presented in Table 9.4. Under the *moderate-growth* scenario, the average yearly increase of GDP in the period 1998–2010 is 4.4 percent, with consumption growing considerably faster than both GDP and investment. As high fiscal deficits prevail, the public debt falls to some 48 percent by 2002, but then starts to grow to almost 60 percent in 2010. The investment to GDP ratio only increases slightly over time; almost one-fourth of the investment is financed by foreign saving (higher current account deficit before official transfers); the lion's share is EU funds.

The *high-growth* scenario leads to annual growth exceeding 6 percent, with a similar increase in consumption and two-digit growth in investment. Fiscal prudence allows for the reduction of the public debt to 25 percent of GDP. The investment to GDP ratio gradually grows, finally stabilizing above 30 percent of GDP. Domestic saving increases to 27.5 percent of GDP and finances the major part of investment. The EU transfers play only a minor role, and the overall efficiency of investment—mainly private—remains higher than in the other scenario (Barro and Sala-I-Martin 1995).

Table 9.4. Growth Projection Scenarios, Key Variables

	MODERATE-GROWTH SCENARIO			*HIGH-GROWTH SCENARIO*		
	1998	2010	**Annual growth rate, 1998–2010**	1998	2010	**Annual growth rate, 1998–2010**
GDP index	100	168	**4.4**	100	209	**6.3**
Personal consumption index	100	197	**5.8**	100	208	**6.3**
Government consumption index	100	156	**3.8**	100	134	**2.5**
Fixed investment index	100	179	**5.0**	100	329	**10.4**
Exports index	100	206	**6.2**	100	253	**8.1**
Imports index	100	270	**8.6**	100	286	**9.2**
	1998	2010	**Average, 1998–2010**	1998	2010	**Average, 1998–2010**
CPI inflation rate (%)	12.1	7.3	**8.4**	11.9	2.1	**5.5**
Percentage of GDP						
Fiscal deficit	-2.5	-5.1	**-3.9**	-2.1	0.7	**-0.1**
Public debt	49.4	58.2	**51.7**	49.1	25.4	**36.3**
Percentage of GDP						
Current account (C/A)	-3.9	-0.6	**-1.0**	-3.8	-1.8	**-1.7**
C/A before official transfers	-3.9	-5.1	**-4.9**	-3.8	-4.0	**-4.0**
Gross foreign debt	32.1	20.8	**26.8**	32.0	19.2	**25.6**
Percentage of GDP						
Total investment	20.9	21.7	**21.4**	21.3	32.1	**28.7**
Financing of investment						
Domestic saving	17.0	16.6	**16.7**	17.5	27.5	**24.4**
Foreign saving	3.9	5.1	**4.7**	3.8	4.6	**4.3**
O/w transfers from EU	0.1	4.5	**3.9**	0.1	2.8	**2.3**

Source: Author's calculations based on CGE Model presented in the appendix.

Both development scenarios lead to various saving-investment balances of the institutional sectors of the economy, and consequently to various financing needs of the sectors (Figure 9.6). The most important differences in the final year of the projection are:

- There are much higher borrowing needs for the nonfinancial enterprises sector under the *high-growth* scenario, caused mainly by the much higher levels of investment.
- Under the *moderate-growth* scenario, the general government is a net borrower that absorbs 5 percent of GDP in yearly financing because of negative gross saving. Under the *high-growth* scenario, high saving in the sector is more than sufficient to cover its investment needs.

- There will be a much higher propensity to save in the households sector.

Figure 9.6. Saving and Investment: Two Scenarios

Saving-Investment Balance by Sector in 2010: Moderate Growth (Percent of GDP)

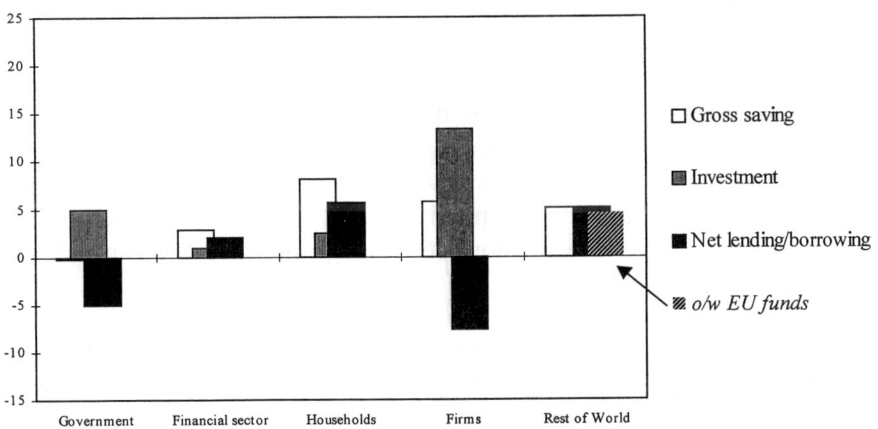

Saving-Investment Balance by Sector in 2010: High Growth (Percent of GDP)

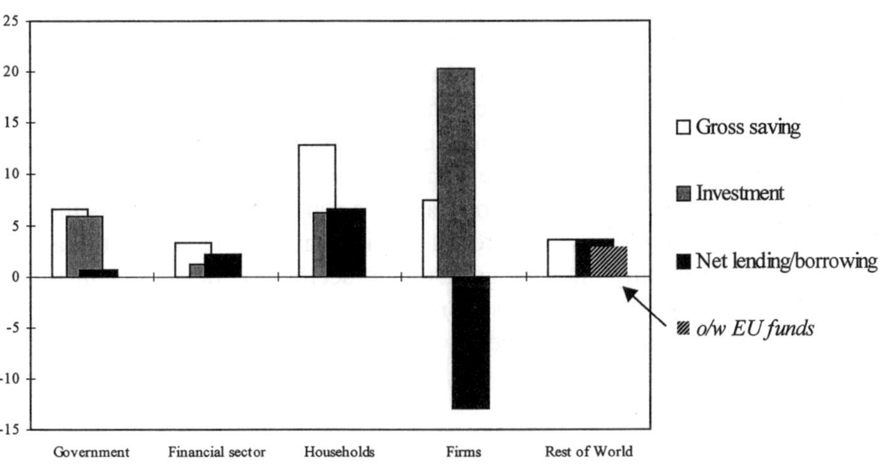

The saving-investment pattern associated with the moderate-growth scenario does not differ substantially from the current pattern. The higher financing needs of the government (5 percent in 2010, against less than 3 percent in 1996) are covered by increased foreign financing, while the saving-investment behavior of the other sectors of the economy does not change substantially.

Under the high-growth scenario, the changes are more profound, and associated with the general increase of saving rates in the domestic sectors (a growth of aggregate saving rates of about 50 percent, with the government tripling its saving). Such growth is the outcome of fiscal prudence, higher profits of the fully privatized banks and firms, restructuring of loss-makers, a more stable macroeconomic environment, and the development of attractive financial saving instruments that promote saving by households (Czyzewski and Orlowski 1995). Greater domestic saving is used to finance higher investment needs. The role of the rest of the world does not change significantly.

In summary, under the moderate-growth scenario, the propensities to save and to invest remain almost constant, and the increased borrowing requirements of the government are covered by the increased foreign saving (mainly in the form of EU transfers). Under the high-growth scenario, the greater investment needs of the economy are matched by increased saving, and the role of foreign saving remains similar to that currently observed.

Figure 9.7 illustrates projected net flows from the financial sector in the year 2010. That the fact that higher borrowing needs of the government under the moderate-growth scenario are matched by increased foreign saving does not mean that the government directly borrows abroad. The major part of the EU funds that come into a country are earmarked for investment, and they cannot be used to directly finance the public expenditure. Thus, under the moderate-growth scenario, the domestic financial sector is still a major provider of financing for the government. In a sense, the sector plays the role of a vehicle that allows the transfer of foreign saving, channeled to various sectors of the economy, into the government sector. EU development funds, instead of adding to the domestic resources used for investment needs, replace domestic financing for the private sector.

Figure 9.7. Projected Financing Patterns: Net Flows from the Financial Sector, 2010
(Percent of GDP)

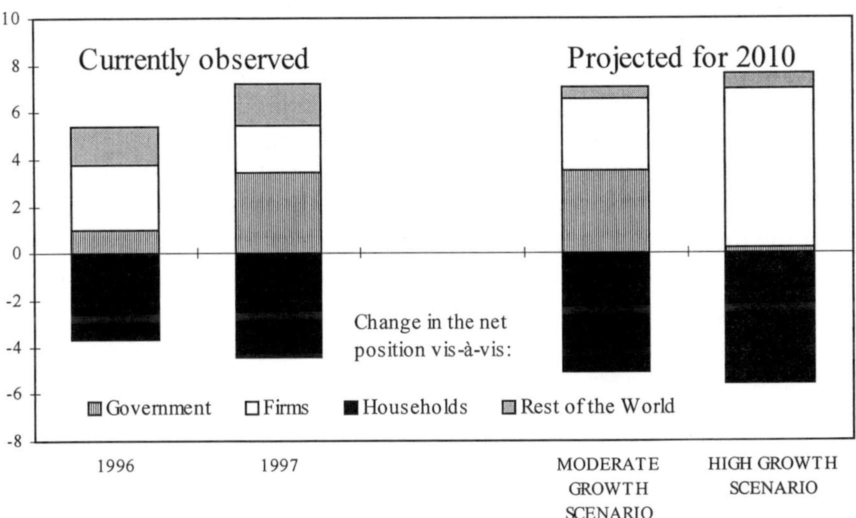

Under the high-growth scenario, the government does not require any significant financing (on a net basis), and the financial sector primarily channels the greater domestic saving into the increased domestic investment of private firms. The efficiency in the use of these resources depends on the development of financial markets and institutions. As the opportunity for safe, highly profitable lending to the government dries up, only a highly competitive and efficient financial sector is able to survive in the market. With the financial market fully liberalized, the mounting competitive pressure will reinforce the necessary adjustment of financial institutions.

Both scenarios change the structure of the financial markets significantly (Figure 9.8). In both cases the stock of loans and deposits in the economy increases (much faster growth takes place under the high-growth scenario). Both scenarios also lead to the fast growth of the capital market. The crucial difference, however, is that while the moderate-growth scenario leads mainly to the rapid increase of the stock of T-bills and T-bonds (45 percent of GDP in 2010 from less than 20 percent in 1997), under the high-growth scenario, the stock of government securities remains almost constant (20 percent of GDP in 2010), and the development of the capital market takes place mainly through the rapid expansion of other financial instruments (shares, equities, commercial bonds, and the like). The nonfinancial enterprise sector does not restrict itself to searching for the necessary resources through financial institutions, but actively uses the capital market for this purpose as well.

In both scenarios there is a significant increase in competitive pressure on the financial sector, after access to the market is fully liberalized for the Western European financial institutions. The source of problems for the domestic banks, however, originates elsewhere. Under the moderate-growth scenario, the problems mainly come from the general slowdown in economic growth, and the competition for foreign supply of funds by the government. Under the high-growth scenario, the pressure comes from the lower banking spreads and elimination of the opportunity of lending to the government.

Figure 9.8 Projected Structure of the Financial Markets in 2010 (Value of stocks of financial assets as percent of GDP)

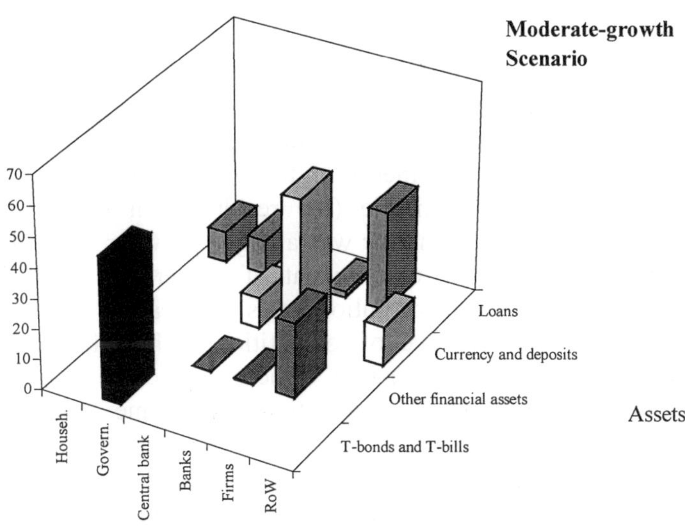

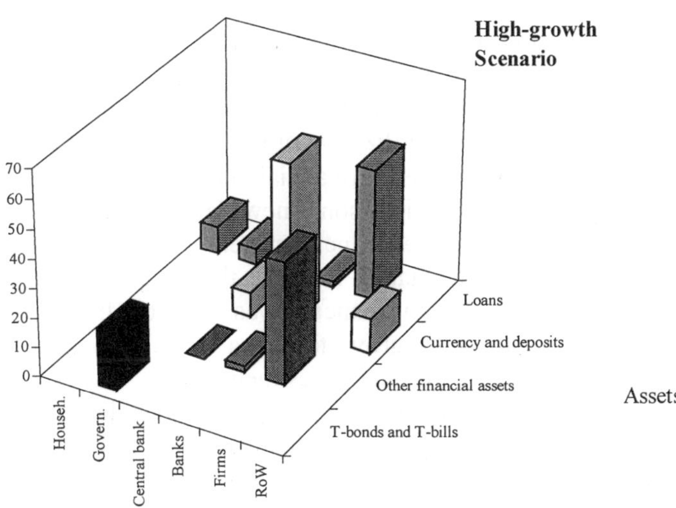

Conclusions

The main conclusions of the foregoing analysis can be summarized as follows:

- The period of transition in Poland should be divided into two subperiods. During the first subperiod, from 1992 to 1994, the development of the financial sector was strongly influenced by the large borrowing requirements of the government. Because foreign financing was not available (the result of an unsolved old-debt problem), the financial sector was a major provider of funds to cover public sector borrowing requirements. Together with limited access to the market for foreign institutions, this was leading to the unhealthy combination of a low level of competition, high banking spreads, and scant pressure to restructure. These unwelcome effects were accompanied by slow privatization and some (albeit reduced) elements of moral hazard.

- The situation changed during the second subperiod, from 1995 to 1997. The general government considerably reduced its borrowing requirements, leaving more resources to finance economic growth. Nevertheless, the net flows from the financial sector remained significant, because the government was continuously replacing some of its foreign debt with domestic debt as a precaution. During the second subperiod, the role of the financial sector as a provider of funds for the private economy increased. The subperiod was also marked by accelerated privatization, improvement of banks' loan portfolio quality, and liberalization of the financial market.

- While the general picture of financial sector development improved during the second subperiod, some new dangers arose. Whatever the rate of development of the financial system and the financial markets, it was too slow to adequately increase the saving rate in the Polish economy. Because foreign financing was available from 1995 on, and the economy started to grow faster, a basic imbalance appeared between domestic saving and investment needs. The gap was filled mainly by the inflow of FDI, leading to a serious deterioration of the current account through a mechanism of real exchange rate appreciation.

- Although the current account deficit did not exceed dangerous levels, the availability of domestic saving began to play a role as a key factor limiting the medium-term rate of growth of the Polish economy in 1997–98.

- Experience, as well as projections for the next decade, point to the crucial importance of availability of domestic saving in determining the potential growth pattern of Poland. Membership in the EU is likely to relax the external limitations on the speed of the expansion, but it is unlikely to eliminate it totally.

- Even the relatively generous development funds from the EU cannot guarantee a high GDP growth. Depending on the quality of economic policy, the new funds may add to the existing saving in the economy and help maintain the rapid expansion of investment, or they may replace domestic saving in financing investment and release resources for consumption. In the latter case, the chances for maintaining a high rate of growth will be traded-off for short-term consumption gains.

- The crucial role in determining the future growth pattern of Poland will be played by the government. Expansionary fiscal policy would depress domestic saving and channel the EU funds indirectly into financing consumption. If such a policy prevails, the financial sector will have to play the role of the main provider of financing for the government. Because access to the Polish market for the Western European institutions will be fully liberalized, however, domestic banks may be replaced in this role by more competitive foreign institutions. A serious handicap for the sector will also be created by the relative economic slowdown, which is likely to lead to deterioration of portfolio quality.

- If, by contrast, a policy of promoting domestic saving is implemented, including enhanced saving of the government and incentives for the other sectors to save more, the financial sector will have to play a more active role as provider of funds to the economy. The economy will be growing faster, but the competition on the financial markets will increase as well, reinforcing the rapid restructuring of domestic financing institutions. A more competitive financial sector is also a precondition for the efficient use of the increased funds spent on investment.

- Independently of the development scenario, completion of the privatization and restructuring of financial institutions appears to be a crucial policy recommendation for Poland. In both cases—the financial sector being the provider of funds mainly for the government, or for the economy—the competitive pressure on the market will increase to such a degree that only the efficient institutions will be able to survive.

Appendix—Model Structure and Data

The projections presented in this chapter were calculated with a computable general equilibrium (CGE) model of the Polish economy. Such models are now commonly used to analyze long-term growth in market economies. They postulate that, over a long period, an economy develops because of continuous adjustment of demand and supply factors: production capacities increase as a result of the cumulative growth of production factors, and changes in the price structure inform consumers about production costs and force producers to allocate production factors in accordance with consumer decisions.

The assumptions: economic agents are rational; producers maximize profits; and, households maximize utility. Prices of goods and services are flexible and clear the market. Wages, however, do not always clear labor markets. As a result, there is some unemployment, both for technical reasons and reasons of labor legislation and institutions. The resulting relative level of unemployment is assumed to diminish over time as labor market reforms proceed. Capital is assumed to be mobile in the medium term, but not in the short term. Capital mobility in the medium term is assured by an investment allocation function that takes into account differences in the return to capital across sectors of the economy. Investment increases the capital stock, only with a one-period lag so that the stock of fixed capital by sector is fixed in any given period. In macroeconomic closure, the model is savings-driven: for a given current account deficit level, investment and output depend on the level of domestic saving. Because the market for foreign currency is flexible, the real exchange rate level that corresponds to any given current account can be calculated.

The model is disaggregated into eight economic sectors and four domestic institutions (households, government, nonfinancial sector, and financial sector). The foreign sector is divided into three groups (EU, CEFTA countries, and other countries).

The equations of the model are presented here in simplified form, omitting parameters and variables that are not significant for an understanding of the mechanics of the model.

- *Household consumption* is given by the indirect addilog system, relating the level of demand in particular groups with the level of disposable income and relative prices:

$$C_i = f_i\,(Y(1\text{—tax})/P, P_i/P)$$

When C_i is demand for product i, Y is income, tax is tax rate, P_i/P is the ratio of price i to average prices.

- *Household savings* (S_g) equals the difference between disposable income and expenditure:

$$S_g = Y(1\text{—tax})\text{—}S_i\,C_i P_i.$$

- *Investment* is equal to the sum of savings (after profit tax) of the nonfinancial sector, households, government (where the "negative savings" of the government is equal to the deficit of the current account of the budget) and the foreign sector (foreign savings is equal to the current account deficit).

- *Exports* depend on the foreign demand and on prices of Polish exports relative to world prices:

$$E_i = \alpha(FDem_c)^\beta [P_i\,XR\,(1 + tar_{z,i})(1\text{—}subs_i)/P_W]^\gamma$$

where E_i is exports of good i, $FDem_c$ is foreign demand in country group c, XR is exchange rate, $tar_{z,i}$ is the foreign tariff on Polish good i, $subs_i$ is the export subsidy (estimated only for agricultural products as the difference between domestic and world prices), and P_W is world price.

- *Total demand* is the sum of demand from households, government (exogenously given), investment, exports, and intermediate demand:

$$Q^d_i = C_i + g_i\,G + i_i Inv + E_i + \Sigma_j\,a_{ij} X_j$$

where Q^d_i is total demand for good i, G is government demand, Inv is investment demand, X_j is gross output of branch j, g_i, i_i, and a_{ij} are coefficients from the input-output table.

- *Demand for imports* is given by "Armington functions" (based on the assumptions of cost minimization by consumers and imperfect substitution of imports and domestic production):

$$M_i/X_i = \alpha\,[P_i\,XR/(P_W(1 + tar_i))]^\sigma$$

where M_i is imports of good i, and *tar$_i$* is the Polish tariff on good i.

- *Production functions* are of the Cobb-Douglas type:

$$X_i = \alpha \, L_i^{\beta} \, K_i^{(1-\beta)}$$

where L_i is employment in branch i, and K_i is fixed capital in branch i.

- *Demand for labor* is derived from the maximization of the profit function of the nonfinancial sector:

$$L_i = \beta \, (X_i P_i \, (1-vat_i) - \Sigma_j a_{ji} \, X_i \, P_j)/w_i$$

where w_i is wage in branch i, which is a constant function of the average wage, and *vat$_i$* is the VAT rate.

- *Capital stock in branch i* depends on the capital stock in the previous period, depreciation, and investment in branch i in the previous period (where investment in branch i depends on volume of production and the return on capital in that branch):

$$K_i = K_{i,t-1} \, (1-\delta_i) + Inv_{i,t-1}$$

where δ_i is the depreciation ratio in branch i.

- *Household income* is the sum of primary incomes (wages, capital income, and mixed income), transfers from government (including old-age and disability pensions), transfers from abroad, and interest payments on the financial assets owned by households.

- *Government income* is the sum of revenues from taxes (indirect and direct, including social security contributions) and tariffs; and *government expenditure* is the sum of government consumption, transfers to households, enterprise subsidies, and net interest payments on the public debt.

- *After-tax profits of enterprises* are calculated residually, as the difference between total revenue of enterprises and their expenditure, corrected for transfers received from other sectors and net interest payments on their debt:

$$\Pi_i = (X_i P_i \, (1-vat_i) + ntransf_i - \Sigma_j a_{ji} \, X_i \, P_j - L_i \, w_i - int_i \,)(1-tax)$$

where Π_i is profits in branch i, *ntransf$_i$* is net transfers from other sectors, *int$_i$* is net interests, and tax is corporate income tax.

- *Net saving/borrowing* by sector is calculated as the difference between investment in the sector and the sum of the sector's gross saving and net capital transfers received.

- *Net debt in each sector* is the sum of the debt at the end of the previous period and net saving/borrowing of the sector in a given period.

- *Market clearing for the product markets* determines the equilibrium price Pi, balancing demand with supply (the sum of production and imports):

$$Q^d_i = X_i + M_i.$$

- *Market clearing for the labor market* determines the equilibrium wage (with a given rate of "structural" unemployment):

$$L^s (1—UR) = \Sigma_i L_i$$

where L^s is total labor supply, determined by demographic factors, and UR is the assumed structural unemployment rate.

- *The balance of payments identity* determines the equilibrium exchange rate equating revenues (the sum of export earnings, transfers, and capital inflows) with expenditures (the sum of expenditures on imports, interest payments, and transfers), plus the necessary increase in foreign exchange reserves. Total capital inflows—equal to the capital account surplus—are exogenously given.

- *Net foreign debt* is the sum of the debt at the end of the previous period and of the current account deficit in a given period, less foreign direct investment and foreign assets held by domestic institutions (which are essentially foreign exchange reserves).

References

Balcerowicz, L., and A. Gelb. 1994. "Macropolicies in Transition to a Market Economy: A Three-Year Perspective." *Proceedings of the World Bank Annual Conference on Development Economics.* Washington, D.C.: World Bank.

Baldwin, R.E., J. F. Francois, and R. Portes. 1996. "The Costs and Benefits of Eastern Enlargement." *Economic Policy* 24:125–70.

Barbone, L., and D. Marchetti. 1995. "Transition and the Fiscal Crisis in Central Europe." *Economics of Transition* 3:59–74.

Barro, R. J., and X. Sala-I-Martin. 1995. *Economic Growth.* New York: McGraw-Hill.

Czyzewski, A. B., and W. M. Orlowski. 1995. "Financer la Transition en Pologne." *Economie Internationale* 62:129–44.

______. 1996. "Disinflation Paths in Polish Economy between 1996–2005." *Research Bulletin RECESS (ZBSE)* 3:19–44.

Dethier, J. J., and W. M. Orlowski. 1998. "Long Term Effects of Fiscal Adjustment." In L. Bokros and J. J. Dethier, eds., *Public Finance Reform During the Transition: The Experience of Hungary.* Washington, D.C.: World Bank.

Easterly, W., C.A. Rodriguez, and K. Schmidt-Hebbel. 1994. *Public Sector Deficits and Macroeconomic Performance.* Oxford, U.K.: Oxford University Press.

EBRD (European Bank for Reconstruction and Development). 1997. *Transition Report 1997.* London.

EC (European Commission). 1997. *Agenda 2000.* Brussels.

Orlowski, W. M. 1998a. *A Road to Europe. Macroeconomics of Joining the European Union.* Lodz: European Institute.

______. 1998b. "Does Maastricht Matter for the Capital Market Development in Poland? (Past Development and Prospects of the Polish Capital Market)." In *Meeting the Convergence Criteria of EMU: Problems of Countries in Transition.* Warszawa: PTE.

Orlowski, W. M., and O. Szczepanska-Maciejuk. 1998. "Old Debt Problems versus New Development Prospects: Capital Inflows to Poland 1990–97." *CEPS Working Papers,* Brussels.

World Bank. 1996. *From Plan to Market. World Development Report 1996.* New York: Oxford University Press for the World Bank.

Quasi-Public Sector Deficits

Lithuania

10.

Lithuania—The Persistent Dependency on the State

John Dawson and Stephen Everhart

In the period since independence, Lithuania has made significant progress toward the creation of a private enterprise market system. While this institutional transition is well under way, in the sense of eliminating price and trade controls and launching privatization, a wide array of sectoral reforms remain to be undertaken. These institutional reforms—largely of a legal and administrative nature—will take time to become effective.

At the same time, the goals of macroeconomic stabilization and the restoration of economic growth have been achieved. Inflation has continued to moderate, with consumer prices increasing only 9 percent in 1997. Real GDP growth began again in 1995 and accelerated to 6 percent in 1997. The budget deficit, which had grown to 2.5 percent of GDP in 1996, was brought sharply down in 1997. And a common accompaniment of restored growth, a rising balance of payments current account deficit, has been recorded in the past two years.

For Lithuania's financial system, the transition period has not been easy. The reform of the banking system—with its 1996 crisis—has been especially difficult, and the establishment of new financial institutions and markets has been slow. Nevertheless, real investment has been revived and it has been financed. This chapter examines the operation of the financial system during the transition period and considers its prospects for the coming decade.

The outlook for the Lithuanian economy over the next decade depends on the vigor of its pursuit of structural reform. On the one hand, moderate policy action can lead to a respectable—but not outstanding—growth path. On the other hand, a stronger and more comprehensive policy initiative can lead to a high and sustainable growth rate. As will be seen, these alternative growth paths have sharply differing implications for the development of the financial system.

Lithuania's Financial Evolution During Transition: A Flow of Funds View

Because of the key role played in Lithuania's financial framework by investment and deficits—government, foreign, and private—it is essential to examine these factors. This can best be done by a review of the financial system as presented in the flow of funds accounts. This section will examine how the major economic sectors have financed their deficits in the 1993–98 period. The analysis will focus on the financing of private investment and its relationship to both the fiscal and balance of payments deficits and the monetary and banking system.

The examination of Lithuania's financial performance begins with an outline of its saving-investment process. In Figure 10.1 the economy is analyzed, and separated into columns for three sectors: the general government,[1] a comprehensive private sector,[2] and rest-of-the-world. For the general government and the private sector, a surplus/deficit or net lending/borrowing curve is derived as the difference between each sector's investment (gross capital formation) and saving. Since the rest-of-the-world does no capital formation for Lithuania, this column contains only its saving (Lithuania's balance of payments current account deficit) and its surplus, rest-of-the-world net lending to Lithuania. The banking sector, which does little saving or nonfinancial investment, is omitted.

---

1. The general government includes the state and municipal government, plus the social security, health insurance, and privatization funds.

2. The private sector is a residual sector, including all sectors other than the general government, banking, and rest-of-the-world. It includes public enterprises, nonbank financial institutions, and nonprofit institutions, as well as households and all private business organizations.

Figure 10.1 Sector Investment, Saving, and Surplus/Deficit (Flow data as percentage of current GDP)

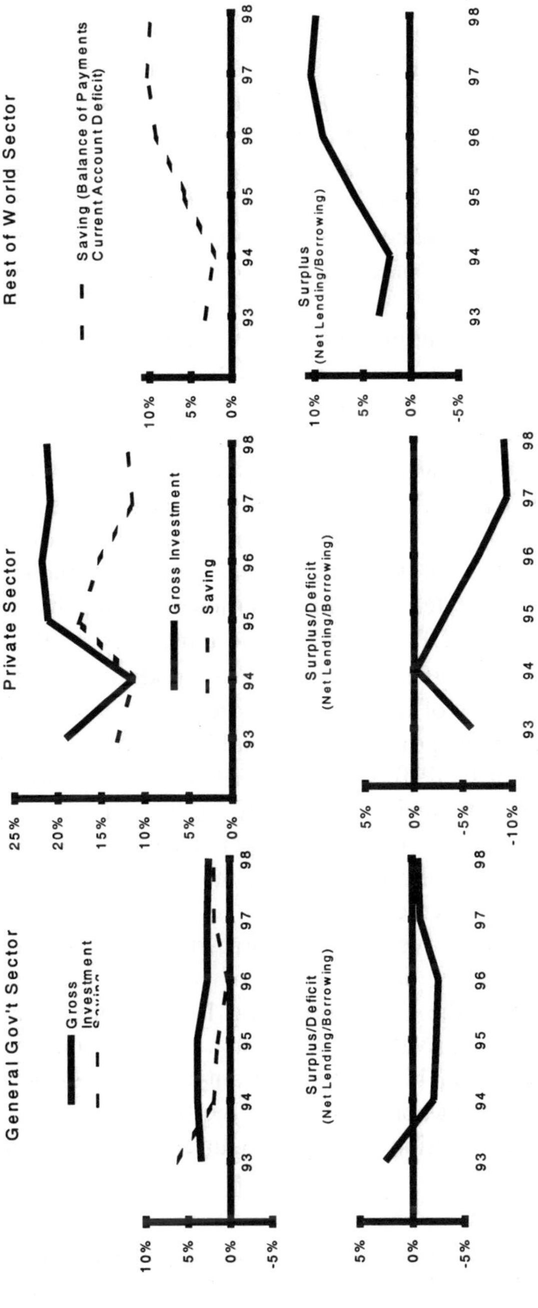

Note: 1998 data are projected.

Looking across the bottom of Figure 10.1 reveals the basic structure of financial flows that has governed the Lithuanian economy: the net lending of the rest-of-the-world finances the net borrowing of the two domestic sectors. The general government deficit has been financed steadily from abroad, and the higher borrowing need of the private sector since 1995 has been financed by the new, higher level of rest-of-the-world net lending. The 1996 and 1997 data suggest a flow structure in which a current account deficit of 10 percent of GDP provides for finance of the government of about 2 percent of GDP, and of the private sector of about 8 percent of GDP. The 1998 projection has maintained this pattern.

These aggregate lending and borrowing flows can be broken down to show a more detailed view of the intersectoral financial process. The government has, since the start of its stabilization program in early 1994 under IMF sponsorship, been implementing a tighter control of the general government deficit. Government policy is aimed at balancing the budget by the year 2000. Control of this deficit has been an essential part of the stabilization program, contributing to the reduction of inflationary expectations and to confidence in the maintenance of the Currency Board—anchored exchange rate. General government saving has been constant at about 2 percent of GDP, except for the temporary 1996 dip. That saving, however, has been insufficient to cover the modest level of investment[3] and the authorities' policy of lending to its satellite institutions. This is shown in Figure 10.2, where the government's total borrowing curve, running between 4 and 5 percent of GDP from 1994 to 1996, is much larger than needed to cover the budget's financial deficit. The additional borrowing provided for the on-lending that has been some 2 percent of GDP in recent years. The recent decline in both the lending and the deficit permit a decline in total borrowing to about 1 percent of GDP.

The bulk of the government's borrowing is from foreign sources, as Figure 10.2 illustrates, in the form of medium- and long-term foreign currency loans. As the total borrowing has declined recently, so has its borrowing from the private sector, which in 1995 and 1996 reflected the absorption of Treasury bills, an important institutional development of the transition. Government borrowing from the banking sector has been notably small since 1995, reflecting Lithuania's Currency Board arrangement.

---

3. A large part of the government investment shown here consists of capital transfers, and only a small part represents actual fixed capital formation.

Figure 10.2 General Government Sector Finance (Flow data as percentage of current GDP)

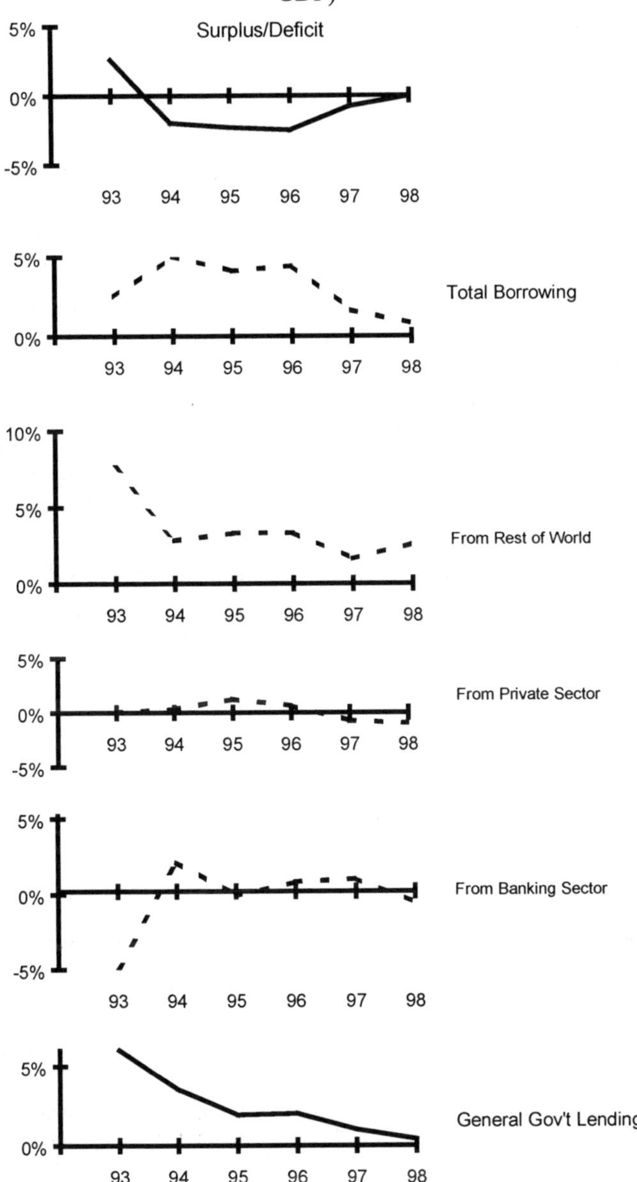

Note: 1998 data are projected.

Figure 10.3 presents rest-of-the-world net lending to Lithuania and its breakdown.[4] Recent data for net lending—the top curve—show a rise to 6 percent of GDP in 1995, continuing up to a sizable 10 percent in 1997. While total foreign lending rises steadily from 6 percent of GDP in 1995 to 13 percent in 1997, the breakdown of this curve reveals the rather steady flow to general government (which was seen as government net borrowing in Figure 10.2), accompanied by a sharply rising flow to the private sector, running up to 11 percent of GDP in 1997. Somewhat more than half of the private sector flow takes the form of direct foreign investment. An improving regulatory climate for such investment, as well as the recent economic growth, underpin the continuing direct investment flow in the 1998 projection. The remainder of the flow to the private sector consists primarily of medium- and long-term loans. This flow has been partially supported by Lithuanian government guarantees (especially in the state-controlled enterprises). A residual pattern—combining the impact of the current account deficit and the inward lending flows—imposes itself on the banking sector's international reserves at the bottom of Figure 10.3. This measures the overall balance of payments surplus/deficit, and in most years it shows comfortable reserve increases of 1 to 3 percent of GDP. The current stock of gross reserves covers about 2.5 months worth of imports.[5]

---

4. Like several of the economies in transition, since 1993 Lithuania has had a continuously growing trade deficit. By 1997, it was up to about 12 percent of GDP. The trade deficit is accompanied by offsetting surpluses in services and transfers, which combined to yield a current account deficit of about 10 percent of GDP for 1997. The movement of the trade deficit, however, sets the pattern of movement for the current account as a whole.

5. It should be noted that Lithuania's external position appears quite strong in comparison with other transition economies such as Latvia, Estonia, the Czech Republic, and Poland. Lithuania's exports exceed 40 percent of GDP and are growing strongly. Lithuania's merchandise trade deficit is lower than that of all these countries except Poland. External debt is only 12 percent of GDP. And in recent years, the exchange rate has been maintained with no great difficulty.

Figure 10.3 Rest-of-the-World Net Lending to Lithuania (Flow data as percentage of current GDP)

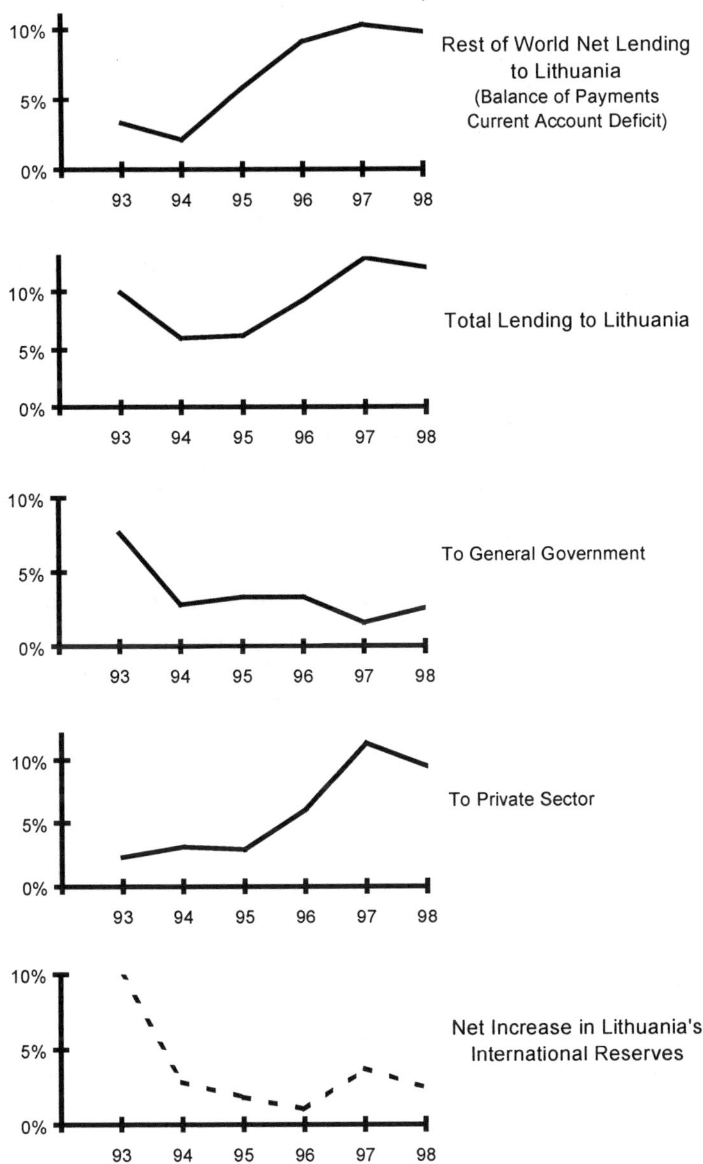

Note: 1998 data are projected.

An analysis of the private sector's financial flows is presented in Figure 10.4. It is here, of course, that the bulk of the economy's capital formation takes place, and here that it must be financed. In order to separate the business activity of this sector from that of its households, the broad assumption is made that the private saving of Lithuania's households is placed entirely in the sector's acquisition of money and other financial assets. The rest of the sector's saving thus represents business saving, the funds retained by enterprises that are used to finance capital formation (the internal finance curve in Figure 10.4). The growth of this estimate of business saving has generally kept pace with the growth of investment until recently. Nevertheless, there is a wide gap between them that represents a borrowing need, a demand for funds that is met by the rest-of-the-world, banking, and government sectors. The curves for private borrowing from these three sectors in Figure 10.4 combine into the total private borrowing curve. The steady decline in the total flow (as a percent of GDP) from 1993 to 1996 is almost entirely attributable to the banking sector curve. The rise in 1997 and projected for 1998 are created by the flow from the rest-of-the-world.

In 1993 the flow of private bank credit—swollen by inflationary needs—was 12 percent of GDP, and the primary vehicle in the financing of private investment. But in 1994–96, that flow grew so little that, as a percentage of GDP, it declined precipitously to zero. The stagnation of bank lending during the banking crisis in 1996 is understandable, but the deterioration began much earlier. Fortunately, the stable flows from abroad (and from the general government) could partially replace the loss of bank lending. Even in the midst of the banking crisis, about a third of private investment was financed from these flows. Bank lending indicates a recovery in 1997. Together with the increase in the flow from abroad (especially in direct foreign investment), total borrowing in that year financed more than half of private investment.

Further analysis of the banking sector's (Bank of Lithuania plus the commercial banks) macroeconomic flows is presented in Figure 10.5. These flows are clearly dominated by the sharp declines in both the broad money increment and the acquisitions of private claims. They both descend into the banking crisis of 1996, and they both suggest earlier roots of trouble.

Figure 10.4. Private Sector Investment and Financing   (Flow data as percentage of current GDP)

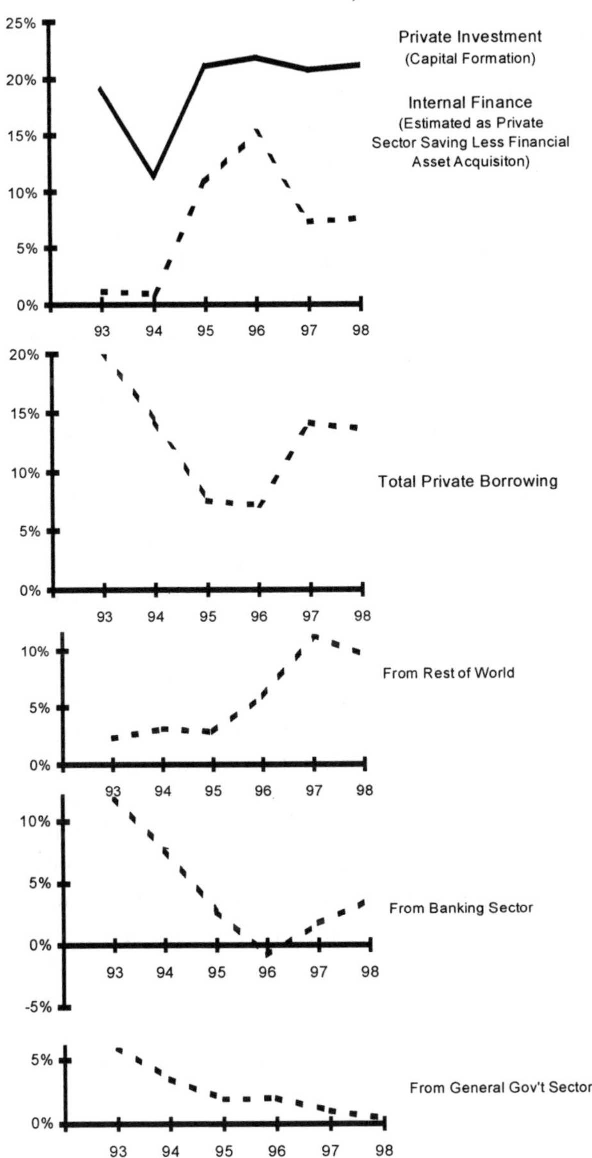

Note: 1998 data are projected.

The commercial banking system of Lithuania is a very recent creation, dating only from the late 1980s. The system has been highly concentrated in a few state-controlled banks. Before the crisis, management had little experience in commercial bank operation, bank capital bases were thin, political intervention in lending decisions was common, and many loans were nonperforming. In the fall of 1995, both liquidity and solvency problems surfaced, and in December a crisis began. During 1996, a quarter of existing household deposits left the system, the interest rates applied nearly doubled, and significant outflows of foreign exchange took place. The reserve outflows led to a contraction in broad money, which was accompanied by a credit crunch in bank lending. All of this lies behind the two sharply declining curves in Figure 10.5. The government and the Bank of Lithuania are still deep in the process of restoring the banking system to health. Nevertheless, the rise in bank lending to the private sector in 1997 suggests that the banks will be able to respond to credit needs in future, and this is shown in the 1998 projection in Figure 10.5.

The sector accounts discussed above can be placed in matrix form for a given year, as is done for 1997 in Table 10.1, to show the horizontal balances of the borrowing and leading flows, as well as the vertical sector account balances. With each of its flows expressed as a percentage of the current GDP, Table 10.1 reveals the financial flow structure of the economy's macro financial system. The table contains some notable features. The gross investment total of 23.5 percent of GDP is a quite respectable figure, reflecting recent data revisions that raised the figure from about 21 percent. The surplus/deficit line shows the sizable rest-of-world surplus of 10.3 percent of GDP financing the small general government deficit of -0.8 percent and the enlarged private sector deficit of -9.5 percent. As our historical analysis has shown, this structure represents a recent major shift by the private sector toward increased borrowing from the rest-of-the-world. The private credit line in Table 10.1 shows private sector borrowing of 14.1 percent of GDP, 11.3 percent of which is from abroad. This high level of borrowing for the finance of private sector investment—a proportion of two-thirds—is made necessary by the decline in domestic saving that accompanies the rise in rest-of-world saving (the current account deficit).

Figure 10.5 Banking Sector Finance (Flow data as percentage of current GDP)

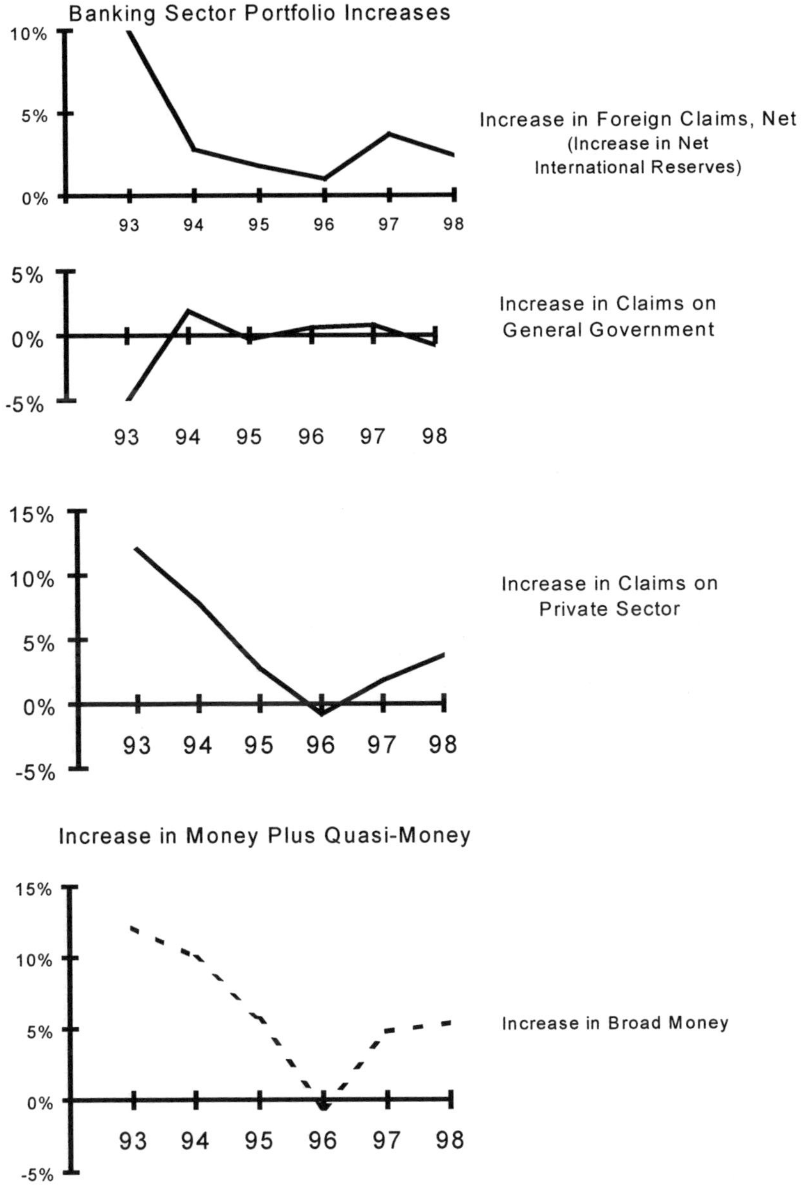

Banking Sector Portfolio Increases
10%
5%
0%
93
94
95
96
97
98
Increase in Foreign Claims, Net
(Increase in Net
International Reserves)
5%
0%
-5%
93
94
95
96
97
98
Increase in Claims on
General Government
15%
10%
5%
0%
-5%
93
94
95
96
97
98
Increase in Claims on
Private Sector
Increase in Money Plus Quasi-Money
15%
10%
5%
0%
-5%
93
94
95
96
97
98
Increase in Broad Money

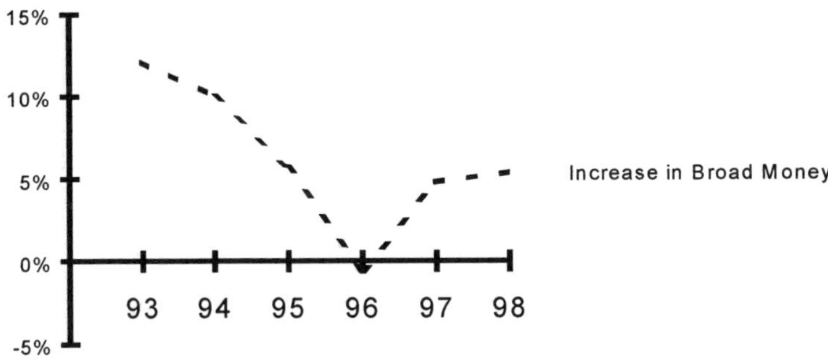

Note: 1998 data are projected.

Table 10.1. Flow of Funds Matrix, 1997 (actuals as percentage of current GDP)[a]

	General government		Banking sector		Private sector		Rest-of-the-world		Total	
	U	S	U	S	U	S	U	S	U	S
Investment	2.7[b]		—		20.8				23.5	
Saving		1.9	—			11.4		10.3		23.5
Surplus/deficit[c]	-0.8		—		-9.5		10.3		0.0	
	ΔFin. Assets	ΔFin. Liab.	ΔFin. Assets	ΔFin. Liab.	ΔFin. Assets	ΔFin. Liab.	ΔFin. Assets	ΔFin. Liab.	ΔFin. Assets	ΔFin. Liab.
ΔForeign claims			3.7					3.7	3.7	3.7
ΔGen'l government debt		1.6	0.8		-0.8		1.6		1.6	1.6
ΔPrivate credit	1.0		1.8			14.1	11.3		14.1	14.1
ΔMoney + quasi-money				4.8	4.8				4.8	4.8
ΔMisc. + discrepancies		0.3		1.5		-0.6	1.2		1.2	1.2
Total	3.8	3.8	6.3	6.3	24.8	24.8	14.0	14.0	48.9	48.9

a. Components may not add to totals because of rounding.
b. Includes capital transfers. General government fixed investment is 0.8 percent of GDP.
c. Sector net lending/borrowing.

Lithuania's Financial System and Economic Policy over the Coming Decade

The Lithuanian economy is judged to be confronting a major macroeconomic choice. It can maintain the moderate speed and coverage of its current reform program, achieving a respectable growth rate, but continuing to face a variety of difficult problems. Or, with a more vigorous and comprehensive reform initiative, it can move into a more rapid and sustainable growth path. In other words, Lithuania could remain on the fringes of the European Union, or become a major performer in the region with enhanced prospects of European integration. Whether Lithuania's growth takes off depends on the effectiveness of its pursuit of the structural reform agenda and whether the private sector can increase its efficiency and boost investment.

To explore the implications of these two contrasting views, this section develops two projection scenarios for Lithuania that look a decade ahead, through 2007. The first scenario, representing the impact of continuing moderate policy action, projects an economy growing in real terms at 3 percent yearly. The second view projects the impact of a more vigorous implementation; the annual growth rate in this scenario is 6 percent. The key factor causing the difference in the projected growth rates is *the size and efficiency of the economy's investment.* In the one case, private investment responds weakly, given persisting constraints in the private sector environment. In the other case, private investment responds with confidence to the new profit possibilities inherent in the reforms, and investment not only grows faster but is also able to incorporate increased efficiencies.

The two projections are derived from a World Bank type RMSM-X model, adapted to Lithuania's current situation. This model is not to be understood as an endogenous-growth econometric model. Rather, each projection begins with assumed growth rates for major economic variables such as production, investment, and exports. These assumptions are essentially judgmental projections. Making use of these assumptions, the model carries the base period national accounts into the future. In the context of RMSM-X, such projections of the government budget, the balance of payments, and the monetary accounts, together with the basic national accounts, permit the derivation of the private sector and its finance. This, in turn, permits an examination of the consistency of patterns of saving, investment, and finance over the term of the projection. The base year for both projections is 1996.

A Moderate Growth Outlook

The moderate-growth scenario is summarized in Table 10.2. The GDP growth rate is assumed to be 3 percent yearly, with inflation projected at 8 percent through the decade. A key factor in setting the 3 percent growth rate is the similar growth rate of gross domestic investment, a pace that maintains—but does not increase—its 21 percent of GDP proportion throughout the projection. A number of elements will retard investment. The slow pace of policy reform and the moderate fiscal tightness suggest a slow development of business confidence in macroeconomic stability, and bank lending rates will decline only moderately. Needed infrastructure improvements will lag as government investment fails to grow from its current inadequate rate. With only a moderate growth in overall investment, and weak structural reform performance, the productivity improvements essential for the modernization of Lithuania's economy will not appear. This is symbolized in the projection by the incremental capital output ratio (ICOR) rise from 5.8 to 6.8 over the decade. Nevertheless, while not stellar, an annual growth rate of 3 percent can be regarded as quite satisfactory; it maintains a per capita consumption growth rate of 2.8 percent in the moderate projection.

With respect to external trade, the projection assumes a continuation of the current robust growth in real exports until the millennium, tapering off to an annual growth rate of 3 percent by the end of the forecast period. Modest economic growth, coupled with robust growth in exports, yields a rise in the ratio of exports to GDP from 54 percent to 62 percent over the forecast period. Imports are expected to increase at a more moderate pace, a result of the slower real GDP expansion, and one positive consequence of this scenario is that the resource-balance deficit (exports minus imports) declines from -10 to -3.2 percent of GDP over the forecast period.

Yet the outflow of net factor income (especially that of debt servicing) will grow rapidly enough to preclude any real improvement in the current account deficit, which will decline as a share of GDP from about -9 percent to -7 percent in 2007. Thus, the rest-of-the-world will continue to be a major lender to Lithuania, supplying an inflow of some 7 percent of GDP annually, which will eventually push the debt/GDP ratio from under 15 percent (in 1996) to over 50 percent by the end of the forecast period. The projection assumes a continuing growth in international reserves (including those of the deposit money banks) of 2 percent of GDP yearly. The stock of international reserves, as expressed in months of imports, will grow from 2.2 to 4.5 months.

The fiscal policy expressed in the projection is only moderately tight; the 1996 general government deficit of some 2.5 percent of GDP continues through the decade. The considerable resistance in Lithuania to raising taxes—despite their low level in international comparisons—is reflected in current revenues that remain at about 30 percent of GDP along with current expenditures. Government saving remains near zero. Lending operations, largely a reflection of the passing on of government borrowing from abroad, have been maintained. In order to keep government borrowing down to 5 percent of GDP, however, capital expenditures have been severely rationed. In effect, the failure of the current budget to generate savings is hindering the government investment effort.

The private sector and the financing of the main portion of the economy's investment should also be examined. The 1996 data on Table 10.2 show private sector investment at 18.4 percent of GDP. As explained above, the growth of private investment is moderate in this projection, and its percentage of GDP remains unchanged over the decade. The growth of saving behaves in the same manner. With the projected current account deficit—that is, the rest-of-the-world annual savings of 7 percent of GDP— the domestic saving available to the private sector in 2007 is only 13.8 percent of GDP (see Table 10.2). Using a crude estimate, the portion of this amount that represents internal business financing might be some 6 percent of GDP, while the capital formation to be financed is nearly 19 percent. If this is so, private sector borrowing to finance such real investment would have to be about 13 percent of GDP. In the moderate projection, the estimated proportion of private borrowing to private investment thus rises from a reasonable 40 or 50 percent in the base years to a quite large 70 percent in 2007. This projection is thus characterized as a heavy-borrowing scenario.

Table 10.2 Moderate-Growth Projection (percent and US$ million)

Indicator	Estimated[d]		Projected									
	1996	1997	1998	1999	2000	2001	2002	2003	2004	2005	2006	2007
Real annual growth rates (1993 prices)												
GDP at market prices	3.6	3.6	3.3	3.0	3.0	3.0	3.0	3.0	3.0	3.0	3.0	3.0
Consumption per capita	2.4	2.2	3.3	1.3	1.4	2.8	2.8	2.9	2.8	2.6	2.9	2.9
External debt outstanding and disbursed and debt service												
Debt outstanding and disbursed (DOD)	1,129	1551	2042	2458	2842	3286	3774	4239	4837	5444	6083	6791
DOD/GDP	14.5	20.6	25.1	28.4	31.0	33.9	36.8	39.2	42.3	45.1	47.8	50.6
Debt service (US$ millions)	139	281	259	248	404	440	513	585	723	817	945	1063
Debt service/XGS	3.2	6.5	5.5	4.7	7.1	7.2	7.9	8.4	9.8	10.5	11.5	12.2
Debt service/GDP	1.8	3.7	3.2	2.9	4.4	4.5	5.0	5.4	6.3	6.8	7.4	7.9
National accounts (percent of GDP at current market prices)												
Gross domestic investment	21.0	21.0	20.8	20.6	20.6	20.5	20.5	20.5	20.5	20.5	20.5	20.5
Gross domestic fixed investment	20.1	20.3	20.1	20.0	20.0	20.0	20.0	20.0	20.0	20.0	20.0	20.0
Gross domestic savings	11.4	12.8	13.4	14.8	16.1	16.5	16.8	17.0	17.3	17.7	17.9	18.1
Gross national savings	11.7	13.2	13.3	14.1	14.8	14.7	14.5	14.3	14.2	14.2	14.0	13.8
Government investment	2.6	2.5	2.3	2.1	2.0	2.0	2.0	2.0	2.0	2.0	2.0	2.0
Government savings	0.1	0.3	0.0	0.4	0.4	0.3	0.2	0.2	0.1	0.1	0.0	-0.1
Private investment[a]	18.4	18.5	18.5	18.5	18.6	18.5	18.5	18.5	18.5	18.5	18.5	18.5
Private savings	11.2	12.7	13.0	13.5	14.2	14.2	14.1	14.0	13.9	14.0	13.9	13.8
ICOR[b]	5.84	5.84	6.36	6.93	6.87	6.85	6.83	6.82	6.82	6.82	6.82	6.82

General government accounts[c] (percent of GDP at current market prices)

Current revenues	29.8	31.1	30.8	30.7	30.7	30.7	30.6	30.6	30.6	30.5	30.5	30.5
Current expenditures	29.7	30.8	30.7	30.3	30.3	30.4	30.4	30.4	30.4	30.4	30.5	30.6
Capital revenues	0.0	0.0	0.0	0.0	0.0	0.0	0.0	0.0	0.0	0.0	0.0	0.0
Capital expenditures	2.6	2.5	2.3	2.1	2.0	2.0	2.0	2.0	2.0	2.0	2.0	2.0
Investment	2.6	2.5	2.3	2.1	2.0	2.0	2.0	2.0	2.0	2.0	2.0	2.0
Overall balance (- = deficit)	-4.7	-4.2	-4.3	-3.8	-3.7	-3.8	-3.9	-3.9	-3.9	-4.0	-4.1	-4.2
External accounts												
Total export volume, annual growth rate (percent)	..	4.0	7.3	6.9	5.7	4.8	4.3	3.8	3.6	3.6	3.1	3.1
Export/GDP (percent)	54.1	55.6	56.5	58.5	59.9	60.9	61.5	61.8	62.0	62.3	62.3	62.4
Total import volume, annual growth rate	..	1.6	6.9	3.9	3.3	4.3	3.7	3.5	3.2	3.1	2.9	2.9
Import/GDP	64.1	64.2	64.3	64.7	64.9	65.6	65.8	66.0	65.9	65.8	65.7	65.6
Current account (US$ millions)	-723	-588	-613	-567	-528	-565	-610	-664	-716	-758	-826	-897
Current account/GDP	-9.3	-7.8	-7.5	-6.5	-5.8	-5.8	-6.0	-6.1	-6.3	-6.3	-6.5	-6.7
Prices												
Inflation rate (period average)	25.0	12.3	9.0	8.0	8.0	8.0	8.0	8.0	8.0	8.0	8.0	8.0%

Note: a. Includes changes in stocks.

b. Fixed investment only.

c. General government includes central government, municipalities, and extrabudgetary funds.

d. Estimates do not incorporate 1998 revisions.

The borrowing and lending relationships become clear if the implicit flow of funds accounts for 2007 are examined in a matrix format that includes the banking sector, as in Table 10.3. The line for the issue of general government debt (4.2 percent of GDP) shows that 2.3 percent is absorbed by the rest-of-the-world and less than 1 percent by the private sector. The remaining 1.7 percent of GDP is taken by the banking sector. Similarly, of the private credit issue of 12.9 percent of GDP that is necessary to finance private sector investment, 6.4 percent is absorbed by the rest-of-the-world, 2.1 percent represents on-lending from government, and the remaining 4.4 percent is bank borrowing. In this projection, the borrowing needs are sufficiently high that even with the large flow from abroad (2.3 percent and 6.4 percent, stemming largely from the current account deficit of 6.7 percent of GDP), major borrowing needs have to be met by the banking sector (1.7 percent of GDP for government and 4.4 percent of GDP for the private sector). The projection thus assumes that the banking sector will be restored to health over the next few years and will be able to accommodate these major credit demands.

If the financial flow structure at the end of the projection (Table 10.3 for the year 2007) is compared with the current structure (Table 10.1 for 1997), it can be can seen how that structure would evolve over the decade.[6] Investment, which had grown up to 23.5 percent of GDP in 1997, would trend back to its moderate level of 20.4 percent. The currently large balance of payments deficit (rest-of-world saving) of 10.3 percent of GDP would decline to a more moderate 6.7 percent. Although this rest-of-world surplus still finances the government and private sector deficits, the unusually large 1997 deficit of the private sector of -9.5 percent of GDP is cut in half by 2007, with a return to more normal, recent levels.

---

6. The revised data for 1997 in Table 6.1 differ from the earlier data for 1996 embodied in the projection base.

Table 10.3. Moderate-Growth Projection, Flow of Funds Matrix, 2007 (percent of current GDP)

	General government		Banking sector		Private sector		Rest-of-the-world		Total	
	U	S	U	S	U	S	U	S	U	S
Investment	2.0[b]				18.4				20.4	
Saving		-0.1		0.2		13.7		6.7		20.4
Surplus/deficit[a]	-2.1		0.2		-4.8		6.7		0	
	ΔFin. assets	ΔFin. liab.	ΔFin. assets	ΔFin. liab.	ΔFin. assets	ΔFin. liab.	ΔFin. assets	ΔFin. liab.	ΔFin. assets	ΔFin. liab.
ΔForeign claims			2.2					2.2	2.2	2.2
ΔGeneral government debt		4.2	1.7		0.3		2.3		4.2	4.2
ΔPrivate credit	2.1		4.4			12.9	6.4		12.9	12.9
ΔMoney and quasi-money				7.7	7.7				7.7	7.7
ΔMisc. and discrepencies		0.0		0.4		-0.2	0.2		0.2	0.2
Total	4.1	4.1	8.3	8.3	26.4	26.4	8.9	8.9	47.6	47.6

a. Sector net lending/borrowing.

b. Includes capital transfers.

The borrowing/lending structure in the lower part of the matrices also shows considerable change. Government borrowing rises from 1.6 to 4.2 percent of GDP. Private sector borrowing maintains its high 1997 rate of 12.9 percent of GDP. The flow of government and private lending from abroad, however, declines from some 12.9 percent of GDP to 8.7 percent. It is the growing banking sector that by 2007 is providing the necessary added financing, domestic credit extension having risen from 2.6 to 6.1 percent of GDP. (The money stock rises in parallel from 4.8 to 7.7 percent of GDP.) Continued heavy borrowing and the shift toward bank finance are key features of the moderate-growth projection.

Lithuania is currently not a highly indebted country, either internally or externally, but the borrowing flows of this projection do carry the debt stock and money stock figures to rather high levels over the next ten years. The continuing current account deficit of some 6–7 percent of GDP causes the external debt stock to rise from 14 percent to 51 percent of GDP, and debt service payments to increase from 1.8 percent to 7.9 percent of GDP. The government borrowing of approximately 4 percent of GDP causes the government debt stock to grow from 7 percent to 39 percent of GDP. The acceleration of banking sector growth leads to the growth of private plus government bank credit from 11 percent to 31 percent of GDP. And finally, the broad money stock grows from 18 percent to 45 percent of GDP.

It should be noted that this projection has not attempted to include any effect of the fiscal pressures stemming from the so-called quasi-public sector deficit. That is, the general government may have to incur additional expenditures—estimated to be as much as 3 percent of GDP—which may be necessary to complete reforms in the banking, energy, and municipal government sectors. Additional fiscal pressure may stem from the implementation of a savings restitution plan and pension reforms. It is important to consider the implications of additional financing for such purposes.

The government debt line in Table 10.1 can provide a summary of the impact of major added borrowing. If the government debt issue were raised from 1.6 percent to 4.6 percent, the added 3 percentage points would have to be placed with the other three sectors. Any additional government borrowing from abroad (assuming no change in the current account deficit) would squeeze private borrowing from abroad, which might well retard investment. Alternatively, the private sector might seek to borrow more from banks—or the government might do so directly—with consequent further growth in the flows of bank credit and the money stock. The latter outcome would compromise the appropriately tight monetary and credit policy in the face of ongoing inflation and a balance of payments current account deficit. It is also unlikely that the government could greatly increase its direct borrowing from the private sector in the current institutional environment.

What is implied by the quasi-public-sector deficit problem is a need for a greater tax effort. As Table 10.2 indicates, the moderate-growth projection includes little growth in general government current expenditures relative to GDP—from 29.7 percent to 30.6 percent—and the growth that does take place is primarily the result of rising interest costs. Current revenue grows about the same amount. Given the low level of taxes in Lithuania compared with its neighbors and the Organization for Economic Cooperation and Development (OECD) countries, there appears to be room for an increase of 2–3 percent of GDP in the value added tax collection (VAT) and/or taxes on companies and individuals. The government has already launched reform measures in tax administration that might add 1–2 percent of GDP over a few years. These resources could finance necessary added expenditures. The government is currently reluctant to raise tax rates, but the likelihood of expenditure increases makes an urgent case for doing so.

In sum, the moderate-growth scenario presents a continuation over the next decade of the current twin deficits—that of the balance of payments current account and that of general government. The posted government deficit that would accompany slow revenue growth makes the financing of any additional expenditures difficult. And the continuing external deficit that would accompany sluggish export growth necessitates a large flow of capital into Lithuania. So far, this flow has been plentiful enough to meet the need, based no doubt on confidence established by the Currency Board arrangements and the government's short-term stabilization policies. Should this confidence diminish, and if foreign borrowing were to become difficult, financing of the foreign deficit could become a major problem. The projection, however, has assumed a plentiful capital flow. Finally, this moderate-growth—but high-borrowing—projection contains strong private borrowing pressure on a banking system that is just now emerging from a very weakened state.

High Growth and Major Reform Impact

Vigorous implementation of needed policy reforms could well place the Lithuanian economy on a sustainable high-growth plateau. This vision is embodied in the high-growth projection scenario. It is characterized by strong export behavior and rapid growth in capital formation, both driven by enhanced confidence and the efficiencies to be derived from improved institutions and incentives. Table 10.4 sets out the main features of the projection.

In the high-growth projection, real annual GDP growth rises from the base year figure of 3.6 percent to 6 percent by 2002, and remains at 6 percent to the end of the projection period in 2007. Gross investment follows an identical path. Both GDP and investment grow at double the rates in the moderate projection. This high rate of investment will be a direct result of energetic sectoral reforms, although a simple quantitative translation is not possible. Nevertheless, for a number of reasons, the policy impact on investment is assumed to be large. The increased pace of privatization, a more favorable (and accountable) private sector development environment (through better tax administration, judicial systems, and mechanisms for corporate governance), sounder and more efficient financial systems (both in banking and in securities markets), and the development of longer-term sources of funding from banks and pension-based investment funds, can trigger a major, permanent improvement in confidence. This, in turn, could drive an increase in investment, and in its efficiency. The major improvements in efficiency are symbolized by the ICOR drop from 5.8 percent to 3.9 over the projection decade. In parallel, real per capita consumption attains an annual 6 percent growth rate, in contrast to the 2.9 percent annual rate of the moderate-growth scenario, making the overall economic framework more socially sustainable.

Both exports and imports rise more rapidly in the high-growth scenario. Export volume grows to 7.5 percent annually, remains at the level through 2005, and ends the forecast period at 6.9 percent yearly, over double the rate used in the moderate-growth scenario. The proportion of exports to GDP rises from 52.4 percent to 63.8 percent. Imports grow more slowly, and end the forecast period at 64.6 percent of GDP, only 1.3 percentage points higher than in the moderate-growth scenario. Consequently, the current account deficit falls steadily, from -8.2 percent of GDP in 1996 to -2.8 percent of GDP in 2007, in marked contrast to the modest decline to -6.7 percent in the moderate-growth projection.

Table 10.4 High-Growth Projection (percent and US$ million)

Indicator	Estimated[d]		Projected									
	1996	1997	1998	1999	2000	2001	2002	2003	2004	2005	2006	2007
Real annual growth rates (1993 prices)												
GDP at market prices	3.6	3.6	4.0	4.5	5.0	5.5	6.0	6.0	6.0	6.0	6.0	6.0
Consumption per capita	2.4	1.8	2.9	2.3	2.7	3.7	5.2	5.1	5.3	5.8	6.0	6.0
External debt outstanding and disbursed and debt service												
Debt outstanding and disbursed (DOD)	1,129	1,461	1,887	2,223	2,449	2,666	2,864	2,936	3,054	3,170	3,294	3,426
DOD/GDP	14.5	18.9	22.6	24.7	25.1	25.3	25.0	23.6	22.6	21.6	20.6	19.8
Debt service (US$ millions)	139	282	255	237	385	405	439	466	542	536	551	554
Debt service/XGS	3.3	6.6	5.4	4.5	6.6	6.3	6.2	6.0	6.3	5.7	5.3	4.9
Debt service/GDP	1.8	3.6	3.0	2.6	4.0	3.8	3.8	3.7	4.0	3.6	3.4	3.2
National accounts (percent of GDP at current market prices)												
Gross domestic investment	21.0	21.5	22.0	22.5	23.0	23.5	23.5	23.5	23.5	23.5	23.5	23.5
Gross domestic fixed investment	20.1	20.8	21.4	21.9	22.5	23.0	23.0	23.0	23.0	23.0	23.0	23.0
Gross domestic savings	11.4	13.0	14.5	16.4	18.4	19.8	20.5	21.3	21.9	22.3	22.5	22.7
Gross national savings	12.8	13.9	14.8	16.2	17.7	18.8	19.2	19.8	20.2	20.5	20.5	20.6
Government investment	2.6	2.5	2.6	2.8	2.9	3.1	3.2	3.4	3.6	3.6	3.6	3.6
Government savings	0.1	0.4	0.6	1.3	1.7	2.1	2.3	2.6	2.7	2.8	2.8	2.8
Private investment[a]	18.4	19.0	19.4	19.8	20.1	20.5	20.3	20.1	19.9	19.9	19.9	19.9
Private savings	12.7	13.5	14.2	15.0	16.0	16.7	16.9	17.2	17.5	17.7	17.7	17.9
ICOR[b]	5.84	5.84	5.38	4.59	4.50	4.18	3.92	3.91	3.91	3.91	3.91	3.91

General government accounts[c] (percent of GDP at current market prices)

Current revenues	29.8	30.9	31.1	31.4	31.7	31.9	32.1	32.3	32.4	32.4	32.4	32.4
Current expenditures	29.7	30.5	30.5	30.1	29.9	29.9	29.8	29.7	29.7	29.6	29.6	29.6
Capital revenues	0.0	0.0	0.0	0.0	0.0	0.0	0.0	0.0	0.0	0.0	0.0	0.0
Capital expenditures	2.6	2.5	2.6	2.8	2.9	3.1	3.2	3.4	3.6	3.6	3.6	3.6
Investment	2.6	2.5	2.6	2.8	2.9	3.1	3.2	3.4	3.6	3.6	3.6	3.6
Overall balance (- = deficit)	-4.7	-4.2	-3.9	-3.5	-3.2	-2.9	-2.8	-2.8	-2.7	-2.7	-2.7	-2.6
External accounts												
Total export volume, annual growth rate	..	6.5	7.3	7.3	7.7	7.5	7.5	7.5	7.6	7.6	6.9	6.9
Export/GDP	52.4	53.8	54.7	56.2	57.7	58.8	59.6	60.5	61.5	62.5	63.1	63.8
Total import volume, annual growth rate	..	4.2	6.1	4.8	5.2	5.9	6.4	6.4	6.7	7.3	6.8	6.8
Import/GDP	62.1	62.2	62.2	62.3	62.3	62.5	62.6	62.7	63.0	63.7	64.1	64.6
Current account (US$ millions)	-641.7	-592.4	-599.5	-566.7	-518.3	-495.2	-486.5	-457.1	-434.8	-438.3	-466.1	-488.6
Current account/GDP	-8.2	-7.6	-7.2	-6.3	-5.3	-4.7	-4.2	-3.7	-3.2	-3.0	-2.9	-2.8
Prices												
Inflation rate (period average)	25.0	12.3	10.0	8.5	7.5	7.0	6.5	6.0	5.5	5.0	5.0	5.0

Note: a. Includes changes in stocks.
  b. Fixed investment only.
  c. General government includes central government, municipalities, and extrabudgetary funds.
  d. Estimates do not incorporate 1998 revisions

The lower current account deficit in this projection, coupled with the increased output of the economy, elicits a sharply lower level of required international financing. As a consequence, the proportion of external debt to GDP rises from 14 percent to only 20 percent over the projection period, less than half the level of the moderate-growth scenario. Not surprisingly, the proportion of debt service payments to GDP increases from 1.8 percent to only 3.2 percent, also less than half the 7.9 percent level of the moderate-growth scenario.

Regarding fiscal policy, a tighter stance is presented in the high-growth scenario. Current expenditures are kept level at 29.7 percent of GDP. VAT increases boost current revenues from 29.8 percent of GDP to 32.4 percent, nearly 2.0 percent more than in the earlier scenario (see tables 10.2 and 10.4). The upshot is a rise in general government saving, which is available to finance growth in government investment. Finally, the general government deficit tapers off sharply in the high-growth projection, from an initial -2.5 percent of GDP to about -1.0 percent from 2001 to 2007. The government deficit, like the balance of payments current account deficit, is considerably smaller here than in the moderate projection.

This tighter fiscal policy should help in the management of the quasi-public sector deficit. This clearly occurs after the year 2000, when the deficit has fallen to -1.0 percent of GDP and an additional 1.0 to 2.0 percent of GDP could be borrowed, if necessary. But there is a timing difficulty in the earlier years, 1997–99. In these years, the posted deficits, although falling, are still large, at 2.1 percent, 2.0 percent, and 1.5 percent GDP. The implication is similar to the finding in the moderate projection. Added tax revenue will be necessary to finance any added expenditures in the early years, but because indirect taxes have already been raised, the burden would fall on direct taxes.

Table 10.5 shows the financial flow structure of the high-growth projection at its end in 2007. (This table can be compared with Table 10.1, the current structure.) As noted, the higher government saving figure of 2.8 percent permits growth in government investment to 3.6 percent. (Government investment declined in the moderate projection.) With the continuing modest deficit of -0.8 percent, the overall government borrowing need would be only 2.6 percent of GDP, largely to cover the on-lending of 1.8 percent. The issue of government debt to be placed is thus much smaller in the high-growth projection. The debt is placed in the following manner:

1.2 percent with the rest-of-the-world, 0.5 percent with the private sector, and 1.0 percent with the banking sector.

Table 10.5. High-Growth Projection, Flow of Funds Matrix, 2007 (percent of current GDP)[a]

	General government		Banking sector		Private sector		Rest-of-the-world		Total	
	U	S	U	S	U	S	U	S	U	S
Investment	3.6[c]				19.9				23.4	
Saving		2.8		0.2		17.7		2.8		23.4
Surplus/deficit[b]	-0.8		0.2		-2.2		2.8		0	
	ΔFin. assets	ΔFin. liab.	ΔFin. assets	ΔFin. liab.	ΔFin. assets	ΔFin. liab.	ΔFin. assets	ΔFin. liab.	ΔFin. assets	ΔFin. liab.
ΔForeign claims			2.2					2.2	2.2	2.2
ΔGeneral government debt		2.6	1.0		0.5		1.2		2.6	2.6
ΔPrivate credit	1.8		1.8			7.5	3.9		7.5	7.5
ΔMoney and quasi-money				4.4	4.4				4.4	4.4
ΔMisc. and discrepencies				0.4		-0.4				
Total	5.4	5.4	5.0	5.0	24.8	24.8	5.0	5.0	40.2	40.2

a. Components may not add to totals beccause of rounding.
b. Sector net lending/borrowing.
c. Includes capital transfers.

Table 10.5 also shows relatively low rest-of-the-world saving (2.8 percent of GDP) being placed into net lending to Lithuania. Even with the 2.2 percent accumulation of foreign reserves, the total rest-of-the-world lending is only 5.1 percent—1.2 percent into government debt and 3.9 percent into private credit. The 5.1 percent of GDP capital inflow represents a decline from the current 12.9 percent over the decade of the projection.

In the high-growth projection, total investment at 23.4 percent of GDP maintains its high ratio, and private sector investment declines modestly from 20.8 percent to 19.9 percent. The private saving figure of 17.7 percent of GDP is high as well, reflecting the projection's high levels of profits. The crude estimate of business saving, or inside financing, is also high, at 12.8 percent of GDP, so that by 2007 only about a third of the private real investment must be financed by borrowing. This proportion of borrowing would leave businesses in a much sounder financial position than the more than two-thirds proportion at the end of the moderate projection.

With the volume of private borrowing in this projection declining to 7.5 percent, even with less foreign lending available, the private sector's call on the banking system is only 1.8 percent of GDP, and does not grow over the projection period. The banking system thus expands much more slowly than in the earlier projection, and the stock of domestic bank credit rises only to some 20 percent of GDP. Similarly, monetary expansion is more modest: the annual increment falls over the projection period from 4.8 percent of GDP to 4.4 percent, and the stock of money rises to only 32 percent of GDP. In this high-growth scenario, with its smaller key deficits, less recourse is made of the financial system.

Conclusions

It has been the purpose of this analysis to explore the policy implications of the two contrasting growth paths expected for Lithuania, a moderate-growth path resulting from slower and less effective sector reforms and a high-growth plateau reached through vigorous and rapid implementation. In this context, the projections have shown the importance of improved government revenue performance, a firm growth path for exports, and the restoration of the health of the banking system as key macro areas in need of attention.

The transition analysis showed a modest level of government saving at about 2 percent of GDP. The projections demonstrated the desirability over the next decade of increasing revenues as a share of GDP in order to finance much-needed growth in public investment, to control the government deficit, and to be prepared for the added expenditures required for the completion of sector reforms. An increase of 2–3 percent of GDP would not be an unreasonable increase given Lithuanian's low level of taxation relative to OECD countries.

Lithuania's exports of goods and nonfactor services have grown rapidly in recent years—in 1997 by some 23 percent. But, will such rapid growth continue? Indicators that suggest sustainability of exports—such as the high and growing export-to-GDP ratio and the lack of persistent pressures on the exchange rate in either direction—appear favorable for Lithuania. The high-growth projection thus assumed a continuous growth in annual export volume of 7 percent, which was an important cause of the reduction in the current account deficit. Continuing export growth is a major force impelling Lithuania's progress on the rapid-growth path.

The Lithuanian banking system—restructured and privatized—will still have had very little experience in commercial banking as a business; that is, in making viable and regular short-term business loans. This commercial bank function will need support and strengthening. In addition, a long-term lending capability is needed. As the projections show, the growing borrowing needs of the private sector will be met largely by the banks. If the banking system is unable to extend the credit demanded over the next decade, would-be borrowers may well not be able to finance desired investment. A high-growth path will require a properly functioning commercial banking system.

Biographical Sketches of the Authors

JOHN DAWSON is a long-time applied flow of funds specialist who has undertaken a variety of consulting missions in Africa, Asia, and most recently Eastern Europe, where he was engaged in both deriving and analyzing flow of funds data. He is the editor of *Flow of Funds Analysis, A Handbook for Practioners* and is Professor of Economics at Grinnell College in Grinnell, Iowa.

STEPHEN EVERHART is an economist in the Poverty Reduction and Economic Management Department of the World Bank's Latin America and Caribbean Region. After a long career as an investment banker on Wall Street, he joined Georgia State University's Department of Economics and has since published in the area of macroeconomics, finance, and development.

ALEXANDER E. FLEMING, a sector manager in the World Bank's Europe and Central Asia Region, has worked on a wide range of financial sector issues in the World Bank encompassing Latin America, the former Soviet Union, and the World Bank's own funding strategy. He covered flow of funds analysis and forecasting for the Bank of England early in his career and was a lecturer in macroeconomics and finance at the University of St. Andrews, Scotland where he deployed the flow of funds framework as a pedagogical device.

MARCELO M. GIUGALE is the Lead Economist for Mexico at the World Bank's Latin America and Caribbean Region. He was previously a Principal Economist in the Eastern Europe and Central Asia Region and a Senior Economist in the Middle East Region. Also, as a World Bank member, he advised the Argentine government on central bank policy management during the 1990 hyperinflation period. He has taught at the London School of Economics and at the American University in Cairo, and has published in the areas of financial econometrics, macroeconomic modeling, applied development economics, and private sector development.

JOHN HOLSEN, a consultant to the World Bank and Professorial Lecturer at the School of Advanced International Studies of the Johns Hopkins University, has held a number of positions in the World Bank including regional chief economist (first for Latin America, and then for South Asia) and director of the country economics department. He has used the flow of funds approach to assist in the analysis of country economic issues in many countries since his initial work on Brazil in 1969.

ANNA KEREKES was an economist at the National Bank of Hungary when her chapter in this volume was prepared.

WITOLD ORLOWSKI is a macroeconomist working mainly on the transition and integration of Central and Eastern European countries into the global economy. In the period 1993–97, he worked at the World Bank. He is currently director of the Research Centre for Statistical and Economic Studies in Warsaw, and advised Poland's Vice Premier Balcerowicz and its chief negotiator for European Union membership. In the early 1990s, he was the author of the first flow of funds and social accounting matrices for Poland.

STEVE PEACHEY is currently a financial sector consultant working on a range of assignments in Eastern Europe. He was previously an economist with the Bank of England where he specialized in flow of funds analysis and modeling, particularly regarding external capital and monetary movements.